Day of Reckoning

Columbine and the Search for

America's Soul

Day of Reckoning

WENDY MURRAY ZOBA

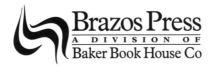

Brazos Press
A DIVISION OF
Baker Book House Co

Published by Brazos Press
a division of Baker Book House Company
P.O. Box 6287, Grand Rapids, MI 49516-6287

Printed in the United States of America

Library of Congress Cataloging-in-Publication Data

Zoba, Wendy Murray.
    Day of reckoning : Columbine and the search for America's soul / Wendy
Murray Zoba.
       p.   cm.
    Includes bibliographical references.
    ISBN 1-58743-001-0 (hardcover)
    1. School shootings—Colorado—Littleton. 2. Christian life—Colorado—Littleton. 3. Columbine High School (Littleton, Colo.) I. Title.
LB3013.3.Z63 2001
343.788'82—dc21   00-049802

For current information about all releases from Brazos Press, visit our web site:
http://www.brazospress.com

To the brave people
of the Columbine community.

Contents

Acknowledgments

I AM INDEBTED to a number of people for their help and support as I undertook this project. My friend and colleague Mickey Maudlin encouraged me to do it and pushed me when I lost the spirit to press on. My agent, Joe Durepos, believed in this project when it seemed few others did. He left no stone unturned until finding the right publisher, and I am grateful. My editor at Brazos Press, Rodney Clapp, offered his editorial recommendations with kindness and graciousness, and his insights elevated this book. My associates at *Christianity Today* have been forbearing with my distractions to accommodate my intense deadline schedule. I thank them for that. My family has been especially long-suffering. I do not feel worthy of the constant expressions of encouragement I have received from my sons, who too often lately have been consigned to Burger King or IHOP for sustenance. I want to thank my son Jon for being willing to share his personal reflections, which appear in chapter nine. My dear husband has carried an extra load in this season of my preoccupation, and I am grateful for his helpfulness and consistency. I hope I can return the blessing. I am also indebted to him for the help he gave me, through his research, in my examination of the Book of Job, which appears in chapter eight.

I am thankful for the assistance I received from my friend Ann Rice, an attorney in Denver who stepped in with legal help and guidance when the going got rough at certain junctures. In the same way, I am grateful for the help of Tom Kelley, an attorney with the Colorado Freedom of Information Council, and that of Byron R. Brown from the Reporters Committee for Freedom of the Press. Keith Pavlischek was very helpful, illuminating for me the nuances and legal intricacies of recent Supreme Court rulings. I am grateful to Nancy Pearcey for getting us connected. Journalist Dave Cullen was my "on-site" guy when big things happened—such as the release of the official report. I thank him for being arms and legs for me when airfares and work obligations made it prohibitive for me to travel. Joy Sawyer, Greg Zanis, Charles Moore, Jill Meyer, Ben McComb, and a few unnamed others (they know who they are) have gone the extra mile for me in one way or another. Their efforts have made a difference, and I am in their debt.

There are so many people in the Columbine community who have given me portions of their lives and hearts. This has been a sacred trust. I hold each of their stories in my heart. I am especially indebted to many pastors in the area who graciously entertained my phone calls and inquiries, and in some instances served as my advocate in securing interviews. For all the frustration many in the community have felt toward the media, I was deeply moved by the grace and good will I received from these vulnerable, welcoming people. It is my prayer that my efforts in this book will be worthy of their trust.

The deepest source of hope for me, in the course of working on this wrenching project, arose from my interviews with the young people, especially the students of Columbine and their friends. They are my heroes.

A note to the reader:

Unless noted otherwise in an endnote, all direct quotations came from the sixty-plus interviews I conducted in the course of my research.

WMZ

Chapter 1

Double Coupon Days

Evil Descends upon the Heartland

ON MY FIRST TRIP to Littleton, Colorado, I arrived on a steamy afternoon in July 1999, two months after the shootings that killed fifteen and wounded twenty-three, at Columbine High School. It took those two months for my magazine, *Christianity Today,* to assign me the task of writing "the Columbine story," in part because we couldn't quite figure out exactly what "the story" was for the magazine. I went to Colorado with a blank slate, expecting to hear "the story" from the people who lived it. In my research and on subsequent trips, I met with family members of those who had been murdered, pastors, students, teachers, friends, and administrators. I spoke with countless others intimately connected to the event. I believe I have heard "the story." This book is an attempt to convey and interpret it as it was told to me.

Amanda Meyer, seventeen, described how it felt to recover from the worst school shooting in United States history: "I wanted to curl up and die. But I couldn't. I found that there is a strange concept called time and it made you keep going. It would be ten o'clock and I'd have to go to bed. The morning would come whether you wanted it to or not, and you'd have to get up. You'd have to go somewhere. I didn't want to live anymore but I couldn't help it. My heart just kept beating and my lungs made me breathe."

She was a junior at Columbine High School on April 20, 1999, the day Eric Harris, eighteen, and Dylan Klebold, seventeen, taunted and massacred twelve fellow students and a teacher before turning their guns on themselves. Amanda lost two close friends that day—Rachel Scott, with whom she had worked at a Subway sandwich shop (the scene, less than a year later, of the killing of two more Columbine students), and Cassie Bernall, who was one of Amanda's best friends.

People like Amanda, Cassie, and Rachel—and Eric and Dylan—took center stage in a cultural drama that "opened a sad national conversation."[1] Something about what happened that day touched more people more profoundly than previous school shootings, horrific as those other tragedies were. The rampage at Columbine was one in a long line of shootings—including urban gang violence and domestic homicides—that have plagued this nation for decades. While homicide rates generally have decreased, however, the phenomenon known as "rampage killing" has occurred with dramatically increased frequency during the past decade.

In the wake of Columbine, the *New York Times* undertook an extensive investigation of rampage killings—"multiple-victim killings that were not primarily domestic or connected to a robbery or gang"[2]—extending back to 1949. In many ways, Columbine carried the marks of the "typical" rampage school shooting (to be addressed in due course). Still, the *Times* called it "probably the most shocking."[3]

At the same time, aspects of this event defied these categories and left the nation, including journalists like me, wondering what *really* had happened that day. In its aftermath, Nancy Gibbs wrote in *Time:* "With each passing day of shock and grief you could almost hear the church bells tolling in the background, calling the country to a different debate, a careful conversation in which even Presidents and anchormen behave as though they are in the presence of something bigger than they are."[4]

Some in the community, perhaps weary of the spectacle made of their once-anonymous existence, couldn't fathom the significance this event carried for anyone other than those whom it had directly touched. One community leader told me, "I have not been persuaded that this is a watershed event. I am not going to say it is not true, but I don't see it."

Outside the boundaries of Littleton, however, stories persisted about people whose lives changed almost instantly when they heard about Columbine. There was the aloof father who raced home to hug his kids and recommit himself to their nurture; there was the mother who sobbed unabashedly in front of her bewildered children as images from Littleton poured from her television. There was the teen who resolved to say "I love you" every time he walked out the front door. People who hadn't darkened the door of a church or synagogue in decades found a way back.

Hearing responses like these made me wonder what it was about this event that generated such emotional resonance. I began to sense that Columbine, at its heart, was a religious story. As the narratives in this book will reveal, many whose lives intersected with the event saw it that way. My research confirmed it. I came across the religious aspect of this story time and again not because I am a religious person and my magazine covers news from that viewpoint. I came to see Columbine as a religious story because, among other reasons, Eric Harris and Dylan Klebold made it one. They brought "God" into this event at almost every turn. In the planning stages Harris documented the rampage in the blue spiral notebook he called "the book of God." On videos they made prior to their rampage, Klebold said, "[W]e're going to have followers because we're so . . . godlike. . . . We're not exactly human." Harris said, "We have a . . . religious war." The videotapes abound with biblical imagery and ravings against God and Christianity. Harris said, "The apocalypse is coming and it's starting in eight days."

Witnesses claim that during the shooting they heard one of the boys ask some victims if they believed in God. Some doubts have arisen about whether this was so in the case of Cassie Bernall (addressed in chapter 5), but, at the very least, this scenario was consistent with the rage against religion the killers exhibited in their videos. In any case, there was no disputing the fact that the gunman posed that question in the library to Valeen Schnurr, who survived.

Then there have been the strange aftershocks that further hinted at a religious aspect. For example, when fifteen memorial crosses were placed on the knoll near Columbine High School known as Rebel Hill immediately following the tragedy, the inclusion of two crosses representing the killers aroused emotional dissent from one victimized family. As a public protest, one member tore down the killers' crosses. Then, in late September, nearby West Bowles Community Church planted fifteen trees on its property to honor the families of those who had died, and the same dissenter, along with a few other people, went onto church property and felled two of the trees. (The church did not press charges.)

There was the story of Garlin Newton, forty-eight, owner of a construction company in Oklahoma City, who believed that the Lord had spoken to him (his words) and told him to carry a cross from Oklahoma to Columbine High School. He walked, arthritic knees and all, the seven hundred-mile journey from Oklahoma City to Jefferson County carrying a white, vinyl, fifty-pound cross over his shoulder, logging about twenty miles a day. (A small wheel at the base helped it along.) Upon his arrival at the school November 20, 1999, he was greeted with the message: "Go Home."[5]

Then there was the spate of untimely violent deaths in the community during the year that followed. Though perhaps not overtly religious in nature, they were inordinate. On October 22, 1999, Carla Hochhalter, forty-eight, mother of paralyzed Columbine shooting victim Anne Marie Hochhalter, committed suicide in a local pawn shop. The body of eleven-year-old Antonio Ray Davalos was found in a dumpster near CHS on February 1, 2000, and on Valentine's Day, two Columbine High School sweethearts, Nick Kunselman, fifteen, and Stephanie Hart, sixteen, were gunned down in the Subway shop where Rachel Scott had worked, a few blocks from the school. A week later a man shot himself in the head a block away from that Subway. Before the first anniversary of the high school shooting, community church leaders felt as if their town was under a cloud of spiritual attack and sponsored a prayer walk. Covering a one-mile perimeter of the area marked by these killings, more than two thousand walked and prayed against the dark forces that seemed to be at war with this otherwise peaceful community. Shortly after the anniversary, the community was shaken again when CHS junior and basketball star Greg Barnes killed himself in his family's garage.

Other religious aftershocks were more positive in nature. Darrell Scott, Rachel's father, has traveled the country speaking in churches and at large youth rallies, often accompanied by Greg Zanis, who displayed the original crosses that stood on Rebel Hill. They have seen young people by the thousands literally fall down before these crosses and commit their lives to service for God. Churches in the Littleton area noted a marked increase in attendance at regular services and youth programs in the months that followed the tragedy. A spokesman for a local church said, "There's a continuing impact on the spiritual receptivity, especially among youth."[6]

During my research, I noticed that, despite the persistent religious overtones attached to this event, much of the reporting did little to note it. This was due, in part, to the insistence of investigators from the Jefferson County Sheriff's Department that what happened at CHS was not "a God-thing." Reporters depended upon the information passed along to them from the sheriff's office, and investigators were inconsistent and selective about what they released and the spin they put on it. Many inside the investigation did not see any religious motivation behind what took place in the school and have said so publicly.

Instead, the tragedy was dissected into many disparate parts: the need for greater gun control; the problem of uncensored access to dangerous information on the Internet; the influence of a violent media culture; the trauma associated with the clique-ish school culture; the issue of parental vigilance; the question of separation of church and state. I understood the desire to "solve" this "problem." Each of these aspects, perhaps in nudges, contributed to the final cataclysmic moments. No parent, myself included, can bear the thought that, in our well-ordered universe, kids can be shot execution-style by their classmates while studying *Macbeth* in the school library during fifth-period lunch. This is America; we *fix* things. Perhaps if there had been more restrictive gun laws, or if Arnold Schwarzenegger hadn't glamorized violence in the Terminator movies, or if the Ten Commandments had been posted in the school hallway, those boys wouldn't have taken in hand their double-barreled sawed-off shotgun, TEC-DC9 semiautomatic assault handgun, sawed-off pump shotgun, and 9 mm semiautomatic rifle to execute their peers.

Perhaps.

But what happened at Columbine High School on April 20, 1999, I came to see, could not be fully understood without giving due diligence to its critical religious dimension. That is the story I heard. It is the story I tell in these pages.

Between Two Worlds

I didn't know what to expect as I made my way from Denver International Airport south toward Littleton. I had heard Littleton was an affluent Denver suburb that could be likened to my hometown outside of Chicago. After checking in at my hotel, I set out on one sojourn I felt compelled to make before doing anything else. It took twenty minutes going seventy miles per hour to drive from the hotel to Columbine High School in the Columbine Valley, which is west of Littleton in unincorporated southern Jefferson County.[7] Columbine is in a series of subdivisions strung together by strip malls and King Soopers supermarkets.

It was west on 470; north on Wadsworth; east on Coal Mine Avenue; north on Pierce Street, and—boom—there it was, on the left.

I immediately recognized the curved two-story glass windows of the high school's cafeteria and library. Rachel Scott and Danny Rohrbough died outside those windows.

I had studied the maps. I knew which door the killers entered, which exits various groups of students used to escape, which window a wounded student named Patrick Ireland hauled himself through and into the waiting arms of SWAT personnel. I knew where to look—though it was a bit of a trick doing so at forty miles per hour going north on Pierce Street. Barricades prevented me from turning into the school parking lot. I could barely slow down enough to catch more than a glimpse.

I drove another hundred yards and pulled into Clement Park, which shares the school's northern perimeter. Entering the park, I saw a walkway that went toward the school, so I was optimistic that I might find a way to get a closer look. The park was abuzz with people, some wandering around, nosing toward the school. Others were oblivious to its haunting presence, tossing Frisbees or lobbing tennis balls. I drove around the outer boundary of the park to get a feel for it.

It's huge. The driveway meandered to the north—parallel to Pierce Street—then turned west, winding around to become parallel to Bowles Avenue. It led me to what, I concluded, had to be Rebel Hill, where the fifteen memorial crosses (quickly reduced to thirteen) had been placed shortly after the shootings. I parked and made my way to the hill—or hills, actually. There are two: a smaller one—more like a berm—to the left of a steeper, more commanding one. A well-worn path connected the two. It was quite a hike from the parking lot, across a lawn, and up the incline to the top of the berm. I thought of Greg Zanis, the carpenter from Illinois, lugging those crosses all that way. The ground was dry; it crackled under my feet. It couldn't have been easy digging holes for crosses in that hard earth.

Three teenage girls were sitting at the pinnacle of the larger hill. Their hands were clenched and their eyes squeezed shut as they bowed their heads in prayer. "Father God, you hear their breaking hearts," one said. "You hear them mourning." Not wanting to give the appearance of being a shameless media person and disturb them, I stepped away. Still, when they finished I was tempted to ask if they were "from around here." I thought they'd be excellent candidates for providing primary-source material.

I had worked the reported events of April 20 over and over in my mind. At 11:17 A.M. that day—Adolph Hitler's birthday—Eric Harris and Dylan Klebold removed duffel bags from their cars and pulled their weapons from the bags. They sauntered up the steps outside the cafeteria, and at 11:19 A.M., started shooting. They shot Mark Taylor, Rachel Scott, Richard Castaldo, and Anne Marie Hochhalter. They walked down the steps and shot Danny Rohrbough, Sean Graves, and Lance Kirkland. They went back to where Rachel lay on the ground crying and shot her through the head. Entering the school by the door outside those steps, they made their way to the second level, shooting as they went. By then all manner of alarms and sprinklers had engaged. Harris and Klebold encountered business teacher Dave Sanders and shot him in the back. They went into the library, shooting people by the computer desks first, then moving to the windows and shooting the people there. Next they moved to the desks nearest the library entrance and shot the people in that section. Then they went to the middle section and shot several before they walked out. They went down to the cafeteria, tossed some pipe bombs, and tried to detonate the one huge bomb they had planted by shooting at it. The rampage ended about forty minutes after it had begun when the killers returned to the library, aimed their guns at their own heads, and fell dead next to their peers.

I had prepared a file for each of the murdered victims; I knew them by name. Cassie Bernall, seventeen, had moved to the school the year before when she was a sophomore, loved Shakespeare, and wore Doc Martens. Steven Curnow, fifteen, loved soccer, which was why his favorite color was green—the color of the soccer field. Corey DePooter, seventeen, gave his best friend's little sister a yellow tulip for her birthday. Kelly Fleming, sixteen, wrote poetry that reflected searching themes. Matt Kechter, sixteen, wore number seventy on the Rebels' football team and played varsity his sophomore year. Daniel Mauser, fifteen, was fascinated by black holes and found loopholes in the anti-handgun Brady Bill. Danny Rohrbough, fifteen, worked in his dad's electronics shop. Dave Sanders, forty-seven, had coached the girls basketball team to a winning season after a twelve-year streak of losses. Rachel Scott, seventeen, liked goofy hats. Isaiah Shoels, eighteen, had undergone two heart surgeries as a child. John Tomlin, sixteen, preferred Chevy trucks over Ford, and Lauren Townsend, eighteen, an artist, had drawn a sketch for her own wedding dress. Kyle Velasquez, fifteen, a special-needs student with a kind heart, was known as "the gentle giant."

I had files for Eric Harris and Dylan Klebold, too. Whatever had possessed them on April 20 to become "killing machines," as one journalist put it, I wanted to keep in the forefront of my mind that they had names, they slept in beds (which, like those of most teenagers, often may have been left unmade), collected baseball cards, and may have had a tube of Clearasil on their bathroom shelves. Eric liked pepperoni and green peppers on his pizza and rolled his eyes at stupid questions; Dylan hung posters of baseball greats Roger Clemens and Lou Gehrig in his bedroom and drank Dr Pepper.

I sympathized with the parents of these boys and the desperation they must have felt upon learning their sons had perpetrated this horror. There was a season in my own sojourn as a mother of teenage sons when I had come to the wrenching conclusion that I hadn't a clue about how to influence their choices. I once saw Elton John's mother in a television interview recalling the earlier days in her son's life when he was engaged in all sorts

17

of destructive behavior. The interviewer asked, "Did you know he was doing all this?" Elton John's mother answered, "Yes, but what could I do?"

I understood exactly how she felt. Elton John's mother and I carried the same sense of helplessness in our mothers' hearts when our sons made choices we could not condone or control. What can a mother do? Chain them to their beds? And since Eric and Dylan had taken their own lives as the final expression of their rage, no more prayers could be uttered for them by their mothers. Eternity came upon those boys before the smoke had cleared.

As I stood atop dusty Rebel Hill, I tried to imagine what it must have looked like before the grieving community made it a pilgrimage site. I was told that the ground used to be green. The throngs of people walking up to view the crosses wore away all the vegetation. Looking out over the school from that vantage point, the scene seemed innocuous enough. The athletic fields were in full view and lent an air of normalcy to the picture. The damage to the library windows wasn't visible. I could see more sky than anything; it was sapphire blue with a lone dark cloud that hung over the valley. Rays of sun sliced through a small crack in the cloud, as though trying to carve its way out. Two monarch butterflies frolicked at my feet, flitting, dive-bombing, retreating, and returning.

I decided not to speak to the girls who had been praying. I sensed from the beginning that you don't just go up to people and start talking about this. I made my way back down the hill to the baseball diamond directly behind the school and sat in the bleachers for a few minutes. Bear Creek junior baseball was in progress. The seats were riddled with discarded Coke and Country Time lemonade cans and Big Gulp plastic cups. Moms chatted in twos and threes, some rocking babies in strollers. Dads sat on the edge of their seats, leaning, cupping their hands over their mouths to yell instructions to their kids in the field. "Choke up on the bat." "Keep your eye on it." Nearby, superhero wannabes rolled down the grassy hills and took flight off retaining walls. It was a good day for baseball.

I made my way closer to the school. It was "two serving five" as I walked passed the volleyball pit and someone on the tennis court had just made an "incredible" serve. I could tell by the grunting and heaving coming from a pick-up basketball game that somebody would be downing ibuprofen before the day was through.

I got as close as I could without entering school property and sat down at a picnic table. Birds in the tree above me were in a singing frenzy. Nature seemed unusually animated. The air was fresh; the grass was dry; clouds hung gracefully over the Rockies. Everything seemed as it should be in this perfect world. Yet, not a hundred feet away, a police officer sat in a cruiser in the school parking lot, poised to turn away gawkers and trespassers. People like me. I had heard locals complain that tourists were making Columbine one of their vacation stops, just like Rocky Mountain National Park or the Chatfield Arboretum. They were indignant, and I could understand it. But I saw us more as pilgrims wandering these grounds, trying to come to terms with what had happened here.

The property line was only feet away. I pondered crossing it. I could see a memorial for the victims over there under a tree. Thirteen small American flags planted in a circle around the tree's trunk and lots of ribbons—some yellow, others silver and blue, the school colors. Evidently people had entered school property to leave dried flowers, cards, notes, and photographs there. I decided to break the boundary, too.

I walked through a small opening in the barricade. The earth did not quake under my feet. It didn't open up to swallow me. Columbine High School seemed no different from the one I had attended twenty-five years earlier, and was no different from the school my sons attend now. Of the nearly two thousand students enrolled at Columbine, about sixty qualified for federally subsidized school lunches. Ninety percent were white. The school had parking spaces for juniors and seniors, some of whose parents had probably bought them cars, and it no doubt sponsored parent curriculum nights, homecoming dances, and Spanish club. The Columbine Rebels brought home their share of state championship trophies. It was, in every way, a typical suburban high school.

Except that on April 20, 1999, the minions of hell had burst out of their confines and temporarily planted a flag on these grounds.

"You're not supposed to be on school property," the woman in the police cruiser said, leaning out her window.

"Could I leave a note at the memorial?"

"It's not a memorial. But go ahead, and then please leave."

I scribbled a note. I wasn't sure what to say or who would read it. The other notes were addressed to the families of the murdered, though I doubted they ever saw them. I wrote: "To the families: Thank you for your strength and faith that has ignited the hearts of a nation"—or something like that. I tucked the note under a sprig of dried flowers and turned back.

King Soopers advertised double coupons that day. I decided to pick up a few groceries before going back to the hotel. Wandering the aisles of the grocery store, I was assaulted at every turn with reminders of my sons. I couldn't help thinking about them and how I would feel if this had happened at their high school and if one of them had been represented by a memorial flag. They prefer Gatorade Frost Glacier Freeze over Cherry

Rush and could down an entire package of Double Stuf Oreos in one sitting. They had recently taken to drinking Lipton Brisk; I picked up a twenty-four-pack each week. Klondike Bars are better than Ice Pops. I couldn't fathom how the families who had lost kids in Columbine that day could ever reach the point where double coupons meant something to them again. I could barely get past the sport-drink section without collapsing into tears, thinking of their losses. There wasn't a corner of that store that didn't derive its significance for me from the primary mission of my life: keeping my boys fed.

I wanted to ask the man mulling over the cantaloupe, *What do you think about the school down the road having temporarily become the epicenter of evil?* There was a mother buying her overweight daughter chocolate milk. *Did you think it possible that kids could get massacred in the school library?*

The checkout girl asked me if I had my Soopers card for special discounts, and I told her that I wasn't from around here. I wondered if she suspected I was a journalist. Her graciousness indicated that she didn't.

"Do you want to use mine?" she asked. She saved me thirty-eight cents by digging out her Soopers card and passing it over the electronic cash register.

"Where are you from?" she asked.

"The Chicago area," I said. *We haven't had school shootings in my town.* Before this happened, they hadn't had school shootings in Littleton, either.

If the locals were tired of outsiders horning in and sniffing around for information, for "primary source material," they didn't show it. The people here seemed to go along as though things were normal, as though the events at Columbine High School, just down the street from King Soopers and right next to the park, were all a bad dream that hadn't really happened. What else could they do? It wouldn't help anything to declare a moratorium on pick-up basketball games or do away with double coupons.

Chapter 2

One More Bus

The Day Their Children Didn't Come Home

THE DAY OF APRIL 20, 1999, started fairly typically for John and Doreen Tomlin. The exception was that they hadn't had their morning devotions, when they read short passages from the writings of the eighteenth-century preacher Charles Spurgeon. Their oldest son—also named John—headed off to school in his trademark brown Chevy truck, chucking his Bible onto the dashboard. Pat and Ashley, John's younger brother and sister, eased into the day at home, the privilege of being home-schooled.

The Tomlins had moved to Colorado from Wisconsin when their son John was twelve. The adjust-ment had been hard on him. In the small-town setting in Wisconsin, John had excelled in soccer and baseball leagues. But being trans-planted into a context where the public schools had as many students as their hometown had citizens, he had retreated inside himself and struggled with friendships and with his identity. There were even signs that John was losing a grip on his strong Christian upbringing. During a summer vacation back in Wisconsin in July 1998, kids in his old neighborhood had heard him using curse words, which shocked them—and his parents, who threat-ened to postpone his driver's test if he didn't clean up his act. He was an example for these young impressionable kids who had always looked up to him, they told him.

Later that same summer, in August 1998, the Tomlins went to Juarez, Mexico, to work on a mission project building a home for a poor family. The trip had a transforming effect on the young John.

"In September, after the missions trip, a boy from work, a pastor's son, invited John to go to his youth group," Doreen said. "About a month later the youth pastor came over here with some kids from the youth group and said, 'I'd like you to know that John recommitted his life to Christ and that he really wants to live for the Lord.'"

A month before he turned sixteen, John purchased his beloved Chevy truck. He had worked at a local nursery since he was fourteen to save money to buy a truck by the time he got his license. He had put away six thousand dollars. The truck cost him three thousand dollars.

"He started to come alive again," Doreen said. "He had been so lonely and was so happy now. He got into weight lifting at school. He was asking kids at work to go to the youth group." And, most notably, he had become attached to a young woman he had met through his youth group, Michelle Oetter, who attended a different high school. She was near him in age but was two grades ahead of him. She became his best friend, as well as his girlfriend, and John quickly bounced back to life. He was the same happy kid he had been in Wisconsin. He and Michelle talked on the phone late into the night, even on school nights (their parents never knew), and frequently ended their conversations by praying together. On the day before John died, he bought Michelle barbecue sunflower seeds. "He said he had been thinking about me and remembered that barbecue was my favorite," she said.[1]

A World Torn Apart

By the middle of the day on April 20 the Tomlins' world would begin to unravel. Their youngest son Pat was watching television in the late morning when the news flashed the headline that there was trouble at Columbine, where John was a sophomore. The newscasters said they thought it was a bomb scare.

"The first thing I did was call my sister [in Wisconsin] and ask her to start praying," said Doreen. "I started getting kind of frantic. I didn't have a lot of composure. Within fifteen minutes the story kept getting worse."

Her friend, Debbie Oetter (Michelle's mother), immediately called the Tomlins. She said, "Doreen, are you there by yourself? Have you heard anything from John?"

Doreen said, "No, we haven't." By this point, Doreen was crying.

Her friend said, "Do you want me to come over?"

"Would you come?"

Meanwhile, Doreen had called her sister three times within a half-hour period.

Parents were told to go to Leawood Elementary School, near the high school, to get word of the whereabouts of their children. Officials posted lists of students who had been accounted for, and students who had escaped were arriving by bus. Doreen's husband, John, returned home from work, and he and Doreen proceeded to Leawood.

"That was difficult in itself," Doreen said, "because you were stuck in traffic, there were sirens going off and helicopters and ambulances. It didn't seem real.

"There was one mother in particular, I remember, I kept asking, 'Did you hear anything about your son?' She doesn't remember me asking her that. We found out later her son died.

"We borrowed someone's cell phone, and we'd call to see if John was home. Cell phones were going off constantly.

"Kids were jumping out of windows of the school. They would get into buses and then they'd bring the buses to Leawood and they would pass on a stage. At the beginning, we were looking for John and he was just never showing up. There were a number of buses. I was getting envious of parents who were finding their kids and screaming out their kids' names. I thought, *If only I could cry out John's name.* But he was never going across the stage.

"I remember sitting in the back of the room. There were still buses of kids going across the stage. I didn't get up anymore. I had no enthusiasm to jump up and look for him. I thought, *Why aren't you getting up and looking? All these other parents are pinned to the stage and you're just sitting here not looking for him.* I think the Lord was already settling it in my heart that John was probably dead."

"You don't want to jump to any conclusions," her husband said. "You don't want to be upset or go off without knowing. So, as every bus arrived, you're hoping that your kid is on the bus. When the buses stopped, when there were no more buses, things didn't look good at that point. I said, 'Doreen, if they ask us to get up and go into a different room, it's not a good sign.' Then they asked us to get up and go in a different room. I knew it then."

Doreen said she will always remember the look on John's face. "It was getting late, about 8:00 P.M. For some reason they had said there was another bus."

"I don't know why they did that," John said, "because there was no other bus."

"There was never another bus," Doreen said. "We were clinging to that hope that one more bus would be there."

"Once we came out of that room and went back to the chairs, they had us fill out the description of our kids," John said.

"Then one mother stood up and said, 'Where is that other bus?'" recalled Doreen. "There never was another bus. It was like a false hope they gave you. When the sheriff came around at our chairs, he said most of the kids that are dead are in the library. I knew it was John. John always went to the library, it never failed. That's where he did his homework. I felt like I was going to pass out. I felt sick.

"I said, 'I've got to go home. I have to be with my other children.' When I came home, his youth pastor and kids from the youth group were there. I said, 'I do believe John's dead.'

"I went up to the shower and prayed with every part of my being. I said, 'Lord, thank you for the sixteen years I've had with John. Let this glorify your name. Let his death not be in vain. Let us not become bitter. Fill us with your Holy Spirit. Let it not ruin our marriage.' I prayed with every part of me that could call out to him. I pictured a fountain when I prayed, 'Fill us with your Holy Spirit.' It was gushing with water, gushing and gushing.

"I believe the Lord has answered those prayers. We have not become bitter. Our marriage is fine. He has revealed himself over and over again through this. I consider us blessed, really, to be used by God in this way. He is walking us through day by day. But right now I do feel like pain is our companion."

The Epicenter of Evil

Other than the cryptic message, "Today is not going to be a good day," that showed up on TV monitors at the school, April 20 at Columbine High School started like any other day. (Those words had been typed in by Eric Harris and Dylan Klebold, who had worked on the school's TV broadcast staff.)

Zach Johnston, a Columbine junior, had awakened with a cold and a sore throat. He almost stayed home. But, by the time he realized how lousy he felt, a friend was already on the way to pick him up, and he didn't want to be an inconvenience. Zach later wrote a lengthy Internet posting that described the events of that day as they unfolded from his vantage point.[2]

"Since April 20 is 4/20 day," he wrote, "it was a day that many students were supposed to love and enjoy for various reasons. Heh." The day was known by some as "weed-smoking day" since 4/20 is the police code designating a drug bust involving marijuana. And since that was the theme of the day for some, they greeted Zach accordingly: "Happy 4/20, Zach. It's 4/20 and I have an important date with You-Know-Who."

The day was just like any other for Zach. He watched "Cyrano DeBergerac" in his World Studies class and did all right on a math test. "After math," he wrote, "I rushed to my locker to meet a friend so we could go out for lunch. As we were driving out of the parking lot to go to lunch, I saw Dylan and his old 325i [BMW]. He was entering the school like nothing was going to happen and looked at me with no emotion."

When Zach attempted to return to school after lunch, he and his friend were unable to get anywhere near it. They saw a police cruiser and cargo van blockading Pierce Street. They thought it was because of a car accident. When they turned around and tried to take a "stealth" route Zach knew about, they were passed by a white Cherokee filled with students waving and honking at them.

"Crap, they wanna beat me up," was Zach's immediate reaction.

He quickly realized they were waving and honking at every car they passed, which allayed his fears about being beat up. Still unable to access any street connecting to the school, Zach and his friend finally realized something was very wrong. Waiting in a crowded intersection, Zach saw "a horde of my fellow students running toward us. I yelled at a girl I knew and asked her what happened. She said, 'Some guys in black charged into school and just shot everyone!'

"I saw hundreds of parents running every which way trying to find their sons and daughters. It was a terribly disturbing sight. I remember specifically one little girl from my choir class crying about how she saw her friend get shot."

Zach decided to return home to call his mother.

"I live about a mile from the school and counted thirty-five police cars passing us as we drove. Ambulances and police cars [were] barging over medians and motorcycle cops [were] weaving through opposite traffic almost killing themselves. It's actually quite amazing that police units can do such wide fishtails and keep control.

"I live on top of a huge hill overlooking the entire Denver metro area and could see the school at a distance," he continued. "I counted five helicopters and two planes circling the premises. I could see Clement Park, where tons of parents desperately searched to find their children. The southwest side of the school is the part that I could view. The library and the cafeteria are both on this side. Apparently, this is where all the action was taking place. The entire southwest side of the school is a huge glass window. Several windows were shattered.

"While I watched [television] and wondered for myself what was happening, I knew in my heart who was responsible for this massacre."

Zach then described in his posting an encounter he had witnessed a month earlier between a friend and Eric Harris: "After lunch we had the same World History class so [this friend and I] would walk together. We would often pass these two kids who wore trench coats. Everyone referred to them as the 'trench coat mafia.' My friend referred to them as 'the Rammstein boyz.' [Rammstein is a German industrial band.]

"One day my friend snarled a remark about Rammstein under his breath as we passed these two guys. The short one, who was named Eric Harris, confronted my friend about it. He said, 'Every day you pass me and make fun of me saying Rammstein sucks. Why do you do this crap, a———hole What did I do to you?'

"My friend replied, 'Oh man, you're so cool. You're my idol!'

"Then Eric's friend Dylan approached us seeming to back up his friend. I really didn't want to get involved in a fight even though I knew these guys wouldn't stand a chance.

"Eric was a short clean-cut looking kid and Dylan was a very tall skinny guy with messed up hair. He always wore a trench coat, hat and dark sunglasses. The bell rang and we went into class. That was the end of the confrontation."

Eric and Dylan didn't go to school on Tuesday, April 20, 1999. According to the official report, Harris's day planner included the following sequence of events:

5:00 Get up
6:00 Meet at KS
7:00 Go to Reb's house
7:15 he leaves to fill propane
I leave to fill gas
8:30 Meet back at his house
9:00 made d. bag set up car
9:30 practice gearups

Chill
10:30 set up 4 things
11:00 go to school
11:10 set up duffel bags
11:12 wait near cars, gear up
11:16 HAHAHA[3]

Zach continued: "They entered the school parking lot at 11:00—Eric in his black Prelude and Dylan in his black BMW325 that the media is trying to say makes him a rich, privileged kid. It's a crappy early eighties one. And if you know what I mean about early Beemers, they do suck."

Brooks Brown, a longtime friend of Klebold and an on-again-off-again friend of Harris, had stepped into the school parking lot for a cigarette. He said something to Eric about missing an important test that morning. "It doesn't matter anymore," Harris replied. "Brooks, I like you. Get out of here. Go home."

Once they were "suited up" with ammunition belts and black trench coats, they walked over toward the cafeteria entrance and opened fire. Details as to the exact sequence are difficult to pin down because every eyewitness has a different description about how it went down. Some witnesses say they saw one of them toss a pipe bomb onto the school roof and felt the ground shake when it detonated. Rachel Scott was hit by gunfire several times. According to Rachel's sister, Dana, witnesses told the family: "Rachel was sitting outside the cafeteria and the gunmen came up the stairs. They opened fire on the group of students that was sitting there. Richard Castaldo was hit—he played dead—and Rachel was hit. She fell." Castaldo had been hit with two 9 mm bullets in his left arm, one in the right arm, and three through the chest, piercing his lungs, kidney, and vertebrae. He remained conscious, but pretended to be dead. He could hear Rachel crying.

Mark Taylor, a student who had transferred to Columbine only three weeks earlier, was talking to some Mormon classmates about his Christian faith when a bullet seared his leg. He dropped and tried to hide in the grass. One of the gunmen came after him and pumped four more bullets into him, collapsing a lung and missing his aorta by a centimeter. He lay motionless, pretending to be dead. Students called to him, but he didn't answer for fear that he would be shot again. Anne Marie Hochhalter, who was eating lunch with some friends outside, was hit in the chest. She fell paralyzed.[4]

Rachel Scott had been hit in the leg, arm, and chest and lay on the ground crying. "She was there for a little while," said Dana, "because after

27

that they went back down the stairs and they shot Daniel Rohrbough. He was killed and lying on the sidewalk."

Dan Rohrbough, a freshman, had just walked outside with his friends Sean Graves and Lance Kirkland. Dan was hit in the back and fell dead into Lance's arms. Lance was then hit in the left foot, right leg, and left knee. A final shot to the chest felled him.

Graves started to run, but was hit in the back. He screamed that his legs didn't work. In the meantime, Kirkland sensed someone nearby and cried for help.

"Sure, I'll help you," the person said. Then that person, Dylan Klebold, aimed his TEC-DC9 semiautomatic handgun at Kirkland's face and pulled the trigger.[5]

"They came back up to where Rachel was crying," said Dana Scott. And lifting her head by her ponytail, "one of them confronted her with the question, 'Do you believe in God?' She said 'Yes' and he took a gun to her temple and killed her. She was shot three times at first, in the leg, arm, and side, and then she was killed after that question."

Confusion and Terror

The early accounts wrongly stated that the gunmen then entered the cafeteria. That was the impression at the time because, when the shooting began, the cafeteria was filled with students who heard the gunfire and soon fled. Kevin Parker, a volunteer worker at the school, was supposed to meet a student at 11:15 at the trophy case. When the student didn't show, Kevin decided to go to the cafeteria.

"I walked down there at about 11:17 and was walking along the side where all the food is sold, toward the window. A freshman saw me and said, 'Hey Parker, come over here.' That withdrew me from that area where the gunmen started shooting. I was with him for about thirty seconds when all of a sudden everything started to go down. Every time I look at this freshman I know he took me out of the path of bullets."

The gunmen's intention was to ambush the cafeteria, without going in, by detonating bombs they had planted. "They had a huge bomb and then a bunch minibombs that were intended to disgorge the west wing of the cafeteria," said Parker. "When the bombs didn't detonate, that's when they started to shoot. None of the main bombs went off. The ones going off in the cafeteria were hand-thrown. Mr. Sanders and a janitor were running around, yelling, 'Get down!' I think, superficially, we thought that it wasn't a big deal."

Many, in the earliest flourishes of the shooting, presumed the popping noise was from construction, firecrackers, paint-ball guns, or—at worst—one troubled kid who might have brought a gun onto school grounds.

Parker continued, "There are five hundred kids lying on the cold cement floor of the cafeteria. There was two to four minutes of silence at that point. We heard gun shots. They were shooting kids outside. That had to have been Danny and Rachel. And then bombs started to go off. There was some sort of panic reaction and all of a sudden students fled up the stairs and took a quick right. But it would have been more intelligent to take a left—that would have taken us by the library where there was an exit. We went through the entire length of the school and ran out some doors. There were five hundred kids that ran across Pierce Street. Traffic stopped dead away."

Dave Sanders, the business teacher who had warned students in the cafeteria to get under the tables, had moved into the hallways and upstairs to shepherd more students out. The gunmen were tossing bombs into the air and shooting at the bombs. Two janitors found refuge in a walk-in refrigerator while twenty students, cafeteria workers, and teachers hid in the pantry.

At some point Eric Harris went back outside, either to reload or to unjam his rifle. Neil Gardner, a Jefferson County sheriff's deputy and school resource officer, exchanged fire with Harris and retreated to Gardner's Chevy Blazer. Harris returned fire and went back into the school.

By this point the school's emergency strobe lights were pulsating and the fire alarm was blaring. Smoke-filled hallways made it difficult to see and a haze of gunpowder and sulfur burned throats and eyes. Bullets ricocheted off lockers as the gunmen moved up the stairs.

Kevin Parker and the other students who fled the cafeteria had made it across Pierce Street to Leawood Park. "For the next ten minutes I was walking around looking, trying to identify kids I knew. Then there was gunfire exchanged outside the school and that precipitated another panic reaction. All of us ran down streets and kids and were piling into houses. At one of the first houses there must have been a hundred-fifty or two hundred kids piled into this house. I saw kids run up to houses and pull doorknobs.

"We were in that house probably for an hour and then reports came on that said people were gathering at the Leawood Elementary School. So I went to Leawood, about two blocks from Columbine."

Shirley Hickman taught Spanish at Columbine and was always amazed when people asked if she was there during the shooting. "Do you think we have a big absentee problem?" she was tempted to respond.

29

"It was lunchtime and my entire fifth-hour class was at lunch," she recalled. There were five of us teachers in the department office, which is close to the cafeteria. Our one male teacher—it is a nine-person department with eight women and one man—had gone to get his lunch in the cafeteria right down the hall. And he came in and said, 'Quick, get on the phone! There are kids with guns.' This is the last place I would have thought there would be guns. I had no discipline problems for a whole year. This was the easiest school I ever taught in.

"One of the teachers said, 'Brandon, quit joking around.'

"He said, 'I'm serious. There really are kids with guns.'

"I got the phone and tried to dial 911 but couldn't get out," Hickman said. "So I tried calling the main office to let them know that there were kids with guns. A student answered the phone. I didn't want to scare the student, which, in retrospect, was kind of silly, so I said that I wanted to speak to an adult. I was on hold and then the shooting started. That was the end of the phone call.

"Under a desk, I tried to call 911 again. Then it dawned on me that where I was hiding I was going to get a bullet in my back if they came along there shooting. So I moved into the closet where the other teachers and four students were hiding.

"The bombs that went off were knocking books off the shelves on the wall. The fire alarm was going this whole time."

In the hallway near the library entrance, the gunmen encountered Dave Sanders who had continued to direct students to safety. One of the gunmen shot him twice in the back. Sanders fell into some lockers, then hit the ground. Bleeding profusely from the chest and coughing up blood, he stumbled into a nearby science room, still directing students away from harm. He collapsed onto a desk, knocking out some teeth.

Aaron Hancey had been hiding in a corner of the science lab down the hall when a teacher burst in to ask if anyone knew first aid. Hancey, a seasoned Boy Scout, stepped forward and the two of them sprinted to the science room where Sanders was sprawled on the floor bleeding.

Hancey checked Sanders's vitals. The teacher was still warm and he was breathing more or less normally. Hancey and other students tore off their shirts and rolled some into a ball to support Sanders's head. They used others as compresses in an attempt to stop the bleeding. They wrapped Sanders in blankets to keep him warm.

Hancey pulled Sanders's wallet from his pocket and found family photos. To keep him from going into shock, he barraged the teacher with questions.

"Is this your wife?" Hancey asked.

"Yes."

"What's your wife's name?"

"Linda."

"What is your name? What do you teach? Are you the basketball coach?"

Hancey and a classmate, Kevin Starkey, alternated applying pressure to Sanders's wounds. They rolled him from side to side to keep him off his back so he wouldn't choke on his blood.

"I can't breathe. I need help. I need to get out of here," Sanders told them in snatches.

"Help is on the way," said Hancey. Some of the students made a sign with a dry-erase board and put it in the window for the SWAT team to see. It read: "1 bleeding to death."

Now and then Dave Sanders would cough and spit blood, clearing his lungs. But time passed and no one came to help. He was turning ashen and his breathing became more labored. "I'm not going to make it." He started to drift off. "Tell my girls I love them."[6]

Conflicting Memories

What happened in the school library once the killers entered has been debated. The library survivors, in the midst of the trauma and chaos, saw the events unfold from differing vantage points and looked back later with differing levels of recall. The scenario as I have reconstructed it here is derived primarily from testimonies of some who were present during the shooting. I have supplemented them with reports that came out in other publications soon after the events.

Joshua Lapp, a sophomore, was in the library during fifth period lunch. "I walked through the commons and then went upstairs to the library, just like every day. My friends and I would meet in the library. Sometimes we'd do homework and sometimes we'd just sit there and talk and make the librarians mad. Nobody was there that I usually sit with, so I sat in front so that everybody could see me. Then everybody showed up—Brittany, Aaron (my best friend), Byron, Craig Scott, Isaiah Shoels.

"I was doing my math homework when Isaiah showed up. He was telling a joke like he usually does. He didn't like to see anybody down or not having fun, so he liked to tell jokes a lot. He would joke around and act like, you know, like he's got all the women. He would loosen everybody up.

31

"He was sitting there probably about five minutes and then got up to go see another friend in the section by the windows. So it was just us five—Byron, Aaron, Brittany, Craig and I. Then Mrs. Nielson ran in and told us to get under the desks, that there were kids with guns."

Kacey Ruegsegger, a sophomore, always went home for lunch with her best friend. But her friend wasn't at school that day, so Kacey decided to spend her lunch period in the library.

"I was sitting reading a magazine by myself when I thought I heard pops outside. It ran through my mind, *What if that's a gun?* But nobody else was reacting, so I went on reading. Then Mrs. Nielson came in."

The teacher on hall duty near the library, Patti Nielson, had been hit in the shoulder before she ran into the library. Joshua recalled: "I heard popping outside, just a rat-tat-tat-tat. I thought it was construction because they are always doing something at the school. The librarian thought it was something for RNN [Rebel News Network, the school's announcement system]. They do little skits every once in a while. A computer technician, Mr. Long, had been in the library looking at one of the computers. [Hearing the gunshots], the librarian asked him, 'What is this?' He went and looked and said, 'This is the real thing.' Mrs. Nielson was already yelling for people to get under the tables when Mr. Long started to run out and told everyone to get out of the library. But, by then, everybody was already underneath their desks and they didn't want to get up. He and, like, four or five kids got out.

"Aaron and I started to walk toward the entrance. We got five feet away from the desks and heard the shooting. Aaron and I are hunters, so we knew that it was gunshots. We turned to each other with stunned looks. He and Byron got up and ran towards the back. Craig went with Isaiah and Brittany was already underneath the table. I hopped underneath the table with Brittany so she wouldn't be alone."

At 11:25 A.M. Patti Nielson dialed 911 on her cell phone: "I've got every student in this library on the floor—*You guys just stay on the floor!* [shots were heard]—My God, the gun is right outside the door. I don't think I'm going to go out there. We're not going to go to the door. I've got kids on the floor. I got all of the kids in the library on the floor."

Then Harris and Klebold walked in.

"Where we were sitting we could see out the main entrance," said Josh. "We could see when they walked in. I saw what they were wearing. When they got close enough to the door, you could hear it, you could smell the gunpowder; I saw the flash of a gun. They had to be using high-powered ammunition if you could see the flash.

"Then I realized, when they walked in, that it wasn't a skit.

"They went behind the librarian's desk and kept shooting back there," he said. "Then they moved in front of the librarian's desk, which was right in front of us. I probably could have reached out and touched their legs if I had wanted to, which, obviously, I didn't. That's when they said, 'All the jocks stand up!'

"I didn't hear anybody say, 'Well, I'm a jock,' or anything like that. Nobody stood up. They went on and said, 'If you're wearing a hat or if you have a sports emblem on your shirt, you're dead.' That Saturday I got my hair cut, otherwise I would have been wearing my hat.

"Evan Todd was behind the librarian's desk when they came in," said Josh. "And—I can't remember for sure—they said, 'Hey look, there's that big fat jock.' He said, 'No, I'm not jock. I'm not a jock. Don't kill me. I'm not a jock.'

"They shot twice behind the librarian's desk. They both had trench coats on. When they came up to our section, Dylan was the only one that had his trench coat on. Eric had a white T-shirt on with black pants. He must've taken his trench coat off somewhere.

"Eric lives just a half a block away. I'd go pick up Aaron—he lives right down there by Eric—and I'd see him drive by and I'd kinda wave and he'd nod his head. And Dylan I knew because he always wore the same hat. He had it on backwards that day. It had a big B on it."

Few Places to Hide

Kacey Ruegsegger had gone under a computer table that formed a cubicle. "I pulled a chair in front and was down on my knees and one shoulder. There was boy named Steven Curnow in the cubicle next to me and he died. On the other side of me was a girl named Amanda. She didn't get shot.

"So everybody got under tables. I got under mine and pulled the chair in and started praying," Kacey said. "They walked in real quick after Mrs. Nielson came in. They shot as they came in.

"They made their way down toward the windows. The first one they shot was Kyle [Valasquez, who was also at a computer desk]. They were laughing and saying how much fun it was and, 'We're going to blow up this library' and 'Today is your day to die.'

"One of them dropped his trench coat [in front of me] and set his gun on a table. The next thing I remember happening was he bent down right next to the chair I had been sitting in and I saw him shoot Steven. I turned around and plugged my ears and shrugged my shoulders. I didn't want to watch that or hear it happen. I was the next one shot.

"After I was shot I made a moaning noise. He told me to quit my b—ing. I thought I was going to get shot again, so I leaned over the cubicle pretending to be dead. After that, I don't know what happened, except for hearing big booms and pops and the comments made toward Isaiah Shoels. But I'm not sure when it happened."

Josh Lapp recalled the shooters walking into the section by the windows first. "There were a few times girls would ask, 'What are you doing? Why are you doing this?' They answered, 'We've always wanted to do this. This is payback. We've dreamed of doing this for four years. This is what you deserve.'

"I think they thought they had the library surrounded good enough that they could have killed everybody in there. They very well could have.

"When they walked over by the windows must have been when they got everybody under the computer desks. They got the people over by the computer desks, then the people in that section by the windows, then the section by the hallway, and then Daniel Mauser.

"The only time that I can remember they talked to each other was when one would say, 'Give me a clip,' or 'I'm out,'" Josh said. "And they would say things to people before they would shoot them, like what they did with Cassie [Bernall].

"They walked up to her and said, 'Do you believe in God?' There was a pause and she said, 'Yes.' She didn't sound timid at all. It was a firm response. She said, 'Yes.' They said, 'Why?' and then they shot her.

"You could hear the littlest noise because it was dead silence. The only thing that broke the silence were the bombs and the gunshots and them talking and taunting people, like what they did to Isaiah before they killed him. One of them said, 'Hey look, there's that little n——.' I knew it was Isaiah because he's short. They shot three times. The other one said, 'Is he dead?' There was a pause and he said, 'Yeah, he's dead.' After they shot him they said, 'Man, I didn't know black brains could fly that far.' I mean, they had fun with it."

Matt Kechter, a sophomore, and Craig Scott, Rachel's brother, also a sophomore, were under the same table as Isaiah. Matt fell dead in a flurry of shooting, while Craig, unhurt but covered in his friends' blood, pretended to be dead.

"Who's ready to die next?" one of the shooters asked.

Seth Houy was under a table with his sister, Sarah, and a friend, Crystal Woodham. He covered their bodies with his. "I told them, 'I don't know what's going on but just start praying.' We decided that whatever's gonna happen, the only way we're gonna get through this is to let God take care of us."

Crystal Woodham said, "We just had to stay calm. That's where our faith came in, just believing that [God] would bring us through. I believe with all my heart that Seth, Sarah, and I were all invisible because they were walking all around us and so many people around us were shot and wounded and even killed."[7]

Dan Steepleton, Makai Hall, and Patrick Ireland waited in dread as the killers approached. Steepleton had known Klebold over the years and looked directly at him with the hope that he might recall their acquaintance. Klebold raised his gun and fired. Dan and Makai both fell, hit in the legs with buckshot. Makai's right leg was gushing blood, so Patrick Ireland tried to stop the bleeding with his hands. He unwittingly raised his head enough for the gunmen to take aim, and Patrick dropped after being hit twice on the left side of his head.[8]

Harris and Klebold left the section of tables by the windows and went around to the opposite side of the library—the side nearest the hallway and library entrance. Under the table closest to the entrance, Lisa Kreutz, Valeen Schnurr, Jeanna Park, Diwata Perez, and Lauren Townsend—all friends and seniors—huddled in terror.

Josh continued, "As they got close to Val's table, they were shooting, shooting, shooting. I remember hearing, 'Oh my God, oh my God,' and they asked her, 'Do you believe in God?' There was another 'Yes' and then they asked 'Why?' and shot again.[9] She was shot in the side. She survived."

Lauren Townsend didn't. Her best friend, Jessica Holliday, was under another table nearby. Jessica recounted, "In that moment all you can do is pray that they won't shoot you, pray that you won't die. You're not ready to die." She used to sit behind Dylan Klebold in their government class. He would pass papers back to her. They used to talk about homework.[10]

"The only people I know that they talked to who made it out alive were Val Schnurr and Evan Todd," Josh Lapp recalled.

Under Josh's table, "Brittany kept saying, 'Where are the cops? Where are the cops? They should be here by now.' She said that so many times, I figured that I couldn't show fear, because if Brittany saw the fear in my eyes or if she saw that I was getting worse, she would be worse. She was bad enough as it was. The more noise she would make, the better chance that we would get it. So the whole time that she would talk, I would hurry up with an answer as quick as I could to get her quiet. Or I'd tell her to be quiet. I played with her thumbnail the whole time."

By this point the killers had reached the middle section of the library, the last place they went before leaving. Harris said, "Who is under the table? Identify yourself!"

"It's John Savage," he said.

John had been a friend of Klebold at one time. When Klebold heard his name, he went over to the table. "Oh, it's you," he said.

"Hi, Dylan. What are you doing?"

"Killing people."

"Are you going to kill me?"

Klebold hesitated. "Run. Just get out of here."[11]

Josh recalled, "Daniel Mauser's desk was one over and back, which was probably about five to eight feet from where we were. When they started coming up the middle section, Brittany was getting really worried. I got up on my side, lying on my side, trying to block her as much as I could with my shoulder and my back so that they couldn't see her. That way she felt a little more comfortable. I don't know if it worked. All I know is that I kept telling her to be quiet. I was looking over my shoulder the whole time. I wasn't going to let them shoot me without looking me in the eyes. I used to watch, like, *Lethal Weapon*—all those action movies. I remember that they say it's hard to kill somebody if they're looking you in the eyes. I don't know if it's true, but, as far as I was concerned, it was real at the time. So I was making sure that if they were going to come over and shoot us, I was going to look them in the eyes.

"Eric shot Daniel," said Josh. Daniel pushed chairs at his killer to try to stop him and Harris shot him again. "Then," said Josh, "they walked on the outside of Daniel's desk, so they were about two desk lengths away. They both looked at me. I made eye contact with them both. They were straight-faced, like I would look at somebody walking down the street. They didn't act like they had hurt anybody a second ago. They acted like it was normal. And for some reason, they kept walking."

Austin Eubanks was terrorized and gripped the arm of his best friend, Corey DePooter, who calmed him: "Stay tight. The cops will come." Eubanks peeked out from under the table to see one of the gunmen reloading. "I looked right into his eyes," he said. One of them leveled his gun and shot, killing DePooter. Eubanks was left with buckshot in his ankle and hand.[12]

"They said, 'I'm running out of ammunition,' and walked out," said Josh. "The only reason why I think they actually ran out of ammunition is because it was quiet for a little while. Then all of a sudden the shooting started again and we knew they were far enough away."

Craig Scott was playing dead as he lay between his two dead friends. He later said that at the moment the killers left the library, "God told me to get out of there."[13] He got up and started yelling to everyone to come with him. Kacey Ruegsegger had been lying in her blood, playing dead under the computer cubicle. She had been shot at close range with a 12-gauge shotgun, blowing a three-inch hole through her right shoulder. Since she was scrunched with her hands over her ears, the bullet passed through her shoulder and severed an artery in her thumb. Her father, Greg Ruegsegger, said, "She was lying in her blood thinking she was going to bleed to death, but she couldn't go anywhere because they were still shooting."

"They left and went down to the cafeteria," Kacey said, "supposedly to try and set off their big bomb because it hadn't gone off yet. That's when somebody said, 'Let's go,' and everybody started coming out. Craig Scott was running past me and I said, 'Somebody help me. Help me get out.' So Craig came and helped me get out of my cubby. He ran beside me holding my arm to my side. We ran out toward the back door."

"All I remember is Seth Houy peeking his head up," said Josh. "He went back underneath the desk to get the girls he was with. I got up and grabbed Brittany's hand. I remember her saying, 'Don't let go of me.' The last thing I remember before getting to the doorway is Brittany saying, 'Don't let go. Don't let go.' I don't remember how I got around that computer desk. The next thing I remember is I'm standing in the doorway pushing Brittany through and telling everybody 'Hurry, hurry, hurry.' Whoever could get up and run got up and ran. I didn't see any of the helicopters above. I didn't hear anything except them shooting and bombs going off.

"At that time," Josh said, "I thought I was going to have to run forever."

"They're Killing Kids"

Patti Nielson had been hiding under the checkout counter in the library, her 911 call connected and recording the massacre. When the two boys entered, she said, she "felt like we were going to die"[14] and started saying the Lord's Prayer. The dispatcher on the phone line told Nielson to "forget about the Lord's Prayer for the moment and talk." Nielson whispered, "They're in here. They're killing kids. I need to go now."

The 911 recording picked up the next seven and a half minutes of mayhem. Alarms were blaring and bombs were going off. Now and then dispatchers could pick up random words the killers spoke to some of their victims. The recording lasted twenty-six minutes. Nielson could not see anything. But she heard it and recalled, "They were saying the most disgusting and vile things." She said they ordered the jocks to stand up but didn't limit their rage to the athletes. She heard what was said to Isaiah Shoels before they killed him and recalled hearing the killers taunt a boy because he was wearing glasses, calling him "a geek." She heard them call someone else "a pathetic fat boy."

She heard one girl saying, "Oh God, oh God," and then she heard one of the boys say to her, "Do you believe in God?" She heard the girl respond that she did, and then heard a shot. She heard another girl, a different girl, crying "Oh God, oh God," but did not hear any shots after that, so she concluded that the second girl must have survived. "Every time one of them would say something, I'd hear shots and I knew kids were dying."

The gunmen were "reloading and talking about watching each other's back to keep anyone from jumping them," she said, and when a student asked them, "Don't you think you've done enough?" she heard another shot.

"They seemed to be acting out some war game. One second they were mean, the next they were laughing. I thought they were on illegal drugs because you can't believe anyone in their right minds would do this. They were crazed.

"I thought the police would show up at any moment. But they didn't." She heard one of the gunmen say, "Let's get down to the commons," but the other one said, "I have one more thing to do." They walked over to the checkout desk where Nielson was hiding. "He stopped in front of me. His black combat boots, with the pants tucked in, were right by my head. I still don't know if he knew I was there. It was pretty open from that side, but I had no place to run or hide." The gunman took a chair and threw it on top of the desk. Then they left.

When the students who were able fled the library, Nielson stayed under the desk in shock. She never realized that the students had fled. She could hear shots in the distance, so she crawled out from under the desk to find a better place to hide. She remembered seeing two tennis shoes sticking out from under a table. Although two students were still alive, she thought everyone was dead. Students lay lifeless amid blood, bullet shells, and backpacks.

She crawled around the perimeter of the library, spotted a cupboard under a sink, and tucked herself inside. "There were no handles on the inside, so I couldn't shut it all the way. There was a crack of light." She heard shots and explosions of pipe bombs in the distance. She later learned that Harris and Klebold had attempted to detonate two propane tanks they had lashed together and placed in the cafeteria as part of their plan to blow apart the southwest side of the school. They shot from a distance and missed their target, so the tanks never ignited.

Nielson tried in vain to feel around the cupboard for a pencil, wanting to write a note to her husband to tell him how much she loved him. She had considered trying to call him from her phone but feared the killers would return and hear her. She thought about her young daughter Mallory and how Mallory probably wouldn't remember her; she hoped her son Josh would get close to his father and that her daughter Elise would be able to remember some of the times they had spent together.

"I could hear helicopters up above, and I wondered why the SWAT teams weren't there yet. I thought at any time someone would come in and say, 'It's all right to come out.'" She had visions of the gunmen returning and pretending to be the police, saying it was safe to emerge. "I was scared to death. And I was thinking about all those students dead in the library."

Being cramped for three hours in so small a space, her limbs went numb and Nielson was afraid that when the time came for her to make a run for it, her legs would give out. "I thought I would have to spend all night in this cupboard and I was determined not to let it make me go insane."

Brittany Weeden, a freshman, was in the cafeteria hiding under tables when the killers arrived from the library. She and the friends with her had not joined the stampede of students who had escaped when the shooting began. "The janitors told us to stay there so we stayed," she said. "We figured out it was real when they came downstairs and we saw the guns. They came downstairs and were shooting down there. We don't think they saw us. Eric was telling Dylan where to shoot. He was saying, 'Go over there.' It looked like they were trying to find something to shoot. We were praying and that was helping us get through it. But it was like everything was down on us. It was like—should we go? We were trying to go, but we didn't know if we should. It was like we had so many decisions. And then they shot something that started the fire. That's when we ran, because there was enough smoke so they couldn't see us."

The first time Patti Nielson was able to read her watch, it displayed 1:00 P.M. She had heard the gunmen return to the library and had heard some commotion, then some shots. "I didn't hear any conversation, any yelling, just rat-tat-tat."[15]

It was 4:00 P.M. before library aides, who had been hiding in an inner room elsewhere in the library, told Nielson it was safe to come out. SWAT officers pulled her into the hallway, ordered her to put her hands behind her head, and frisked her. She didn't look around to see the dead bodies and didn't realize that the killers were lying among the dead. She and the others eventually were told to leave the building.

"I could see hundreds of backpacks scattered everywhere." She ran outside and was directed to a police car. "I still didn't feel safe at that point. I could barely see out the window. We were driving through the park.

"The paramedic who treated me asked me if I believed in God, and I told him I did. He said it was a good thing, because only God could have saved me."

"A Moment Will Bring Us There"

John Tomlin's memorial service was the first of what became "a heartbreaking procession of funerals and memorial services," as one writer noted. It snowed that day. His friend Jacob Youngblood recalled, "The first thing John ever said to me was, 'Ford or Chevy?'"

"I said, 'Ford' and immediately got on his bad side. John always set the example. He worked hard and made sure the work was done and done right. He was kind and respectful."[16]

More than a thousand people showed up at John's memorial in Littleton. The following week his parents took him back to Wisconsin to bury him.

When the Tomlins returned from Wisconsin, Nicole Nowlan came to visit them. She had been trying to figure out the identity of the boy who had hidden with her under the table that day in the school library. She had seen John's image on the television and thought he might have been the one.

They confirmed that John had been under the table with Nicole when his father, John, went into the library with other families a few weeks after the shooting. The bodies had been removed, but peoples' locations had been marked with name tags.

Doreen Tomlin said that even during their visit, Nicole was still "traumatized."

"She had seen kids die. She saw John die before her eyes and others lying in blood. She still had five bullets in her."

Nicole described to the Tomlins what happened to their son that day. She had first hidden under a table near John's, but didn't want to be alone. So she asked John if she could join him under his table.

"She was talking and talking, and John put his hands over her mouth, saying 'Shhhh,'" said Doreen. "But she would keep talking and John had to do it again. She said they held hands. They saw the legs coming. She knew by hearing their voices who they were. She said that they were evil and wicked. And then it happened."

Nicole told the Tomlins that if it hadn't been for John, she wouldn't be alive. Doreen, in her words, "wondered why she said that. She didn't elaborate. She said John was totally calm through the whole thing. I just know the presence of the Lord was there with them."

John and Doreen Tomlin eventually looked up the devotional reading from the writings of Spurgeon they had not read the morning of April 20. This is what they found:

> Child of God, cease to fear dying. Living near the cross of Calvary you may think of death with pleasure. . . . It is sweet to die in the Lord. . . . Death is no longer banishment. It is a return from exile. . . . We are not far from home—a moment will bring us there. . . . When the eyes close on earth, they open in heaven. . . . It is true that the battle is turned against us. . . . But let us be of good courage. . . . Do not look so much at the battle below, for there you will be surrounded by smoke and overwhelmed by garments rolled in blood. But lift your eyes to where your Savior lives and pleads.[17]

41

Scandal of the Crosses

"The Cross Is a Dangerous Symbol for Vicious Murderers"

I RETURNED TO CLEMENT Park to assimilate the stories I had heard. The accounts of the private horrors of these hurting people haunted me. Doreen Tomlin had said the sound of a cell phone ringing caused her to break out in a cold sweat because of her association with the scene at Leawood school while waiting for word about John. She said a friend's daughter, who was in the high school when the shooting began, had to leave a parade abruptly because the sound of the flags snapping in the wind reminded her of pipe bombs going off. Doreen hadn't read a newspaper in months. She told me I probably knew more about some aspects of this event than she did.

Shirley Hickman, the Spanish teacher, had remained hidden with her colleagues and students for more than two hours. When they finally decided to make a break for freedom, they armed themselves with three-hole punches and a coffee cup. Hickman lost three students who had been in her classes: Cassie Bernall, Matt Kechter, and Steven Curnow. "In my fifth hour class, Cassie and Matt probably had the two highest averages," she said. "You have to figure that the kids who were in the library studying at lunch, rather than eating, were

42

some of your more studious students. Steve was a freshman, a neat kid, real quiet. They were all kids you would have wanted to take home with you. I'd go in to class and sit down, and the kids would sit and be facing forward, and [I'd] teach them. It didn't matter if you were boring or interesting; they were respectful."

Once school resumed, she said, "I took some flowers and we put them on the empty desks to represent the kids who were killed. In the class where Steven had died, one girl was having a real hard time dealing with the whole picture of things. Every day she wanted me to put a flower. She said, 'I don't want us to ever forget Steven in class.'"

Joshua Lapp said he knew five of the people who died that day. "I knew Isaiah had died, so I had dealt with that, and I knew Daniel had died because I saw it. But when I heard that John Tomlin and Matt Kechter and Mr. Sanders died, I was mad. If there's anybody who didn't deserve to die it is those five. I knew Daniel and had been in the same grade with him. I had been in classes with him. He probably would have been a politician. Isaiah probably would have been a comedian of some sort. Matt could have been anything he wanted because he had the biggest heart out of anybody. Somebody said, 'He's not going to make varsity football.' Well, guess what? He suited up for varsity. He had that kind of heart. John Tomlin had everything going for him. He had good grades, he had a girlfriend, his truck. Those were the things that meant the most to him, with his family. Mr. Sanders had his life the way he wanted it. He was working with kids. When I had him in my business class, he always found a way to make us laugh even when he was mad at us. He always talked about his girls. He talked about his family."

After Kacey Ruegsegger escaped with the help of Craig Scott, they were quickly separated. Kacey ended up behind a police car with a girl named Sarah, who was helping her. She and Sarah were told to get into a second police car, and did so, but then the officer couldn't find the keys. They waited for yet another car. By that point Kacey was weak from loss of blood and could barely move. An officer told her to get into a third car "over there." Kacey replied that she didn't think she could make it, but the officer said, "Let's go." Kacey's father Greg described it: "They made her get out of one car and then open doors and then get into the next car." This car then drove across the field, with its "bumps and hills" into a neighborhood where Kacey then went to lie down in a grassy area. "That was all I had left in me," Kacey added. An ambulance arrived shortly after that.

Kevin Parker, the school volunteer who also served as a leader in a local Christian outreach ministry, said that after April 20 he and his wife "had kids at our house every night until midnight, sometimes till 2:00 in the morning. The first week and a half, our house was full of kids just bawling. We must have had forty crying kids in there. A lot of times kids were at our house twenty-four/seven—during the day, at night, you name it. We've been intentional about keeping an open door."

A Carpenter and His Crosses

From where I was sitting in the park one particular day, I couldn't help being distracted by a group picnic under one of the shelters. A rousing game of hula hoop kiss was in full swing ("the longer the hula, the longer the kiss"), animated by Paul McCartney's "Band on the Run." A fortress of grills and coolers separated the cooks from the game mavens, who were armed with Velcro paddles, bubbles, hula hoops, and balloons. My eye caught sight of an Asian man and his two children, maybe ages six and seven, walking around the perimeter of the school, just as I had done the day before. They obviously were exploring to find a way onto the property. He, too, apparently had been stopped by the police in the parking lot. He was undeterred. With his kids scampering behind him, he walked with full strides along the barricades and past the tennis courts to the back of the school. I marveled at his brazenness. At the same time, I wanted to follow him.

I decided, instead, to return to Rebel Hill. I ascended the hill and again was assaulted by two butterflies. Looking out over the campus, I noticed a footpath that traced the perimeter of the track below and seemed to wend closer to the school. I followed it and, sure enough, it led to the school—at least as far as a chain-link fence that faced the southwest side, what some had called the "hot zone" during the rampage. Two men walked toward me from the other direction. I assumed they were guarding the property and would tell me to turn back. Instead, one walked past, while the other stopped and asked, "Is that the hill where the crosses were placed?"

I told him it was, but that the original crosses were back in Illinois with the carpenter who built them. This led to an in-depth discussion about "the cross controversy."

I explained to my fellow pilgrim that Greg Zanis, the carpenter, had been vacationing in Florida when he received a phone call from a friend in Illinois on the Friday after the shooting. She had been contacted by students from Littleton who had seen on national newscasts the crosses that Zanis had built and placed on the lawn of a home in Naperville, Illinois,

44

where a woman had murdered her three children. Through a set of inquiries, the students had traced those crosses to Zanis's homespun ministry, Crosses for Losses, and had called to request fifteen crosses for those who had died at Columbine.

Zanis and his family left Florida the next day. "There were three messages on my recording machine. They all wanted fifteen crosses on Rebel Hill," Zanis said. By 5:00 P.M. on the following Monday, he had purchased the lumber and, by midnight, the crosses had been built and he was ready to hit the road for Colorado with the crosses in the back of his pickup truck.

When Zanis arrived at Columbine late in the afternoon on Tuesday, April 27, he saw people sitting on the hill.

"I don't think they realized who I was," he said. "I went around the back of the hill and staked it out, marking the holes with a string and a tape measure five foot apart, and dug the first hole. When my son carried up the first cross, they figured it out. After that, all the rest of the holes were dug and the crosses installed by the people there. They grabbed shovels and started digging.

"When the crosses started coming up the hill, I asked that each one be put in by a different person and that a different person write each name. You can see each style [of writing] is a little different. I asked if they would place the crosses in a particular order. I wanted Mr. Sanders to be in the middle, and I wanted the killers to be like the [fangs] of it."

Zanis said his son warned him not to place the two crosses for the killers. "Don't do it, Dad. You're going to get in trouble." But Zanis wanted to honor the request, and it had come to him asking for fifteen. He wanted to put up the full number for the sake of the parents of the killers, who also had suffered losses. To Zanis, including the two crosses for Eric Harris and Dylan Klebold was his way of extending love to all of the grieving families and friends in the midst of their heartache, despite the circumstances of the tragedy. "I just want people to know one person loves them— Greg Zanis. I don't care where they're at. It's very simple: Jesus' arms are open for you and he loves you more than I do. He cares about you. That's the point."

Besides, Zanis believed the community bore some of the burden for what had become of those boys. "The government has failed our children. Our kids are at school five days out of the week, and they don't teach them about God, but they teach them their religion, called evolution." Zanis felt that the government, through public schools, forced people to "tithe to their religion" and brainwashed students with the "survival of the fittest" mentality. "The boys who did this were young. They were educated to become 'the fittest.' When you took God out of the picture, we've taken out accountability."

Zanis, with his crosses, wanted to make Rebel Hill like "sacred ground," as he put it. "We were trying to make this sort of like Mount Calvary or in the movie *Spartacus,* when they come out of Rome and all the crosses were there with people hung on them."

The image of the fifteen crosses, looming over the school in the days following the massacre, appeared in newspapers and magazines throughout the country. Somehow these crosses bore the regrets of a grieving nation. So many people made a pilgrimage up Rebel Hill to leave notes, flowers, teddy bears, pictures, school pins, candles, rosaries, and other tributes that, at one point, the piles of mementos made the crosses indistinguishable as crosses. More than 125,000 people ascended that hill over those few days, some waiting in line for hours in pouring rain to reach the crosses.

Some left mementos that were personalized. Kyle Velasquez's cross had a Denver Broncos banner draped across it; Lauren Townsend's bore a red, white, and blue volleyball medal; Steve Curnow's held a plastic "Friday Star Wars celebration" badge picturing Obi-Wan wielding a light saber. Several had dogtags that read "God Is Awesome" or "Jesus Lives."

Zanis had left pens at each cross so visitors could write expressions of grief. The resulting messages covered almost every inch on each cross. Many included general thoughts of shock and grief, such as this sentiment on Matt Kechter's cross: "I never knew you but you will always be remembered by me and 1000s of others." And this on Corey DePooter's: "We pray that this tragedy will encourage our community and our nation to remember our children." Someone wrote on Daniel Mauser's cross: "We are sorry this happened. Sorry you died." Many writers thanked Rachel Scott for the way she had reached out to them: "You accepted me for me and kept me determined to keep my individuality." "You made me laugh." "You kept me inspired to keep believing." Dave Sanders's cross read, among other things: "You saved many and died for them. Thank you." Kyle Velasquez's cross displayed the simple message, "God is still God." Someone else promised Kelly Fleming: "We will change the world." To Isaiah Shoels, a friend wrote: "You have overcome," and someone penned to Cassie Bernall, "You were very brave. You did the right thing." Steve Curnow's father wrote, "May the Force Be With You, Love, Dad." On Lauren Townsend's cross was the message, "Our hearts cry for those you left behind." Daniel Rohrbough's carried the note, "You are missed. . . . We love you." John Tomlin's read, "All of Wisconsin's prayers are with you and your family. We're sorry."

46

Writings on the crosses of Eric Harris and Dylan Klebold ran the gamut from such sentiments as "Shame on you" and "Hate Begets Hate" to "I'm sorry I didn't realize your pain" and "Sorry we failed you." Someone's message on Dylan's cross read: "I weep for your families and those who knew you—or did they? Did we fail you? Or do you only want us to think we did?" A girl wrote to Eric: "I'm sorry I didn't talk to you on April 17th. Would it have made a difference if I would have?"

The crosses provided an outlet for the expressions of grief and initially had a healing effect on the community. Many residents from Littleton wrote Zanis to thank him for the effort he had made in constructing the crosses and delivering them to Colorado from Illinois. One woman described to him how she and her husband had inched along in a line up the hill, in a downpour, for more than two hours. It was a trek, she noted, that normally would have taken only two or three minutes. "Despite the fact that there were so many people, the tone of the crowd was so hushed and so very reverent. Your beautiful cross memorial has helped so many with forgiveness and healing," she wrote.

Another woman from Littleton wrote to tell Zanis that she thought placing all fifteen crosses was a good idea. "I think Dylan and Eric had enough separation in life that they shouldn't have it in death, too. Sorry that not all people could accept them. Maybe it was too quick for some. It's all so sad, but I know some things can't be changed."

She was referring to the controversy that had erupted after Brian Rohrbough reacted to the inclusion of the killers' crosses. His son Dan had been killed outside the cafeteria early in the rampage. To Brian Rohrbough, the presence of those two crosses was an affront. He posted signs on them that read: "Murderers burn in hell."

Dan had been Brian's only child. He had worked with his father in his electronics shop after school and on weekends for years. He had saved his work money to buy everyone in his family Christmas presents. He had given his father a cordless drill, which he used at his shop.

Someone had told Brian Rohrbough's ex-wife, Sue Petrone, that Dan was holding the door for others to escape when he was shot. Rohrbough said, whether he was or wasn't, "It is irrelevant. I was proud of him, and he was important to me, and it would not have any significance whether or not the story is true. I know that Dan and his friends wouldn't have been standing there if they had thought they were in danger."

Dan had worked with his father at the shop on the Monday before the shooting. "I dropped him off at Sue's house about 6:30 and was planning to see him again the next day." On Tuesday, Brian Rohrbough's cellular phone rang on three occasions, each time with no one on the other end.

47

The fourth time, the call connected. "It was Sue. It was probably 11:45 A.M. She said, 'Do you know what is going on? Have you heard from Dan?'"

Rohrbough recounted: "I said no. I jumped in the van and headed for the school. It was mass chaos. We walked over where we could see Columbine and the SWAT teams. At about 2:00 P.M. I knew he was gone. I would assume it was God telling me, preparing me. I hoped I was wrong. We waited for busloads of kids, but I knew he wasn't going to be on it. I told Sue, 'You know, he's gone.'

"They were still lying to parents. I use the word 'lying' because there is no other word that can fit. The school people, the police, and all the counselors who were there had assembled and were saying, 'Don't give up hope. There's one more busload to come.' This was hours after the last busload. I told Sue, 'There are no more buses.'"

Rohrbough said the district attorney and the sheriff introduced the coroner before anyone had been informed of which students were feared dead. "They didn't say, 'Listen folks, kids have been killed here and we're very sorry but the fact that you're here may mean that your kids are victims.' Instead, they said, 'We want to introduce you to the coroner.' But you never introduce a coroner before you say, 'Look, there have been kids killed here.'

"The coroner came up and said, 'Well, we don't know when we are going to be able to get the bodies, and we don't know if we will be performing autopsies or not. But don't worry about using your phones and all, because when we need to inform you we will have an officer come to your house. We won't do it by phone.'"

Rohrbough said before calls came from the coroner, or anyone else confirming Dan's death, a photo of him lying dead on the sidewalk appeared in the *Rocky Mountain News* the next morning. "There was no question about who he was," said Rohrbough. What made matters worse, because the site was a crime scene none of the bodies was removed right away. Dan "was dead there twenty-six hours or thereabouts before they picked up his body," said his father.

The Crosses Come, the Crosses Go

When Brian Rohrbough learned that crosses for the killers had been placed on the hill along with crosses for the victims, he contacted the park district and asked them to remove the two crosses. When the crosses remained, he consulted family members, including his ex-wife and her husband, and they decided to take matters into their own hands. Rohrbough called CNN, and with the television cameras rolling, on Friday, April 30, he went to Rebel Hill: "We don't build a monument to Adolf Hitler and put it in a Holocaust museum—and it's not going to happen here," he said, and then he tore down the killers' crosses.

"We cut them into pieces and threw them in the dumpster," he said.

By that time, Greg Zanis had returned to Illinois. "I had heard on the radio that this guy had torn down these crosses and I didn't know what it was all about," he said. Zanis quickly learned what it was about. Several people called from the Littleton area to tell him that some people were spitting on the crosses, defacing them with messages of hate (like "murderers burn in hell") and that one girl had been pushed off the hill into the mud. "All she did was put a flower there. She bought fifteen carnations," said Zanis.

He turned around immediately to return to Colorado. "I was planning to remove the controversy. This is not what I put them up for. We put them up for closure and other reasons, not for people to find a target."

Rain fell the Sunday Zanis arrived to reclaim his crosses. The mud on the hill sucked at his boots and the rain crackled against the cellophane wrappers of the dried flowers and laminated poems attached to the crosses. The crosses pulled easily from the soaked earth.

"In forty-five seconds they were lying there on the ground," said Zanis. "I was carrying them down two and three at a time. I was gone in about four minutes. I was angry because it got to be so controversial. I was angry at everybody in Littleton. I didn't see where this was going to work."

Murder Spurs a Ministry

Greg Zanis launched his cross ministry in 1996, which was a defining year for this quirky, Lone-Ranger carpenter. In January of that year, he went to the home of his best friend and carpentering mentor, who also happened to be his father-in-law, and found him dead in a pool of blood, shot through the eye. Zanis offered a twenty thousand dollar reward to help find the killer, and within a week the murderer's sister turned him in. The loss devastated Zanis, who became suicidal and lost fifty pounds. He attended a support group for families of murder victims, where he met a woman whose six-year-old son had been killed. When she learned he was a carpenter, she asked if he would build a cross for her son. "At that meeting, fourteen people, including her, asked for crosses and signed a paper giving me permission to put them on their property," he said. "It was a breaking point in my grieving process to have a mission instead of just going to work and coming home and locking myself up in my bedroom. He taught me how to be a carpenter. I'm building crosses in his honor."

That was also why Zanis took it so personally when two Columbine crosses were defaced. It is why he responded so emotionally by retrieving the remaining thirteen. This, however, only fueled the controversy, and Brian Rohrbough grew more indignant. "He should have left the thirteen other crosses standing," he said. "Instead of doing the right thing to honor the victims of those two murderers, he comes back and tears down the whole thing."[1]

After Zanis returned home with the crosses, he was besieged by requests from people in Littleton to bring them back. "I was very embarrassed about having to take this action," he said. "It wasn't easy to do. I'd pick up the phone and someone would say, 'Greg, please bring those crosses down' [or] 'Greg, you can't do that. We want those crosses back.'" The mother of one the victims called to tell Zanis that she had wanted to go to Rebel Hill to see the crosses, but hadn't made it before he took them down. "She wanted to see her daughter's cross and never got the opportunity," he said. "She said she didn't really want to go out in public because people knew who she was. It was very emotional."

Zanis felt he needed to resolve the conflict with Brian Rohrbough before he could return any crosses. He wanted to set up a meeting, but could not get Rohrbough's phone number. Through a convoluted set of contacts, he arranged a meeting with Rohrbough at a Denny's restaurant. As they approached one another, Zanis recalled, "He was yelling at me, 'How dare you honor a murderer! How dare you put up a murderer's cross by my son's cross! How dare you put a cross up for somebody that's going to hell.' One time I was sure he was going to hit me. It was quite a scene.

"Anyway, the Lord blessed me, because I didn't provoke him any further. Finally he calmed down. I said, 'I'm sorry.' He said, 'Sorry's not enough.'"

Zanis continued to ask Rohrbough for forgiveness and Rohrbough continued to rebuff him, saying things like, "I'm not going to forgive you. You were crazy when you did that." The two went back and forth for some time. Zanis described the end of their discussion: "I said, I'm asking you to forgive me as a Christian. I just want you to know that I'm here with thirteen crosses and I'm going to put them up today.'

"'I don't care what you do,' he said. Right there I said, 'Listen, I've asked you as a Christian brother to forgive me and you haven't. I'm tired of you yelling at me. I put up with all I can take. I'm going to pack my crosses and go back to Illinois. But I want to ask you one more time, are you or are you not a Christian brother? And are you going to forgive me or not?'

"I don't know what hit him," Zanis said, "but he broke down and we hugged and cried together. He was a changed man. We went inside and ordered food, but none of us ate it." Zanis assured Rohrbough that he would not memorialize the killers in any way with his crosses, and the two found common ground. After the reconciliation, Brian Rohrbough said, "Greg didn't do any of this to cause a problem. It took tremendous courage for him to come back."[2]

Greg Zanis's attempt to replace the crosses on Rebel Hill did not last long. The Foothills Park and Recreation District promptly removed them and placed them in storage, citing the principle of separation of church and state. Soon thereafter, Zanis set up two more sets of thirteen crosses; one set on the property of a local resident who donated some land for it, the other at Chapel Hill Memorial Gardens near the graves of Rachel Scott and Corey DePooter.

The goodwill between him and Brian Rohrbough was also short-lived. Greg, in time, reneged on his agreement not to remember the two killers with crosses. Occasionally, over the course of the first year after the massacre as he traveled with the crosses, he displayed two smaller crosses near the other thirteen. He never did so when he was in Colorado or when any family members were present. "It wasn't three weeks later when he was saying in the paper that he believed in his heart that fifteen crosses should be up," said Rohrbough.

The Offense of the Cross

Brian Rohrbough objected to the crosses that had been placed on the hill for the two killers because, he said, it was "a dangerous symbol to use for vicious murderers." "You don't cheapen what Christ did for us by honoring murderers with crosses," he said. To better understand why the symbol of the cross became a lightning rod for controversy, it is necessary to gain an appreciation for what Christ accomplished when he died on the cross.

"Christ was killed for us, that His death has washed out our sins, and that by dying He disabled death itself. That is the formula. That is Christianity." So wrote C. S. Lewis in his book *Mere Christianity*.[3] The cross in Christianity, in other words, is the epicenter of God's saving activity.

Jesus suffered on three levels in the event of his crucifixion. On the judicial level, he was condemned and executed as a criminal under Roman law for a crime he did not commit. The religious leaders of the day accused him of blasphemy against God because he forgave sins, a prerogative, they said, that is God's alone. But such a charge does not merit execution, so they took their case to the Roman court. They fabricated the testimony of witnesses to say that Jesus was leading a rebellion against Caesar. The official charges against him were that of inciting insurrection.

Because of the barbaric nature of crucifixion, this form of execution was practiced only by the state—in this case, Rome—and not by any religious community. The Romans were known for their expertise in the rule of law. It could be expected, and indeed came to pass, that Jesus' trial under Pontius Pilate, the governor at the time, would flush out the flimsy nature of the charges against him and show the trial to be the sham that it was. In the end, Pilate thought Jesus should go free, and he tried in vain to convince the assembled crowd of as much. Having been stirred up by propagandists dispatched by the religious elite, the crowd would hear nothing of it and demanded that Jesus be crucified. Pilate let it be so, but washed his hands of it.

Jesus' suffering also was on a physical level. Crucifixion was a particularly cruel and inhumane form of execution and was reserved for society's worst criminals. It was a slow, excruciating death, so gruesome that prisoners frequently would be scourged first—beaten with a whip of several leather cords with metal balls on the ends—in part, as an act of mercy to hasten death. The sites for crucifixions often were public roadways in order to make a greater spectacle out of it and to maximize the humiliation of the punishment.

The crucified suffered for hours. If they relaxed their arms, the weight of the body against their nailed metatarsus sent bolts of pain shooting upward. As their lungs compressed and they tried to snatch air by pulling up, more bolts of pain went through their arms and down the back. In time, their lungs filled with fluid and breathing became labored. Death finally would be caused by asphyxiation.

The third level of Jesus' suffering possesses for Christians the greatest and most mysterious significance. "The central Christian belief is that Christ's death has somehow put us right with God and given us a fresh start," writes C. S. Lewis.[4] But what does he mean, "a fresh start"? A look at the thought world of the Columbine killers may help answer that question.

There was a corner of their hearts that whispered to Harris and Klebold: You are your own masters; you don't have to serve anybody but yourselves. They were convinced, as Dylan Klebold noted on one of the videos, "We're gonna have followers because we're so . . . god-like."

"We're not exactly human," he said. "We have bodies, but we've evolved into one step above you. . . . We actually have . . . self-awareness." They called their murderous plan their "own little judgment day." They were going to bring judgment upon the masses who, from their point of view, deserved to die. That corner of their hearts that whispered that they were their own masters convinced them, in other words, that they could be like God. And they assumed the prerogatives of God in their massacre.

Human history attests that Jesus' suffering did not remove that part of the human heart that whispers such things. But it did, in a mysterious way, compensate for the suffering that wayward inclination metes out in the world. There is so much that is wrong in the world, so much that is unjust and unavenged. These unanswered injustices, and the judgment due them, come together on the cross. Listening to and obeying the heart when it whispers that we can be "like God" wreaks havoc and impedes our ability to know God and be loved by him. The cross, in Christianity, is God's way of coming to terms with that impediment. When Jesus bore the full force of all three aspects of his suffering, he incurred the judgment God must pronounce against injustices. In so doing he availed to all fallen human beings the "fresh start" Lewis noted. "Jesus knows he must go, solo and unaided, into the whirlpool, so that it may exhaust its force on him and let the rest of the world go free," writes theologian N. T. Wright. "Jesus was called to throw himself on the wheel of world history, so that, even though it crushed him, it might start to turn in the opposite direction.[5] . . . We are at the brink of the great mystery."[6]

By the Christian confession, this is not a sadistic gesture on God's part. To the contrary, it reflects the extent of his love toward those he is reconciling and the seriousness of the heart's rebellious inclinations. "Evil is real and powerful," writes Wright. "It is not only 'out there' in other people, but it is present and active within each of us. . . . When human beings worship that which is not God, they give authority to forces of destruction and malevolence; and those forces gain a power, collectively, that has, down the centuries . . . caused wise people to personify it, to give it the name of Satan, the Accuser. . . .

"Jesus' victory over evil is also real and powerful," Wright continues. "It, too, is not only 'out there,' a fact of history two thousand years ago, but it is available here and now for each of us. Where human beings turn from idolatry and worship the God they see revealed on [the cross], they are turning from darkness to light, from the Strong Man to the one who has bound the Strong Man. To pray 'deliver us from evil' or 'from the evil one' is to inhale the victory of the cross, and thereby to hold the line for another moment, another hour, another day, against the forces of destruction within ourselves and the world."[7]

In other words, as heinous as were the deeds of Harris and Klebold, these in themselves did not necessitate the cross. The cross was necessitated before the first shot was fired, in fact before the first murder in human history was registered. The cross was necessitated because of the part of the human heart, theirs and ours, that inclines us to go the wrong way, to become like God. The impulse is the same, only in lesser degrees, in us all when we convince ourselves that we don't have to serve anyone or answer to anybody as we live our own God-likeness and assume his prerogatives. The cross is the great equalizer in that regard, which is why the apostle Paul talks about "the offense of the cross" in one of his New Testament letters. He was addressing the Jewish believers in a church in the province of Galatia (in modern-day Turkey), who resented the fact that the *goiim*, or Gentiles, could also be recognized as "God's people" because of what Jesus did on the cross. These Jewish Galatian believers believed that, as Jews, they had special standing before God, a status the Gentile believers did not enjoy. Paul wrote, "In Christ, there is neither Jew nor Greek." In other words, neither religious heritage nor lack thereof secured or denied anyone standing before God. The only way anyone, Jew or Greek, had access to God was by means of the cross of Christ, the great equalizer. It was the dark side of the human heart, not lack of religious affiliation, that kept humanity out of sync with God.

So it offended the Jewish Christians in Galatia that their religious standing merited them nothing and that the enemies of God won equal standing before God without any religious heritage. This is the "offense of the cross." And it is the same sentiment that sparked the controversy over the Columbine crosses.

"Any cross that I put up shows that Greg Zanis cares for them and loves them and that the Lord loves them and he's there for them," said Zanis. "It's very simple. Jesus' arms are open for you. He loves you more than I do; that's the point."

Yet Brian Rohrbough argued: "The cross is a visual symbol of what repentance is about. The only thing, apparently, the killers regretted is that they did not kill more. So I'm very offended by people who try to paint them as victims or who put up crosses for them. They are not victims. They were never victims."

As will be evident in subsequent chapters, the cross controversy weighed heavily in the minds of many in the community throughout the tortured journey toward healing.

Parents at a Loss

The Reverend Don Marxhausen, former pastor of St. Philip's Lutheran Church in Littleton and the one who buried Dylan Klebold, said Dylan's parents, Tom and Sue, didn't have a clue that their son possessed so much rage. While some have laid the blame at their feet, the Klebolds sincerely attested that they never saw this coming. Marxhausen told me the Klebolds had shown him a video that was filmed on prom night, the Saturday before the shooting. He described how an awkward and flustered Dylan, pulling his cuffs and straightening his tie, was receiving his boutonniere. He said into the camera: "Dad, we're going to laugh about this in twenty years." On the Monday before the shootings, April 19, Sue Klebold had sent in the deposit for Dylan's enrollment at the University of Arizona.

The family lives of both Columbine killers, while not perfect, exhibited the qualities of stability and parental love. Neither set of parents had been divorced; there was no evidence of abuse; conversely, both sets of parents possessed obvious affection for their sons.

The Klebolds, natives of Ohio, came from differing backgrounds. Sue was born into privilege, the granddaughter of the renowned Leo Yassenoff, a Jewish builder and philanthropist from Columbus, where a Jewish center bears his name. Tom lived through a childhood marked by tragedy. His mother died when he was six, his father when he was twelve. He was raised by a half-brother who was eighteen years his senior.

Tom and Sue met at Ohio State University, where both were studying art, and they married in 1971. Tom went on to receive a master's degree in geophysics from Marquette University in Wisconsin. He later took the family to Oklahoma and then to Colorado. The Klebolds' first son, Byron, was born in 1978 and their second, Dylan, came along in 1981.

People who know them described them as excellent parents. "Sue was more patient and gentle and kind with her kids than I was able to be," says Vicki DeHoff,[1] a family friend. She and Sue Klebold had made a pact always to tell one another "if our kids got into trouble." The Klebolds tried to instill in their sons "the value of money and work," says another friend, Judy Brown.[2] They didn't allow the boys to play with toy guns when they were little and didn't keep a real gun in their home.

In 1989 the Klebolds purchased a rustic but elegant home in Deer Creek Canyon, nestled into the hogback in the shadow of the Rockies. These rounded rock formations, older than the Rockies, look like the backs of hogs and lean east, the direction in which they erupted during the earth's early stages.

"It's Always People"

So, I explained to my fellow pilgrim as we stood behind the school chatting, the original crosses remain in the possession of Zanis, who has been traveling around the country and displaying them at various youth events.

I changed the subject and expressed my surprise at being permitted to get this close to the school. He said, "Well, now you see the trouble spot of the world. Everything happens for a reason. It's people; it's always people."

We said our good-byes, and I made my way closer to the school. Kitschy accoutrements still adorned the chain-link fence. The library windows remained boarded. This image stood in stark contrast to the teddy bears, dried flowers, and religious poems people had left.

A young woman approached me as I stood behind the school. "Have you been to see the crosses?" She was referring to the additional set of thirteen that Greg Zanis had built and erected at the cemetery. "It's really quite moving," she said. She was from Albuquerque, New Mexico, and was visiting a friend who lived next to the cemetery. This friend, she said, had kept tabs on the Columbine funerals at that cemetery. "Dylan Klebold is supposed to be buried in there in an unmarked grave," the visitor said.

Storm clouds were forming over the mountains. I decided to scramble out to the cemetery before the rain started.

Chapter 4

"Men Without Chests"

The Rise of the Gun-toting Antihero

THE THIRTEEN CROSSES WERE impossible to miss upon entering the cemetery. Identical to the original fifteen that stood on Rebel Hill, these crosses—also made by Greg Zanis—formed a semicircle on a grassy median between entrance and exit driveways. There were no trees on the median and the grass was brown and dry. Beyond, on the main grounds, evergreens, oaks, and maples lent a bucolic quiescence to the picture.

Rachel Scott and Corey DePooter were buried side by side within the semicircle of the crosses. The graves, like everything associated with the deaths of these young people, had become personalized memorials. Rachel's grave was replete with silk flowers in bunches or vases, pinwheels, and teddy bears placed under clear plastic umbrellas. Two small crosses marked Corey's grave. One bore his name and the other was draped with his fishing vest, sunglasses, and a baseball cap. Silk flowers also adorned his grave, and teddy bears and sports banners had been left in a plastic box. Someone had placed there a live columbine plant, Colorado's state flower. The only indication that these plots were graves—other than the small crosses with their names—were the strips of sod, lain the approximate length of a casket.

Like the originals, these memorial crosses were covered with heart-felt sentiments. Dee Fleming found a poem her daughter Kelly had written before her death. It was laminated and tacked to her cross. It was my first exposure to Kelly's voice. The latter portion read:

> I walked to the window and pulled on the long string.
> What a surprise to see the sunrise.
> In the distance were children with laughter and happiness,
> that was the thought that I like to see!
> But of course can that really be?
> Or can this be another dream?

A person named Kami wrote to Dave Sanders that she would play "110 percent" at basketball this year, and someone noted on Dan Mauser's cross that he had lived 5,778 days. Someone else left tickets for an 8:00 P.M. showing of *Star Wars—Episode 1: The Phantom Menace* at Steven Curnow's cross.

Standing amid these crosses, thinking about the lives they represented, I was haunted by the notion that Dylan Klebold, a killer and their peer, might be buried somewhere nearby. I was wandering around on the off chance I might stumble onto his grave when I glimpsed a scrap of paper on the ground. I was surprised to discover that it was lodged between two fresh sod rolls that looked like those at Rachel's and Corey's graves. This grave had no flowers, sports banners, poems, teddy bears, or markings of any kind. But it was clearly a grave. The blankets of sod extended the length of a casket. The scrap of paper was a portion of a note that had been torn; only the words "sample," "memory," and "family" remained. It looked like the writing of a young girl; the 'i' was dotted with a bubble.

I stood over this strange grave, figuring that whoever lay here had to have been buried at the same time, more or less, as Rachel and Corey. The sod had the same not-yet-integrated-into-the-lawn look. There was not so much as a stick to mark it—not even a makeshift flower vase. There was no way I could know whether it belonged to Dylan Klebold, but I couldn't help thinking that in death, as in life, this young man remained beyond the fray, cut off from his peers.

I thought about the controversy over the memorial crosses. Some felt confident that the destiny of the killers was eternal banishment, and that by their own choosing, and that they had forfeited the right to be memorialized by a cross. Others were less resolute about how to deal with the memory of two killers.

Dylan grew up pitching for his Little League baseball team and "threw harder than everybody on the team."[3] He excelled in math in the talented and gifted program he attended during elementary school, and he collected baseball cards. He grew to become a spindly six-feet, three-inches tall and possessed a commanding look, especially when he wore the black trench coat that was to become his trademark. He was a master at anything technical and used to be able to hack into the school's computer to find the locker combinations of people he wanted to intimidate.[4]

But he possessed a softer side. He feared that his cats, Rocky and Lucy, might get eaten by cougars in the hogback, and he hung posters of Roger Clemens and Lou Gehrig in his room. He was known to be able to eat an entire bucket of Kentucky Fried Chicken in one sitting and used to eat cereal from a metal mixing bowl. He found a niche in the sound booth in the school's drama department and sometimes put in twelve-hour days supporting the cast in rehearsals. A few weeks before April 20, a girl drove her car into the back of his black BMW and was crying and shaking for fear of how he was going to respond. "Don't worry about it. It's all right," was all he said to her. "Dylan did not learn hate in that home," said friend Randy DeHoff.[5]

According to the *New York Times,* after the shootings Sue Klebold told her hairdresser that the "killer depicted in news reports was not the Dylan she knew."[6] In the letters Sue promptly wrote to the families of all of the victims, she said, "We'll never understand why this tragedy happened, or what we might have done to prevent it. We did not see anger or hatred in Dylan until the last moments of his life, when we watched in helpless horror with the rest of the world."[7]

Despite Dylan's bantering with his father on the evening of the prom, we know that he didn't expect to laugh about that moment with him in twenty years. On one of the videotapes he and Eric Harris made during the weeks prior to the shooting, he said to his prom date: "Robyn, I didn't really want to go to prom. But since I'm going to be dying, I thought I might do something cool."

Talent, Brains, and Sparky

Eric Harris's upbringing was more mobile than Dylan's but still possessed elements that would predispose normalcy and stability. His parents, Wayne and Kathy, were born in Colorado. They were married in 1970 and, three years later, Wayne joined the U.S. Air Force and was sent to Oklahoma for pilot training. From then until 1993, the Harrises crisscrossed the country, moving every couple of years. Their oldest son, Kevin, was born in 1978 and their second, Eric, was born in 1981. Kathy stayed home with the boys to lend stability to their otherwise itinerant lifestyle while Wayne rose through the ranks of the military. He won the Meritorious Service Medal for his work on B–1 bombers and served on some prestigious test programs before retiring with the rank of major. When Plattsburgh Air Force Base in New York was closed in 1993, Harris returned to Colorado and took a job at Flight Safety Services, which makes military flight simulators, in Englewood. The Harrises bought their home south of Columbine High School in the spring of 1996 as Eric was ending his freshman year.

Eric, too, played Little League baseball, and fellow players recall him being tentative about swinging the bat. They said he was afraid he would strike out. He was more talkative than Dylan, and many of his female classmates said they thought he was cute. Terra Oglesbee, an African-American, shared a creative writing class with him and remembered him being "a really good writer." She said, "he would help me cheat sometimes, pass me answers in tests and stuff."[8] Another friend from his childhood, Mike Condo, who used to play with him on Plattsburgh's Sun Foods Little League team, said he "couldn't believe it" when he had heard that part of the killing may have been racially motivated. "His best friends back then were . . . an Asian kid and . . . a black kid."[9] Eric's dog, Sparky, used to have seizures, and sometimes Eric would take time off from work to be with Sparky when he was sick.

Eric was high-strung and prone to depression, which precipitated his being put on the antidepressant drug Luvox. He was an eloquent speaker, well-read, witty, and brilliant. He is remembered for his ability to carry on an intellectual conversation for hours and used to have discussions with a classmate about Ayn Rand's "objectivism" which "sees man as a 'heroic being' whose happiness is the purpose of his life."[10]

A few days before the shooting he had been rejected by the U.S. Marines because of his need to be on Luvox, and he was told he would have to be off the drug for six months before he could reapply.

Searching for Answers

We are left to ponder how Eric Harris and Dylan Klebold, two seemingly normal upper-middle-class boys from two-parent families, came to a place where their fantasies of revenge crossed the line to become a bloody rampage of executing their peers.

Don Marxhausen told me a story he had heard about an incident that had taken place a year or so before the shooting. A senior who was a "certifiable bully" started throwing ketchup packages at Eric and Dylan in the dining hall, "and he and his friends would say, 'Why don't you fags kiss? You guys are sweethearts.' [The bully] was an all-state wrestler in the heavyweight division. Those kind of things fed into a rage that built up over the years of being different and outcast and shamed."

Zach Johnston described on his Internet posting an occasion when a coworker of his, a member of the "trench coat mafia," also felt the abuse of tormentors:

"About a year ago I worked at a movie theater with one of the Trench Coat Mafia kids. He would constantly complain about rich jocks and other stuff that is common to hear. I figured to myself, 'Just an angry kid venting some anger.' Then one night he came into work and told me he had been chased in his car by so and so. Well, it turns out 'so and so' were athletes from my school who don't seem to have anything better to do than torment this dude. I can see why the fellow I worked with hated Columbine High School."

Eric Harris and Dylan Klebold, wrote Johnston, "were two outcast kids that were constantly made fun of and they finally snapped. What they were thinking before they performed this horror will never be conceivable to anyone. I saw Dylan and his old 325i. He was entering the school like nothing was going to happen. Then I made eye contact with him for a split second and he looked at me with no emotion. I truly had no idea he was soon going to perform the most horrible school massacre in history."

Some have speculated that the Luvox triggered Eric's manic episodes. Doctors who were interviewed by the *Washington Post* and CNN said there is no link between the drug and aggressive behavior. Yet one study has indicated that the drug can produce rage and other forms of mania in some patients.[11]

Recurring episodes of being taunted and demeaned fueled Eric and Dylan's anger. At some point the hostility reached unmanageable levels, which gave rise to their fantasies. I remember as a child of seven or eight also nursing a fantasy of revenge when my sisters and I conspired to create "Poison for Dominic," our neighborhood bully. We scrounged around our backyard and raided the cleaning supplies under the kitchen sink to concoct our elixir of three parts water, one part dirt, and a dash each of Comet cleanser and Tabasco sauce. Our fantasy carried all the elements of indignation and lust for vengeance that Harris and Klebold's did, with one critical difference. The culture of my early years availed neither the resources nor the model of vigilante activism I needed to spur me on and translate my plot into reality. In television's quintessential small town of Mayberry, Andy Taylor would have helped Opie find another way to deal with the local bully. In the case of the gunmen at Columbine, their culture set up the standard of the vigilante gunman and gave them the tools to move their fantasy into possibility. It empowered their rage. "Online, your imaginary friend really talks back. The realness, or potential realness, is part of the compulsion here: Whenever you want, you can take this unreal world and make it real," noted Michael Wolff in *New York* magazine. "It is sci-fi in its dimensions. You have this fantasy; you've developed it, plotted it, played it out. Now you have the power to keep it a fantasy—or make it real."[12]

While cultural conditioning was not the primary agent that precipitated the actions of the Columbine killers and does not absolve them of culpability, it molded their thinking and distorted their judgment. At any point they could have snuffed out the fantasy and put down their arms. But the boys had plenty of help from their culture which, at the least, gave their fantasy arms and legs. Social and cultural influences among peers are leaving an imprint on the souls of today's young people. In extreme cases, these forces accelerate emotional deterioration and predispose some to act upon destructive impulses.

"The hardest thing for me sitting with [the Klebolds]," said Marxhausen, "is to turn off that switch in my head and not pursue the *why*—to just listen to how they are processing what has happened to them. The mother is almost afraid to grieve because it means giving up her son, and she doesn't want to give up her son. The father is trying to deal with his rage. He wants to know: Who put a gun in my son's hand? Why is there a culture in which he was an outcast?"

Negative External Forces

During the year before the shooting, the school had sponsored a talent program in which Rachel Scott performed a mime routine based upon Simon of Cyrene, the man who carried Jesus' cross to the hill of crucifixion. With jarring abruptness her music went out. But before the interruption could linger into awkward restlessness, the sound technician slipped in a replacement tape, cued it up, and rescued her performance. A year later, Rachel lay dead outside the school cafeteria, shot through the temple, while that sound technician, Dylan Klebold, was doing some of the shooting. What happened to reduce Dylan Klebold to a killing machine?

The respected church historian Martin Marty has said that today's youth "stand between later modernity and postmodernity." He defines modernity as "principled use of reason aided in discriminating and coming through critical inquiry to truth." By postmodernity he means, "relativism at worst and relativity at best. . . ." To illustrate the latter, he told of a teacher who described what a student had written: "'Hitler had his ideas and way of life, and I have mine. How do I get to judge what he lived by?'"[13]

In either case, God is considered irrelevant. The "godkillers of modern times," as Marty calls them—Nietzsche, Darwin, Marx, and Freud (among others)—"issued their devastating challenges to faith" that resulted in human reason triumphing over a mysterious faith. Scientific skepticism displaced Christian assurance, and the lordship of Christ was overtaken by the notion of "progress." Religion was made "a private affair" and remains so today, even as modernity has metamorphosed into postmodernity.

It is too daunting a task to walk the reader through the revolution known as the Enlightenment that, more or less, brought us to this place. Suffice it to say that, post-Enlightenment, God was dethroned. Human rationality, in the case of modernism, and—some might argue—irrationality, in the case of postmodernism, gained assent. For the purposes of understanding the forces in today's teen world that converged at Columbine, these are more easily tracked by a brief look at the past fifty years.[14]

The Big/Small Inversion

When I was a teen in the early 1970s, Baby Boomers (of which I was one) were rewriting the rules of American culture. Many social factors contributed to this: the Vietnam War, which began in the fifties; a steady stream of political assassinations in the sixties; the Kent State University shootings and the Watergate scandal in the seventies. In due course, these and other events shattered Baby Boomers' trust in conventional institutions such as politics and the military. This mistrust predictably carried over into the realm of the church. Baby Boomers left institutionalized religion by the droves.

This spawned a cultural revolution that rallied around personal expression and the shedding of inhibition; individual rights and freedoms; and the questioning—and sometimes ridicule—of authority. Sheer numbers made this generation a force to be reckoned with. The cultural mindset of the time became so radical and self-referring that *Time* magazine ran a cover story that posed the question, "Is God Dead?"[15]

Concurrent with the Baby Boomers' social revolution was another, less overt but no less insidious, assault on American culture. It came by way of television. My grandmother used to sit in her living room and listen to President Franklin Delano Roosevelt talk on the radio about World War II. She felt small in the big world around her. She wondered what she could offer "to do her part" for the greater good. Time marched on. Radio gave way to television, and it did not take long for the visual medium to become a standard feature in nearly every American home. Marketing forces quickly recognized the television as a boon for reaching huge numbers of potential buyers, and this spurred the advertising industry. Americans started believing what marketers, through television, told them— such as that living the good life depended upon owning the right car, smoking the right brand of cigarette, or wearing the right kind of tennis shoes. Almost without our noticing it, "wants" took on the characteristics of "needs" because we, the consumers, "deserve the best."

The confluence of these two revolutions—the Baby Boomers' new rules and the mainstream dissemination of TV—created an environment in which peoples' perception of reality began to change. The revolution of the sixties and seventies celebrated the right of every individual to come up with his or her own version of happiness. In the eighties, Baby Boomers traded a self-centered pursuit of happiness for a self-centered pursuit of material things. Ronald Reagan won his presidential election not by asking, as John F. Kennedy had, "Ask not what your country can do for you..," but by asking, "Are *you* better off today ... ?"

All the while, the television culture, through advertising, perpetuated this fantasy and defined the terms of that happiness. Soon individuals stopped viewing themselves the way my grandmother viewed herself—as a small player in a big picture—and instead *became the picture.* Individual wants, opinions, and cravings became the epicenter of a self-focused universe. Instead of approaching life with a view toward what one could contribute to the larger world, this forced the question: What does the larger world offer me? Individuals no longer were small and their world big. The opposite became true: Individuals were big and their respective worlds small. Their worlds existed to serve *them.*

This might not have been bad had the Baby Boomers' revolution actually played out along the lines of its utopian vision. But many social observers are coming to terms with the fact that much of this revolution has ended in disaster. It has been a "social experiment gone awry," notes Susan Littwin in her book *The Postponed Generation.* "Some of this was wonderful" and "much of it was inevitable," but "a lot of it was delusional." "It is hard to say when all the experimenting started to turn sinister."[16] It could be argued that part of the culpability for this sinister turn rests at the feet of the electronic media, the next aspect of youth culture that contributed to Columbine.

The Electronic Media

Michael Wolff is right when he writes in *New York* magazine that it is hard to bring "intelligent analysis" to this topic. Those who broach it—myself included—tend to come off sounding like Dana Carvey's church lady in the old *Saturday Night Live* skits. But that doesn't make it any less true.[17]

To understand the impact of the media culture on this generation of teens, some definitions will be helpful. Today's teens have been called the Millennial Generation,[18] which, in broad strokes, includes those born between 1977 and 1992. They are second only to Baby Boomers when it comes to sheer numbers, composing 26 percent of the U.S. population (numbering about seventy million), compared to the Boomers' 29 percent. They are the second wave of the Boomers' offspring, the first wave being represented loosely by those born between 1965 and 1976 (numbering around forty million) and known as Generation X. Both sets of offspring have inherited the fallout of their parents' revolution, but Generation X has borne the brunt of it.[19] The Millennials have faced the same troubling social demographics, but stand apart from Gen X in one critical difference. Gen Xers came of age enmeshed in their parents' revolution; the Millennials are coming of age *reacting to* it.

Nearly 2,000 representatives of this new breed attend Columbine High School. (In 1999, sixteen students were black and one hundred and twelve were Hispanic.[20]) The students enter the hallways at 7:30 A.M. and are bolting to freedom by 2:30 P.M. The CHS Rebels, donning silver and blue, have boasted several state sports championships. In the year that followed the tragedy of April 20, 1999, the baseball and football teams brought home first-place trophies from state competitions. The school's mission statement reads, "At Columbine High School we will teach, learn, and model life skills and attitudes that prepare us to: work effectively with people; show courtesy to others; prepare for change; think critically; act responsibly; and respect our surroundings." The school motto is "Stretch for Excellence."[21] In every respect, CHS seems a typical suburban American high school populated by typical teens. But, as we will see, what's "typical" in today's teen world can take on astonishing nuances.

Michael Wolff continues in his article, "If you can't appeal to teens, you don't have a mass-media business model. You need teen obsessiveness, the market power of teen compulsion. To get at it, you have to offer something forbidden; some taboo has to get broken." All mass media are teen media, he concludes.[22] The problem is, the media culture today has moved beyond the notion of a single living-room television set for family viewing of *The Ed Sullivan Show*. It is far more pervasive—some have called it inescapable and omnivorous[23]—and what is considered taboo keeps reaching new levels.

At every point and in each medium the shock and speed levels are ratcheted up to win and sustain media consumers whose attention spans are becoming shortened and fragmented. All of it is predicated upon a worldview that keeps the self at the center of the universe, divorced from any higher law. This has led, predictably, to a cultural ethos of nihilism—the sense that life has no ultimate meaning.

Roberto Rivera, in an essay titled "Nothing, Nihilism, and Videotape," argues that the nihilism pervading today's youth culture is the offspring of Friedrich Nietzsche's death of God philosophy of the nineteenth century. Rivera draws upon the work of Thomas S. Hibbs, professor of philosophy at Boston College, who defines nihilism as "the state of spiritual impoverishment and shrunken aspirations" and "the growing sense that no religion or moral code is credible."[24] Without God who orders the universe, the argumentation goes, "definitions of good and evil are 'arbitrary.'" The subsequent "spiritual impoverishment" leads the human spirit to one of two places: to despair or to "creative boldness," the latter of which found expression in the Columbine killers. This creative boldness, according to Hibbs (and Rivera), results when a person "declares independence from outmoded notions of right and wrong" and "considers [himself] as transcending such considerations."[25] In Nietzschean terms this means they see themselves as being "beyond good and evil," which Dylan Klebold echoed when he said on the video, "we've . . . evolved into one step above" humans; "we're so . . . god-like"; "we have . . . self-awareness."

We are seeing the rise of the antihero, Nietzsche's "beyond good and evil" cult figure, depicted in many of today's movies and music. Before Michael Carneal took aim at his classmates in Paducah, Kentucky, he had been watching Leonardo DiCaprio act out a similar fantasy in the movie *The Basketball Diaries*. After Luke Woodham opened fire at his school in Pearl, Mississippi, he wrote in a letter, "Murder is not weak and slow-witted, murder is gutsy and daring."[26] Rivera concludes that Nietzschean nihilism means "no one cares, no one is in control, no one is innocent, and even if they are, there's no one around to vindicate their rights."[27] It is every man for himself, like Ayn Rand's "heroic being" that inspired Eric Harris.

Web pages and chat rooms on the Internet reveal the troubling fact that, for some, Harris and Klebold have assumed this cult-hero status. One Web site labeled them "Colorado's Thrillkill's MVPs" and another proclaimed, "Support Eric Harris and Dylan Klebold, Our fallen heroes!"[28] Shortly after the Columbine shootings, young people were seen in malls wearing T-shirts bearing the slogan, "We're still ahead, 13–2."[29]

The nihilism of youth culture and its attendant banality, individualism, and amorality are being woven into the fabric of our children's souls. "If children are living in pop culture, and a good part of it is ugly and stupid, that is effect enough; the sheer cruddiness is an affront," writes social critic David Denby. "The kids pick up this devaluing tone, the sense that nothing matters."[30] This has led to a third component that marks our teens' world: the loss of childhood.

The Loss of Childhood

School psychologist Richard Lieberman, quoted in *Time,* said, "Increasingly, we're seeing the high-risk population for lethal violence as being the 10-to-14 year-olds. Developmentally, their concept of death is still magical. They still think it's temporary, like little Kenny [who dies a bloody death in each episode] in *South Park.*"[31] The very vocabulary of that statement defies logic: High-risk for 10-to-14 year-olds? In America? This sounds like the conditions of childhood in Sierra Leone, where prepubescent boys are forced to pick up arms and fight a civil war. It would not come to mind as a condition of childhood in the most prosperous and powerful nation on the planet. The fact that children of that age remain at "high risk" for "lethal violence" says something about the state of childhood in America.

The *New York Times* recently ran an article titled, "No Room for Children in a World of Little Adults." In it, the writer, Peter Applebome, highlights how the roles of children in America and their adult counterparts are being reversed. "At a time when a Texas legislator can propose the death penalty be extended to 11-year-olds (and be taken seriously), when children commit ghastly murders and adults struggle to get in touch with their inner child, when first graders run on schedules as rigid and focused as CEOs, and CEOs go to camp to bond and climb mountains together, the blurring of the lines . . . reflects the blurring of the stages of life."[32] This blurring begins and accelerates with the media culture. That is where young people confront adult themes and situations and, many times,

67

receive little guidance as to how to interpret these confusing narratives. The "family hour" in television, which draws millions of young viewers, has included shows like *Friends* and *Seinfeld*. These offer plenty of laughs but little in the way of moral fortitude (the last episode of *Seinfeld* notwithstanding). Children as young as eleven or twelve attend R-rated movies[33] and the age of the average reader of *"16"* magazine is nine to fourteen.[34]

Joan Jacobs Brumberg, in her book *The Body Project,* traces the evolution of the lives of young girls over the twentieth century by studying their journal entries. She observed that in the 1900s, girls were preoccupied with sublime thoughts about virtues such as honesty and self-discipline. By the late 1990s, those concerns had given way to the more mundane: weight, hairstyle, and what brand of makeup to wear. In her review of Brumberg's book, Peggy Orenstein writes: "The average age of menarche has dropped so low that a girl today is likely to be sexually active before the age at which her great-great-grandmother began to menstruate. Yet since there is no equivalent acceleration in psychological development, these sexually mature youngsters are still little girls, children who are given scant help in coping with such a confusing mismatch."[35]

The highly sexualized environment of today's media culture (with a little help from a scandal in the White House) has prompted prepubescent kids all over the nation to ask about things like oral sex and how to find the G-spot,[36] and worse. A sixteen-year-old, who became sexually active at fourteen, said she learned everything she needed to know about sex from cable television. "It's all mad-sex stuff," she said.[37] A study conducted by a Rhode Island Rape Center involving 1,700 young people between sixth and ninth grades revealed that 65 percent of the boys and 57 percent of the girls believed it was acceptable for a male to force a female to have sex if the couple had been dating for six months.[38]

Dr. Robert W. Blum, a physician, is the director of the division of general pediatrics and adolescent health at the University of Minnesota that analyzes data on teenage sexual activity for the federal government. In an article in the *New York Times,* he said, "There are significant numbers of youngsters who are engaging in sexual activity at earlier ages. Besides intercourse, they are engaging in oral sex, mutual masturbation, nudity and exposure as precursors to intercourse." Dr. Richard Gallagher, director of the Parenting Institute at New York University's Child Study Center said elsewhere in the article, "I see no reason not to believe that soon a substantial number of youths will be having intercourse in the middle-school years."[39] But even more troubling is the "new, casual, brazen attitude" these children exhibit toward sex. "I call it body-part sex," said Dr. Marsha Levy-Warren, a psychologist on New York's Upper West Side. "The kids don't even look at each other. It's mechanical, dehumanizing. The fallout is that later in life they have trouble forming relationships. They're jaded."[40]

The sexual content of the media also reinforces false and superficial standards of beauty and virility. This, too, is taking its toll on young people of both genders in other ways. Roughly 90 percent of teenagers who are treated for eating disorders are female, but recent findings demonstrate that boys may be catching up in terms of insecurity and even psychological pathology when it comes to their view of self through the lens of physical appearance, according to Stephen Hall in an article in the *New York Times Magazine*.[41] "Young girls have suffered greatly from insecurity about appearance and body image, and the scientific literature on anorexia and related body-image disorders depicts a widespread and serious health problem in adolescent females," he writes. But "the cultural messages about an ideal male body, if not new, have grown more insistent, more aggressive, more widespread and more explicit in recent years."[42] This has precipitated what some psychologists are calling a "national crisis of boyhood."

The spate of recent books about young boys and masculinity, such as *Raising Cain* (1999) by Daniel J. Kindlon and Michael Thompson (et al.); William Pollack's *Real Boys* (1999); and Jonathan Kellerman's *Savage Spawn* (1999), highlights the rise of a generation of sad, angry, and increasingly violent young men. In his article, Hall examines how some adolescent males undertake a grueling, near-obsessive and self-abusive regimen of weight lifting and bodybuilding to achieve the perfectly sculpted male body with the appropriate "buff quotient." He cites many studies, but one that is especially telling is the informal study conducted by Roberto Olivardia and Harrion G. Pope Jr., of Harvard Medical School, tracing the body proportions of action figures over the years. "Once Pope and Olivardia gathered new and 'vintage' action figures, they measured their waist, chest, and biceps dimensions and projected them onto a 5-foot–10 male. Where the original GI Joe projected to a man of average height with a 32-inch waist, 44-inch chest and 12-inch biceps, the more recent figures have not only bulked up, but also show much more definition. Batman has the equivalent of a 30-inch waist, 57-inch chest and 27-inch biceps. 'If he was your height,' Pope told me, holding up Wolverine, 'he would have 32-inch biceps.' Larger, that is, than any bodybuilder in history.

"'People misinterpreted our findings to assume that playing with toys, in and of itself, caused kids to develop into neurotic people as they grew up who abused anabolic steroids,' Pope said. 'Of course that was not our conclusion. We simply chose the toys because they were symptomatic of what we think is a much more general trend in our society.'"[43]

"Males are getting the same medicine that women have had to put up with for years, which was trying to match an unattainable ideal in terms of body image," Hall concludes.[44]

The pressure applies to athletes and nonathletes but is especially galling to the latter. The unreported subtext of Eric Harris's hostility, Hall notes, was that he "apparently felt dissatisfied with his height, repeatedly complaining that he was smaller than his brother."[45]

In the same issue of the *New York Times Magazine,* Adrian Nicole LeBlanc tracks life on the other side of this struggle: the plight of those nonathletic types who forego the obsession with weight lifting but who feel similar pressure and inadequacies. They are the ones who operate "below the popular kids [the jocks] in a shifting order of relative unimportance"—"the druggies (stoners, deadheads, burnouts, hippies or neo-hippies), trendies or Valley Girls, preppies, skateboarders and skateboarder chicks, nerds and techies, wiggers, rednecks and Goths, better known as freaks. There are troublemakers, losers, floaters—kids who move from group to group. Real losers are invisible."[46] The author notes that being bullied goes with the territory.

The homicide and suicide rates of boys in the last forty years has seen a fivefold jump, "a rise some experts attribute to increasing male depression and anger as well as access to guns, among other factors," she writes. LeBlanc describes a boy named Andrew, fourteen, who is relentlessly bullied by "R.," fifteen, weighing two hundred pounds. On a routine day, Andrew says, he is body-slammed and shoved into chalkboards or dropped into a trash can headfirst. "At a school dance, in the presence of chaperones and policemen, R. lifted Andrew and ripped a pocket off his pants. 'One day I'll be a "faggot," the next day I'll be a "retard,"' says Andrew. Andrew joined the cross country team but the misery trailed him on the practice runs. He won't rejoin next year although he loves the sport."

Andrew used to earn straight As but now receives mostly Cs and Ds and was recently suspended, along with some friends, for suspected drug use. "He could understand the Columbine killers, Dylan Klebold and Eric Harris, if their misery had shown no signs of ending," writes LeBlanc.

The saddest part of Andrew's tale was that he did not expect to be helped by the adults in his world. The teachers and parents at the school dance, who witnessed R. roughing him up, took no action. He says he cannot talk to his mother and father about it because, "If I try to explain it to my parents they'll say, 'Oh, but you have plenty of friends.' . . . They don't really get it."[47]

This touches upon one of the most troubling components of our teens' world—that is, how adults have abdicated their role as moral guides, leaving young people to flounder like a rudderless ship on a tumultuous sea.

Adult Abdication

This is a touchy subject because I, being a Baby Boomer, understand the impulse behind it. I saw a cartoon once that showed a young person coming to his Boomer parent, asking for moral guidance. The parent clammed up and said, "You'd better go talk to your grandmother." For all the negative repercussions of the revolution of the sixties that I have touched upon, I am loathe to be too hard on one aspect of this revolution that, in many ways, has been healthy. That is, Baby Boomers have brought a more relational and interactive dynamic to the parent-child bond than many experienced with their own "establishment" parents. Many from that generation, heroic though they were in surviving the Great Depression and storming the beaches of Normandy, were also preoccupied with their before-dinner highballs and after-dinner bridge clubs to the neglect of their soon-to-be-revolutionized sons and daughters. The concept of a "soccer mom" did not exist when I was growing up. "As teenagers, boomers rebelled against all things authority," notes Jeff Brazil in *American Demographics*. "That's a strong quality that remains at their core even as they age. As parents, many boomers display a strong desire to be a friend to their child rather than an authority figure."[48]

Brazil measures this tangibly in the amount of cash teens generate in a year. A recent study of teens' allowances sponsored by Jay Zagorsky, a research scientist for Ohio State University's Center for Human Resource Research, revealed that allowances for kids between the ages of twelve and sixteen averaged $50 a week.[49] A study conducted by Teenage Research Unlimited revealed that in 1998 teens spent $141 billion, a 16 percent increase over the previous year. "On a per capita basis, they do have more money than prior generations," says TRU vice president Michael Wood.[50] Michael Kitei, president of the marketing consulting firm Small Talk, says studies show that children spend, or influence the spending of, $500 billion a year.[51]

Kitei and Wood suggest parental guilt is one motivating factor that has spurred teen spending. "Parents who are so time-tapped, what with two-parent working homes and chock-full calendars, they may be using money as a substitute for time." The kids don't seem to mind.

Dan Acuff, president of Youth Market Systems Consulting, says, "We've gone from a patriarchy to a matriarchy to a filiarchy, where [a lot of] power is ceded to the kids. It's whatever you want, Johnny."[52]

In the 1950s, 20 percent of mothers worked outside the home. Today, that figure has reached 70 percent.[53] This absence of parental oversight in the home has left many young people growing up in homes with no adult

71

presence for the bulk of the day, sometimes into the evening. Studies have shown that input from parents, even more so than the influence of peers or the media, goes a long way toward guiding the choices young people make, but many parents are either unavailable, aloof, or too tired. Partnership for a Drug-Free America conducted a survey of nearly ten thousand parents and teens in 1999. The survey revealed that teens who received antidrug messages at home were 42 percent less likely to use drugs. But many parents aren't taking the initiative to convey those messages.[54]

What's worse, while drug abuse among teens has dropped precipitously in recent decades, adult drug use has increased. According to a study done by the National Center for Health Statistics, the death rate for teenagers due to drugs fell 66 percent from 1970 to 1996 "but rose 113 percent among their aging baby-boom parents." "It is drug abuse among parents, not teen-agers, that is a crisis today."[55]

Some have called it a "new generation gap," not resulting from differences in morals and social outlook, as was the case for Baby Boomers and their parents, but from "career-driven parents [and] the economic necessity of two incomes."[56] The pace of this way of life has left little in the way of time and emotional reserves for lingering conversations with struggling kids. Author Patricia Hersch, in her best-selling book, *A Tribe Apart*, says the "most stunning change for adolescents today is their aloneness."[57]

> Today's teens have grown up in the midst of enormous social changes that have shaped, reshaped, distorted, and sometimes decimated the basic parameters for healthy development. They have grown up with parents who are still seeking answers about what it means to be an adult man or woman. . . . At a time when adolescents need to emulate role models, the adults around them are moving targets. . . . The effects go beyond issues of rules and discipline to the idea of exchanges between generations that do not occur, the conversations not held, the guidance and role modeling not taking place, the wisdom and traditions no longer filtering down inevitably. How can kids imitate and learn from adults if they never talk to them?[58]

Many studies have shown, and experts agree, that teen violence, in many cases, easily could be preempted by more parental vigilance. Many youths send plenty of signals when they are racked with violent thoughts and impulses. But they aren't taken seriously, says Dewey Cornell, a psychologist at the University of Virginia. "We need to take violence threats as seriously as we take threats of suicide," he says.[59]

Even where there might be some healthy give-and-take between parents and teens, many times parents, being Boomers, equivocate when it comes to asserting a clear moral voice. In the survey by the Partnership for a Drug-Free America, 68 percent of parents said that if they found a pound of marijuana in their kids' rooms they would talk to them about it, while only 12 percent said they would ground or punish their teen.[60]

Baby Boomers have been called the Peter Pan generation: "[We] became the first in human history . . . that imagined we might never grow old. Prolonged adolescence became the point of us."[61] The writer who coined that term, Richard Rodriguez, describes a wedding he attended at which the bride's seventeen-year-old daughter was giving her away. Her mother had been divorced three times. "The mother is dewy with liquid blush. The dry-eyed daughter has seen it all before."[62]

Moral equivocation has spilled over into our institutions. A recent study about the way marriage is presented in high school textbooks reveals that textbooks "generally treat marriage respectfully" and present it "as an important institution." But the study concluded that what these textbooks *didn't do* was more compelling:

> Trapped within the restrictive confines of a "health" paradigm, with its related psycho-therapeutic emphasis on individual self-actualization, these textbooks seldom even attempt to convey any broader understanding of marriage as a complex institution with many dimensions, including natural, legal, moral-religious, economic, and social. As a result, these books simply cannot address the core questions confronting today's teenagers. . . . The story of marriage and family life contained in these textbooks is not so much wrong . . . as it is empty: intellectually, emotionally, and morally vacuous. Many of today's teenagers, themselves children of the divorce revolution, are uncertain and even anxious about their own chances of achieving a loving marriage. . . .
>
> Finally, these textbooks provide fascinating insights into the overall state of our society, a window through which we can glimpse the current fault lines of the broader cultural debate. . . . These books clearly expose our often excessive reliance on health, self-actualization, and self-esteem as the main categories for understanding life. In turn, this one-dimensional vocabulary surely reflects a deeper ambivalence as to how, or even whether, in our pluralistic society, we might properly speak to one another in directly communal and moral terms about sexuality, marriage, and family life.[63]

Textbooks advance an "intellectually, emotionally, and morally vacuous" presentation of marriage so as not impose one person's version of morality upon someone who might embrace another version. Martin Marty notes that most youth "are overwhelmed by [this] relativism" and "tolerance and mere indifference are not attitudes and expressions that will do justice to their dreams and passions."[64] We, as a society, have tolerated so much that we have stripped the culture of clear lines between right and wrong. In the eyes of searching and struggling young people, this looks like a lack of belief in anything in deference to upholding dutifully a lot of little meaningless rules. Essayist Lewis Lapham puts it this way: "Absent a unified field of moral law that commands a sufficiently large number of people to obedience and belief, with what else do we fill in the blanks except a lot of little rules—rules about how to address persons of differing colors or sexual orientation, about when to wear fur and when not to eat grapes, about what to read or where to smoke?"[65]

Oddly, Eric Harris expressed frustration along these lines in one of his Web postings labeled "Society."

> I live in denver . . . people with their rich snobby attitude . . . like, yeah do 50 situps and 25 pushups each morning and run a mile every day and go to the gym and work out and just push yourself to be better and you can achieve anything and set high goals and have great expectations and be happy and be kind and treat everyone equal and give to charity and help the poor and stop violence and drive safely and don't pollute and don't litter and take shorter showers and don't waste water and eat right food and don't smoke or drink and don't sell guns and don't be a bad person. . . . phew. I say . . . shut up . . . and die

Baby Boomers are looking into the faces of their children and seeing a harvest of young people who have eaten of the tree of the knowledge of good and evil and don't know what to do with such knowledge. It is a burden the adults in their world have placed upon them. And, in many cases, adults have left them to figure it out on their own in a world bereft of a higher law.

The big/small inversion has instilled the sense that one's feelings are the center of the universe; the electronic media have glorified the vigilante antihero and made killing "gutsy"; the loss of childhood and crisis in boyhood have shared equally in robbing young people of innocence; adult abdication has left a vacuum in the realm of guidance and, by default, given youths the green light to nourish destructive fantasies and act on irrational impulses without anyone calling them to account. David Denby goes so far as to say that young people today "are shaped by the media as consumers before they've had a chance to develop their souls."[66]

America seemed shocked that the evil at Columbine could have emanated from "our kids." Yet Harris and Klebold's "war against the human race" was merely the final expression of the self-referring philosophy of our market-driven culture. There is no "higher law." Every person's individual belief *is* that person's law, even if it is Eric Harris's. He wrote in another Web posting under "Philosophy":

> My belief is that if I say something, it goes. I am the law, if you don't like it, you die. If I don't like you or I don't like what you want me to do, you die. If I do something incorrect, oh . . . well, you die. Dead people can't do many things, like argue, whine, b——, complain, narc, rat out, criticize, or even . . . talk. So that the only way to solve arguments with all you . . . out there, I just kill! God I can't wait till I can kill you people. I'll just go to some downtown area in some big-a— city and blow up and shoot everything I can. Feel no remorse, no sense of shame.

The cover copy on a special issue of the *New York Times Magazine* in 1999 read: "We put ourselves in the center of the Universe. Now, for better or worse, we are on our own."[67] Richard Russo wrote the lead essay and makes the point:

> Science, technology and humanist philosophy, by not allowing us to see the universe as operating according to moral principles overseen by God, have conspired to inflate our individual stocks in the absence of anything like an exchange. Each of us has the authority to print his own currency.
>
> Rather than proceeding from assumed truths that God must be at the center of things and that when we looked toward the skies we were observing a moral order, modern science insisted we observe the facts that were observable and reason *from* them, rather than *toward* them from assumptions that had not been tested. . . . Replace God with a machine (as Copernicus, Kepler, Galileo, and Newton did, without exactly meaning to), and right away you've got problems.[68]

Climbing Body Count

The body count from school shootings gets higher, while the age of some perpetrators gets lower. On October 1, 1997, in Pearl, Mississippi, Luke Woodham, then sixteen, stabbed his mother to death then took a .22 caliber rifle to school and killed two classmates. Michael Carneal followed suit a few months later, on December 12, in West Paducah, Kentucky. Then age fourteen, he said he was going to do "something big" and took a .22 caliber Ruger pistol and killed three girls at his school as they stood in a circle praying. A few days later, on December 15, Joseph "Colt"

Todd, fourteen, randomly shot two schoolmates with a .22 caliber rifle (there were no deaths). A few months after that, in Jonesboro, Arkansas, March 24, 1998, Mitchell Johnson, thirteen, and Andrew Golden, eleven, armed themselves with three rifles and seven other guns, tripped the fire alarm at their school, and stood in wait outside, killing four students and a teacher as they exited for the fire drill. Kip Kinkel, fifteen, two months later on May 21, 1998, in Springfield, Oregon, killed his parents and then went to his school with a .22 caliber rifle and shot twenty-four fellow students, killing two.[69] As noted by *U.S. News and World Report,* "It wasn't even the only school yard killing *last week.* "[70]

Perhaps the most wrenching school shooting was the death of six-year-old Kayla Rolland in March 2000. She died in room six at Buell Elementary School in Mount Morris Township, near Flint, Michigan, after a classmate, also age six, pulled a gun and shot her.

Homicides committed by young people age seventeen or younger have declined in the last decade, down by nearly a third.[71] But they have been nearly always perpetrated by disaffected adolescent males who have struggled with feelings of powerlessness[72] and, in many cases, feeling "physically or emotionally abandoned by those who should love them."[73] When the assistant principal finally subdued Woodham during his shooting spree in Pearl, he asked him, "Why? Why? Why?" The boy answered, "Mr. Myrick, the world has wronged me."[74]

The Columbine killers echoed similar complaints. Klebold blamed his troubles on the people he knew in day care. Harris blamed the government for the military life of constant relocation, putting him back on the "bottom of the . . . ladder again and again." Klebold blamed his family: "You made me what I am. Actually, you just added to what I am." Harris blamed the handful of girls who never returned his phone calls: "You know who you are. Thanks, you made me feel good. . . . Think about that for a while." Klebold said, "If you could see all the anger I've stored up over the past four . . . years. I hope we kill 250 of you." Harris said, "If you get p—ed, well, go kill some people. Take out some aggression." They proclaimed it was payback time when they entered the Columbine library. Feeling victimized and exacting revenge arises from the sense of being empowered to act upon one's own version of truth as the master of one's destiny. It gets messy, however, when one person, in mastering his personal destiny, cuts short the destiny of someone else. Then, as Russo aptly puts it, we've got problems.

Most young people slog through the troughs of adolescent despair to emerge relatively unscathed as healthy adults. But some—in a season of mental or emotional crisis, lacking moral constraints or accountability—defer to lower instincts propelled by notions of the antihero that have been drummed into them. You make a plan, as in the video game "Doom," and write your own script, just as Harris and Klebold did when they worked out the details of their rampage. Why are we surprised to see young people acting on the impulses and the values-free paradigm that our culture has taught them? Why are we shocked that they bring a consumer nonchalance to moral issues such as sex, drugs, and even killing?

Loss of Magnanimity

Perhaps the horror that reverberated nationwide after Columbine echoed our fear that this event signaled the rise of a generation of "men without chests" (gender issues aside), described by C. S. Lewis in his book *The Abolition of Man*. Lewis argues that when young people are reared in an environment that jettisons "objective value" (what he calls "the belief that certain attitudes are really true and others really false"[75]) the result is a system that creates young people bereft of magnanimity and driven by visceral cravings—his men without chests. "Without the aid of trained emotions the intellect is powerless against the animal organism. . . . The head rules the belly through the chest—the seat . . . of Magnanimity, of emotions organized by trained habit into stable sentiments. The Chest—Magnanimity—Sentiment—these are the indispensable liaison officers between cerebral man and visceral man. It may even be said that it is by this middle element that man is man: for by his intellect he is mere spirit and by his appetite mere animal." Lewis concludes: "The practical result of [such an] education . . . must be the destruction of the society which accepts it."[76]

Don Marxhausen said Harris and Klebold mixed their rage with a plan and somewhere in the plan they crossed a line and "got lost." In a world that presumes there is nothing greater to serve than our cravings, and nothing to which we must give an account except our own inclinations, we are all destined to get "lost." Russo asks in his essay: "If God is out of the picture, where do we turn for wisdom and purpose: To ourselves? Or to our 'self'?"[77]

The answer to that question lay beneath my feet in that solitary unmarked grave. It was the saddest one of all.

Chapter 5

Cassie's Yes

Her Final Moments: Martyrdom or Myth?

THE ACCOUNT OF THE death of Cassie Bernall introduced the first overtly religious element to the Columbine story. Cassie quickly became a central figure whose reported confession of faith in God at gunpoint captured the imaginations of the religious and jaded alike. Young people nationwide (perhaps worldwide) saw the story as a rallying cry to commit their lives to God, and more, to be willing to die for him, if necessary, as Cassie did. One person wrote on Cassie's cross on Rebel Hill, "You made me believe."

The transcendence of this story was quickly overtaken by the crass marketing of Cassie's death in all manner of key chains, bumper stickers, and other paraphernalia, as if she had become the patron saint of the Christian Booksellers Association. It did not take long for the nonreligious to turn a cynical eye toward Christians who seemed to exploit this tragic death to advance a key chain version of what it means to follow God. It was only a matter of time before the image of "Saint Cassie" fell from grace, and the cynics pounced.

As a Christian, I too had been inspired by the account of Cassie's confession before death; as a mother of teens, I was especially heartened to see its effect on my own sons, who were equally moved. But when questions emerged in September 1999 about whether an encounter between Cassie and her killer had taken place, my journalistic instincts to get to the bottom of it went full throttle. Painful as it would have been to concede that the Christian community had embraced a fabrication, I was ready to go down that road to get to the truth about what had happened to Cassie that day.

Where that road led unfolds in the following pages. But even beyond her last moment, Cassie Bernall's place in the Columbine story remains at the center of its religious resonance.

Descent into Darkness

It seems implausible that Cassie Bernall was born with dark hair, given the silky blond locks that became one of her defining features. Her hair quickly turned from dark to light, her parents said, and her blond locks, along with her crystal blues eyes, button nose, and duck feet, made her an irresistible daddy's girl.

Brad Bernall wasn't thrilled when he first heard that his young wife, Misty, was pregnant with their first child. "I had visions of doing things and going places before we settled down," he said. He admitted he was hard on Misty during the early going of the pregnancy: "I couldn't understand why she was so tired and getting so big.

"Anyway, when I saw Cassie come out of the womb, it did something to me. Cassie was everything. I changed her first diaper. I wanted to do everything for her. She was always at my side. Even when I was cutting the grass, I would drag her and, later, her [younger] brother [Chris] around in the playpen from one section of the yard to the other."

Misty has vivid memories of the "terrible twos." "Cassie would have fits. She was strong-willed. Chris was a little bit easier to deal with than Cassie. She really was a difficult baby—but she was so cute. I remember when she used to lay her head down on the bed. We had a crib right next to the bed, and when Brad would come in and talk to me, she would lie there and pretend to be asleep, but her eyes were rolling around. When he would leave for work, she used to run to the window and cry as if to say, 'He left! He didn't want to be with me!'"

"She was always a little bit stubborn," Brad added. "She always had a mind of her own, and sometimes she would try to execute her own little will. She was probably three or four when I taught her how to adjust the bathwater herself. She was probably in kindergarten when I sat her down at the table and started showing her fundamentals of algebra and sets using things like forks, spoons, table knives, toothpicks—whatever I could get my hands on. We soon substituted A, B, and C."

Cassie's life lessons would, too soon, take a different turn. Before she hit adolescence she made friends with a girl whom the Bernalls call "Mona" (not her real name), who quickly monopolized Cassie's attention and pulled her into a sphere that would test their parent-child bond. "Cassie gravitated more and more to her, and before you knew it, so much time had elapsed that Mona was her only girlfriend," said Brad. "That's when things started getting a little hard."

The girls had become friends in the fifth grade, but things didn't begin to deteriorate until Cassie reached junior high. "Seventh grade was hard," said Misty, "Her attitude was getting worse. There was a season in eighth grade when she started coming back out of it, and she was a little easier to deal with. But once they hit ninth grade and high school, things deteriorated very quickly."

The Bernalls began receiving phone calls from the school informing them that Cassie had been missing several classes during the day and that her grades were slipping. "We knew there was something wrong. Her attitude was very rebellious," said Misty. "That's when we began to question what was going on with her."

The Bernalls later found out that when Cassie skipped class, she and Mona would either wander the halls or go to the parking lot to drink or smoke pot. On many occasions they told their parents they were going to stay after school to work on special projects. Instead, they experimented with drugs.

In December 1996, Cassie's freshman year, Misty took matters into her own hands. She quit her full-time job to be home more and decided to take the initiative in confronting what was wrong in her daughter's increasingly troubled life. "I remember trying to figure out why her friends didn't like us. They didn't like that we had rules and didn't respect us. I went into Cassie's room at one point to snoop around, to see if I could find her teen Bible, to see if there were any insights there that could help me figure out if this was normal or if we should be alarmed," she said.

"I came across a drawer full of letters from Cassie's friend, Mona. They gave us a major indication about what was going on. The essence was that Cassie should kill her parents and then all her problems would be over. They had drawings about how they should do this. There was also a teacher they didn't like and there was a drawing of how they should end her life. They talked about sniffing glue and smoking pot and drinking during lunch, and the occult, and about getting this other boy involved to help kill us so that Cassie could do what she wanted to do."

Her friend, it turns out, had been feeling threatened because the Bernalls had told Cassie that if she didn't straighten up, they were going to take her out of the public school and put her in a private school.

"I took the letters," said Misty, "and when Brad came home he called the minister and the sheriff's department. If something did happen to us, we wanted them to know that we thought it was serious. When this girl would sign the letters, she would draw a monkey that had a pentagram and vampire teeth and, many times, a knife dripping blood—as a symbol for herself."

"We never recovered any of the letters Cassie passed on to Mona," said Brad, "but we know they were very similar."

The Bernalls photocopied the letters, making one set for the sheriff's office, one set for Mona's parents, and one set for themselves. When Cassie came home from school that day, they confronted her. "The first thing she said was, 'Well, we didn't mean anything. Why are you taking this so seriously? This is ridiculous.' She got very, very angry with us," said Misty. "As the weeks continued, her hostility toward us grew. It was suggested by the sheriff's department that we have a meeting with this girl and her parents.

"When we went to this meeting and first walked in, Brad went to the father to shake his hand. He said, 'Don't bother.' Then, when they sat down, it was the girl and her parents—and Cassie sat with them. It felt like it was us against them. The sheriff said that these were some of the worst things that he had seen in his ten years of juvenile work and that these parents should take it seriously. The only thing the father said was that this was our way of breaking up a five-year friendship."

The Bernalls intervened decisively when they realized the extent of Cassie's rebellion. They broke off Cassie's ties with all her friends and pulled her out of the public high school to put her in a Christian school. There she met a girl named Jamie, who remembers a dark, troubled rebel: "When I first met Cassie [in the winter of 1997] she was like really closed off, really bitter and hopeless, and she wallowed in that hopelessness. . . . A few times we talked about God, but she told me that she had given her soul to Satan through one of her friends. She said, 'There's no way I can love God.'

"She was really struggling with suicide. She'd write these really dark, suicidal poems. She also had a problem with cutting herself and hurting herself. I don't know how deep that problem was, but I know she did it frequently. She'd bring this metal file thing to school with her, and she and another friend would cut themselves. She also said she'd been doing marijuana."[1]

Cassie described this painful season of her life in an essay she wrote for her English class: "Throughout this time I hated my parents and God with deepest, darkest hatred. There are no words that can accurately describe the blackness I felt."[2]

Beyond cutting off her old friendships and changing her school, the Bernalls also made Cassie a prisoner, more or less, in her own home. "We took all of her privileges away," said Brad. "She could go to youth group, that was all. We answered the phone when we were home, and we put a phone monitor on the lines so that when we weren't there, we could find out what she was doing."

"I had made the decision not to go back to work, and we stayed with her constantly," said Misty. "We would go through her backpack and through her bedroom. . . . Life was not any fun for Cassie. During that time she was so angry with us that she was threatening suicide. She would go through bouts where she would scream and yell at us. I remember one incident where she was sitting on her bed screaming and yelling at me. I was sitting on the floor and I put my hand on her knee and started to pray for her until she subsided. We knew it was a battle of wills. But it was also a spiritual battle."

"We told her that she had lost all the trust we had invested in her and she had to earn it back," said Brad. "And the only way she could do that was to start being obedient. It was very hard at first, because we'd catch her and we'd call her on it. Sometimes we would walk around the block and take the wireless phone with us. When we were back behind the house across the street, we would turn it on and catch her talking. She finally saw that we were going to be as relentless as she was."

"She threatened to run away and we'd say, 'You can go with these people, or Grandma and Grandpa in Texas,'" said Misty. "I told her, 'You know that if you run away they'll probably put you in a foster home.' I think that deterred her. I remember one day she said, 'I'm going to live with Grandma and Grandpa Bernall' and I said, 'Fine. I'll call them tonight.' Then, by that afternoon when she got home from school, she had changed her mind. I think Cassie knew deep down that we loved her and that home was a good place to be."

Rather than suffer with self-doubt and recriminations, Brad and Misty were secure in their parenting and were not shaken from their position when Cassie would lash out at them. "I remember feeling an incredible sense of betrayal," said Misty. "We loved her so much and were trying to be good parents, and she totally rejected our love and betrayed her family by agreeing with this girl that her parents were bad. Brad and I raised our kids in church, and we toughed it out through some rough times in our marriage because we felt like it was important for kids to have both parents. I would get the kids out in the morning, and Brad was there for them in the afternoons. We were there for them."

"I felt like we were pretty good parents," said Brad. But, he said, just as many children do when they reach the point of making decisions for themselves, "she started trading our rules, our morals and values for those of the girl she was with. She started making some bad decisions."

The Bernalls' tenacity slowly turned the tide with Cassie. She began to realize that life was indeed more pleasant when she stopped trying to out-maneuver her parents and simply did what they said. She was developing more friendships at her new school and at church, and she slowly won back some privileges. Brad and Misty were put to the test, however, when Cassie approached them one day in March 1997, and asked if she could attend, with Jamie, a weekend youth retreat sponsored by Jamie's church. Misty's first impressions of Jamie were mixed. "She had real short bleach-blonde hair and these bead necklaces and kind of a grunge look. I thought, 'Oh Lord, what are you doing?' But then she got in the back seat of the car and Cassie introduced her to me, and I turned around and looked at her. She had the shiniest, brightest eyes and the love of the Lord was evi-dent. She wanted Cassie to go on this weekend retreat with her church. We just didn't trust Cassie enough to be able to do that. We figured she'd leave and run away.

"Then Jamie wrote us a letter saying, 'I think this would be good for Cassie, and I wish you would trust her to go with me.'

"We finally agreed," said Misty. "I remember we prayed all weekend for God to take care of her. When we picked her up on that Sunday, I saw all these kids getting off the bus and standing around smoking. A lot of them had that rebellious look, and I thought, 'Oh boy.' Then Cassie got out of the car that she was in. The kids in the car had been smoking. And I thought, 'What is going on?'"

Brad continued: "When I saw Cassie start to come toward us, I knew something was different. There was a spring in her step, and as she drew closer I could see a sparkle in her eyes. She was smiling. Her eyes were open and bright. When she left, her head was down and she was depressed. When she came back, it was like she had been in a dark room and a light got turned on and she saw what was around her and realized the beauty of it. She was radiant. She walked up to us and said to both of us, 'I've changed.'"

Reflecting on that day, Misty repeated her daughter's words. "'Mom, I've changed. I know you're not going to believe me. But I'll prove it to you.' And from that time forward," Misty said, "she stuck to her guns. She was lonely, and it was a hard road for her, but she never turned back."

According to Jamie, while they were at the retreat some of the group had prayed for Cassie. They went outside and placed their hands on her and prayed for her, and Cassie said that she physically felt a burden being lifted from her body. "She said it was a physical sensation," said Brad, "and she knew that the Lord had released her from the dark powers that she knew held her."

That is not to say that Cassie did not still struggle with her newfound faith and her understanding of God after this dramatic turnaround. She told Jamie one time: "I go through the motions of faith, I go to all the Bible studies, and everyone at youth group thinks I'm all right, but inside it's like I sometimes feel really disconnected and far from God."[3]

Zach Johnston described Cassie in his Web posting: "When I was a sophomore I noticed a new girl in class. She was very pretty and quiet. At the time I didn't take much notice to her since my attention was usually drawn to Ms. Haggard, who always caught me mouthing off or doing something I shouldn't have been doing. Then we were given an assignment where you had to pick a partner and write about something I cannot remember. Each group of two had to stand up and read their paper. I read mine and, as usual, was yelled at by Ms. Haggard for screwing around and not writing about the correct topic. Then Cassie stood up and read her paper alone because she didn't have a partner. It was about how she was new at Columbine High School and she tried to explain how unfair it was to have to do a partner assignment when you don't know anybody. She read her paper with great confidence and didn't care what anyone thought. After she sat down some students grumbled and whispered negative comments, but not I. There was something about this girl that caused me to stay quiet. I wanted to approach her and talk to her everyday of that semester after that, but I never did.

"Then a few months ago, a girl I knew, who is friends with Cassie, told me I should talk to her because she said Cassie is really nice and an overall cool person. I still had this fear of talking to her. I didn't understand it. I could probably go up to my principal and recite every bad word I knew, but I couldn't even say 'hi' to this girl.

"Well one day I was in the photo room after school making up work and she walked in. I figured, 'What the heck' and went over and talked to her. She turned out to be one of, if not *the* coolest person I have ever spoken with. I could tell she was nervous because she probably thought I was some sort of freak for telling her I remembered [her] paper that she [couldn't] even remember writing."

On the Friday before the shooting, CHS held its annual preprom assembly in which, according to Amanda Meyer, "they get the whole school together and say, 'Don't drink and drive after prom because you're gonna die,' blah, blah, blah." That day, school principal Frank DeAngelis said to the student body, "Look at that person sitting next to you and imagine your life without that person." Amanda was sitting next to Cassie. "I looked at her and I shook my head and I'm like, 'No way; I would die without you.' And she gave me the saddest smile I have ever seen in my entire life."

That Sunday, April 18, Cassie's youth group at West Bowles Community Church created video snippets of the kids sharing, in a few sentences, how they see themselves as "furthering the kingdom" of God in their lives. Cassie stood outside, in front of an evergreen tree. It must have been fairly warm, because she wore no coat, only a black Hard Rock Cafe T-shirt. Her hair was down, and the wind brushed it back and forth over her shoulders. She seemed comfortable in front of the camera, sometimes looking straight into it, other times allowing her eyes to wander as she gathered her thoughts. She said: "I think that the way I'm furthering the kingdom is just being a loyal friend and a good example to nonbelievers and also Christians, um, just trying to not contradict myself and get rid of all hypocrisy and just to live for Christ."

Cassie had been crying on Monday, April 19. Amanda said, "Cassie, why are you crying?" Cassie answered, "I don't know. I can't put it into words." Later that day, Amanda saw Cassie at her locker and said, "Cassie, I just love you so much. What would I do without you?"

On Tuesday morning, Cassie handed Amanda Meyer a note that read: "Honestly, I totally want to live my life completely for God. It's hard and scary, but totally worth it!!" It was signed with a smiley face. Zach Johnston also saw Cassie that day: "I would greet her in the hall for the last time a few minutes before she entered the library on April 20, 1999."

Cassie was supposed to meet Amanda in the school library during lunch hour so they could study *Macbeth* for their English class. During the hour before, Amanda accompanied a friend to Taco Bell and spilled taco sauce on her new white silk shirt. The friend talked Amanda into going home to change before returning to school. Amanda never made it to meet Cassie. Cassie was studying *Macbeth* when Eric Harris and Dylan Klebold walked into the library. She was shot early in the killing spree that lasted about seven and a half minutes.

By the time Amanda and her friend drew close to the school, she said, "kids were running down Pierce and a girl was screaming, 'Don't go to the school. Don't go to the school.'"

Ominous Early Reports

"I came home early that day," recalled Brad Bernall. "I wasn't feeling well and thought that before I went to sleep I'd do a little bit of work." It was a nice day and Brad opened his windows. The Bernall's home shares the southern perimeter of the school—they can see it from their yard—which is why he heard popping sounds coming from the school grounds around lunchtime that day. "I thought the kids were out lighting firecrackers. I didn't pay it any mind," he said.

Meanwhile, Misty had received a call from a friend who was the first to tell her there had been a shooting at Columbine. She promptly called Brad, who still hadn't realized the seriousness of what he had heard, and he went outside to see if he could see anything.

"There were sheriffs all over and I could hear gunfire exchanged. I realized what was going on. I knew there was nothing I could do, so I turned on the TV. The news bulletins were fully geared up," he said.

Misty left work and, like everyone else who was trying to get to the school, she was caught in a web of traffic and blocked streets. "When I came down the hill to our street it was blocked off," she said. After trying to get home by another route and finding it also blocked, Misty identified herself to the police and said that she had to be able to get to her house. Finally she was allowed to pass.

"I went to the back yard and climbed the fence and saw the SWAT team members. We were about a hundred yards from the building," she said. "Brad and I took off and tried to drive over to the school. They wouldn't let us through. We came home and heard they were having parents meet at the [public] library. I grabbed the cell phone and Brad stayed here, because we hadn't heard from either of the two kids. We had two kids in that school.

"We kept calling back and forth, and finally I got a call from Brad that [our son] Chris had called. I knew something was not good, because Cassie was our more responsible child. I knew she would call. There was another meeting place over at Leawood Elementary School, which was across our neighborhood on the other side of Pierce. They had lists being faxed in of the names of kids that were safe. Then they were starting to get lists of the injured. I scanned the lists. Nothing. I finally left the library and went across the park to the parking lot just north of the school. They had it cordoned off, but all the media were starting to come in. Police were there and the buses were starting to come out of the school—they would load up kids and bring them out.

"By that time our youth pastor [Dave McPherson] found me and some other members of our church, and we ran across the parking lot and started checking the buses for Cassie. I asked everyone I saw if they knew or had seen Cassie. There was a bus that came out and Craig Nason, from our youth group, was on that bus. He was reaching out and grabbing my hand, and I said, 'Craig, have you seen Cass?' He said, 'No.' Then the bus took off. We learned later that that was the last bus to come out of the school."

Misty returned to the public library, which was on the northern end of Clement Park. By then it was early evening, between 5:00 and 6:00 P.M. She saw one of Cassie's friends, Erica, and asked her if she had seen Cassie. Erica said she hadn't. Misty told her that Cassie had been in the library, and Erica's eyes widened and she said, "Oh my gosh, that's where the worst of it took place."

The parents who remained, whose loved ones had not been accounted for, were told to congregate at Leawood. So the Bernalls snaked their way through the blocked roads and again returned to Leawood. Once they were there, as Misty described it, "We sat and waited." Amanda Meyer waited with the Bernalls to hear word of Cassie.

"Somebody had said there was going to be another busload of kids. So we kept looking," said Misty. "We'd go to the sidewalk, we'd look, we'd check the streets to see if any bus was coming. Then pretty soon the SWAT team members started showing up at the school. I remember seeing them carrying their gun cases in, and one guy had his semiautomatic weapon. I remember thinking, 'What are we dealing with here?'

"They started getting physical descriptions of the kids," said Misty. Amanda had to tell the coroner what Cassie was wearing because Misty couldn't remember. Earlier that morning, around the time of second period, Cassie had complained to Amanda about how bad she thought she looked in her outfit, a turquoise shirt with a black tanktop and blue jeans. The last thing Amanda said to Cassie before they parted was, "Never forget that you're beautiful."[4] That's why Amanda remembered what Cassie was wearing that day.

"There were quite a few families there, because there were a lot of kids that weren't accounted for, including kids that had been injured," said Misty. "They weren't giving us any information, so we finally gave up at the elementary school and came home. We still had hope that maybe Cassie was hiding in a closet, someplace in there, still alive."

About 10:30 that night, the Bernalls heard a huge explosion coming from the school. They ran up to Cassie's room on the second floor to see if there were flames or smoke.[5] "We're thinking, 'My gosh, what if she is in there and she's injured,'" said Misty. They thought that at any moment they would get a phone call telling them some news of Cassie's whereabouts. No one called. Exasperated that their daughter was still unaccounted for, Brad took binoculars and stood on top of the shed in their backyard in an attempt to see through the windows of the school. "We saw the ATF [agents of the Bureau of Alcohol, Tobacco, and Firearms] walking around the library, but that was about all we could see."

As that first night wore on, the Bernalls tried to sleep. "Brad slept a little, but I couldn't sleep. I remember lying there thinking, 'She's over the fence a hundred yards away from us and they won't let us get to her. It was such a sense of helplessness. It was agonizing. I got up at 3:00 A.M. That would have been Wednesday morning."

Brad also got up. They showered and decided to try to walk to the school. They encountered a police officer at the end of the street.

"We tried to get information out of him," said Brad. "I told him our child was still in there and we just wanted to know what the truth is. We just want to know if there is anyone still alive in there. He paused and said, 'No. There is no one left alive.'"

Brad said, "Thanks."

Misty said, "We appreciate your honesty."

Still No Word

Later that Wednesday morning one of Misty's friends came to the house and they tried to go to the school. "They wouldn't let us through," said Misty, "so we went across the stream and over as close to the school as they would let us get. I wanted to know—are they taking care of her? Are they removing her?

"I then went down to the end of the street to see if they were starting to bring people out. They hadn't identified anyone yet, so you can't give up. You can't give up.

"There was an officer there that said they wanted all the parents to meet back at Leawood. So we went back over to the elementary school, and they met us there, and we proceeded to sit and wait and wait.

"At about 1:30 P.M. the district attorney gathered all of us around and said, 'We can't let you people wait any longer. We've got unofficial IDs.' It was 1:30 Wednesday afternoon when he said, 'Yes, Cassie had been identified by her clothing and by our description.' But it wasn't official. One of the families, Danny Rohrbough's family, found out that Danny was one of the dead because the *Rocky Mountain News* had his picture on the front page. It was very difficult.

"We came home and we were still waiting for them to get her out of there and to give us absolute positive identification. We felt she might be dead, but held on to a shred of hope. I just wanted her out of there. I wanted someone to start taking care of her. It was 2:00 A.M. Thursday when we finally got a call from the coroner's office saying that they had her. They had just brought her in. They didn't start the autopsy until late Thursday afternoon."

The first time the Bernalls were able to see Cassie was after her body had been sent to the funeral home later that Thursday. Brad had spoken to the people there and told them that he wanted to see her right away— "before you do anything to her," as he told them.

"We had been told that Cassie had been shot in the head with a shotgun," he said, "so I expected the worst. I went in first and looked her over and, surprisingly, she looked pretty good, considering. It was our Cassie.

"I kissed her toes. I kissed her cheek. She was cold. I cried on her chest. I covered her face with my jacket, and then Misty came in."

"She had those little baby duck feet," said Misty. "When she was born, Brad looked at her and said, 'Oh, you've got duck feet just like your mom.'"

Someone Said "Yes"

Word began to spread the day of the shooting that a girl had been asked if she believed in God and then was shot dead for answering yes. As the Bernalls wandered between the public library and the school with many in their church trying to help them locate Cassie, a girl, a stranger, ran up to youth pastor Dave McPherson and said, "Oh my God, they asked her if she believed in God, and when she said yes, they shot her." Dave instantly thought, *Who else could that be but Cassie?*

"Then," said Misty Bernall, "We heard it through Craig Scott and, later, through Joshua Lapp," both of whom she said identified the speaker as Cassie.

The situation in the school library as the killers went from table to table taunting and shooting people was "generally a lot of noisy pandemonium," as one investigator described it. Students were huddled under tables and desks, some were crouched in the fetal position and curled on their backs under study carrels with wooden sides. Once the shooting started, gunshots, screams, and moans only confused the picture. Some had their hands over their ears and eyes. Others heard echoes from the hardwood sides of the carrels. Still others would have been so traumatized that they would have experienced "tunnel vision," as described to me by Gary Muse, who then was a Jefferson County Sheriff's department investigator. He said that in a crisis situation the body reacts in several ways. The digestive tract shuts down (which sometimes causes vomiting), the circulation slows down (which sometimes causes fainting), and the part of the brain involving peripheral vision blanks out. "You're only focusing on the danger," said Muse. "You only see or hear what you're focusing on. Anytime you have a traumatic situation, even if only one person is killed, every single testimony is different."

As people got together and started to piece together their stories, they concluded that two girls in the library had been asked if they believed in God—Cassie Bernall and Valeen Schnurr. Valeen was shot *before* the gunman posed the question, and she survived; Cassie was shot *after* answering yes, and she died.

"Kids started comparing notes in the park that evening," said Jill Meyer, Amanda's mother. "The kids that were in the library, before the account had been reported [in papers] and before they knew that Cassie was dead, were saying that's what happened."

According to Jill Meyer, the Bernalls insisted on not allowing the account of Cassie's last moments to become exaggerated. "They would say things like, 'Are you sure that's what she said? Don't embellish anything. We want only the truth,'" said Jill. "They said, 'Don't say that she said "Yes, I believe in Jesus" or "Yes, I'm a Christian" if that isn't what was heard.'

"The consistent story was just that she had said 'yes' and that he said, 'Why?' and she was shot before she had time to answer. It would have been easy, if that hadn't been the case, to substantiate it. The Bernalls were diligent about that from day one."

It didn't take long for the story to get picked up by the press. The earliest published accounts of what had happened in the library appeared on April 21. Evan Todd, who was in the library, told the *Denver Post,* "I saw them shoot a girl because she was praying to God."[6] The *San Jose Mercury News* reported, "Emily Wyant and Cassie Bernall were both shaking under another library table. 'Who's going to be next in line to die?' one of the gunmen asked, then headed toward Emily and Cassie. The gunman glanced past Emily, who buried her head in the floor, then took a closer look at Cassie. He shot her point blank in the temple, just inches from Emily. Cassie grabbed her head and looked at Emily, bewildered, then slumped to the floor and died."[7]

On April 25, the *Rocky Mountain News* included a story with this account: "They walked through the library asking the kids why they should live, laughing and hooting as they shot them. If someone quivered or yelled after the first volley, they'd shoot them again.

"'Peekaboo!' one of them said to a student hiding under a table. And then came the blast of a gun.

"'Do you believe in God?' one of them asked Cassie Bernall as he trained his gun on her.

"'Yes, I believe in God,' she answered.

"'Why?' he asked.

"He didn't wait for an answer."[8]

One week after the shooting, the *Rocky Mountain News* ran a story about Valeen Schnurr: "She heard other students being shot, some pleading for their lives. The screams coming from her end of the room drew the gunmen's attention, and they came back her way, guns blazing.

"When the bullets and shrapnel hit Valeen, she slumped and clutched her abdomen. 'Oh my God, oh my God!' she remembers saying.

"'God!' one of the gunmen taunted her. 'Do you believe in God?'

"Moments earlier, Valeen saw what happened when Cassie was asked the same question and answered yes.

"'Val was scared to say, "Yes,"' says Valeen's mother. 'But she was scared to say "no," because she thought she was dying.'

"Finally, she told the gunmen, 'Yes, I believe in God.'"[9]

In due course, national media also picked up the story. A week after the shooting, the Bernalls appeared on the television show *Oprah* and the first question host Oprah Winfrey asked them was, "Do you wish she had said 'no'?"

"After knowing that a girl begged for her life and was released," said Misty, "as a mom you would have wanted her to beg for her life. So, on the one hand, you're like, 'Yeah, I'd have wanted her to beg.' But I can't think of a more honorable way to die than to profess your faith in God. We were very proud of her before her stand for Christ. She said 'yes' to Christ every day of her life, and it wasn't always easy for her."

Time and *Newsweek* ran covers stories on Columbine in their May 3 editions, both of which reported that a girl had died confessing her faith. *Time* identified her as Cassie Bernall.[10] *Brill's Content* later evaluated both magazines on the accuracy of their reporting. Under the heading "Test of Faith: A gunman asked a girl if she believed in God. After she said she did, he shot her dead," *Brill's* said both magazines had reported it accurately.[11]

The *Weekly Standard* ran two articles on Cassie alone May 10. Matt Labash wrote one called "'Do You Believe In God?' 'Yes.'"[12] and J. Bottum wrote "A Martyr Is Born." Bottum wrote, "Eight of the murdered students at

Columbine high school were serious Christians, four Catholics and four evangelicals. The killers went after 17-year-old Rachel Scott and 18-year-old Valeen Schnurr apparently for no other reason than that they had Bibles. The central image of Littleton, however, is that of Cassie—the 17-year-old with a gun to her head being asked if she believed in God."[13]

On May 15, Dave Cullen wrote in the electronic magazine *Salon.com* of Cassie Bernall, "a modern-day Christian martyr,"[14] while *Time*'s May 17 issue reaffirmed the account: "In ever widening circles the story that lingers is the tale of Cassie Bernall."[15]

In June, the *Denver Post* ran an extensive story relating in meticulous detail the account of Patti Nielson, the art teacher who had been huddled under the checkout desk in the library throughout the rampage, who had finally broken her silence about that day:

"'You'd hear them yell something terrible,' Nielson said. 'Then, boom.

"'When one girl said "Oh God, oh God," an assassin asked her, "Do you believe in God?' When she said she did, she was shot. But another girl also cried "Oh God, oh God," and I didn't hear shots, so I knew she was alive.'"[16]

A day later, in the June 13 edition of the *Denver Post*, another major article spelled out what had happened with equal attention to detail:

"Nearby, a killer waved a gun at Cassie Bernall.

"'Do you believe in God?'

"'Yes, I do believe in God,' the girl replied.

"Boom.

"'Why?' the killer asked the dead girl.

"Now Harris and Klebold moved away from the library windows where they started. Beneath a table huddled Lauren Townsend, Lisa Kreutz, Val Schnurr, Jeanna Park and Diwata Perez. A shotgun fired and hit Townsend, Kreutz, Schnurr, and Park. Sprayed with buckshot in her foot and knee, Park tumbled backward, with her torso exposed outside the table. Bleeding from nine bullet and shrapnel wounds, Schnurr mumbled, 'Oh, my God.'

"Harris stopped her.

"'Do you believe in God?' he demanded.

"Schnurr had heard the result when Bernall professed her faith. Still, Schnurr answered truthfully.

"'Yes, my mom and dad brought me up that way,' Schnurr replied.

"She fainted and fell to the floor."[17]

By late May, the story of Cassie's confession had inspired a revival, of sorts, in teen spirituality. David Van Biema wrote a piece in *Time* titled, "A Surge of Teen Spirit," in which he highlighted the near-mythic status Cassie's martyrdom had won her: "Teen evangelicals have their own rock concert circuit, complete with stage diving; their own clothing lines, like Witness Wear; and in the omnipresent WWJD ('What Would Jesus Do?') bracelet, their own breakthrough accessory. And now their own martyr. Cassie Bernall's life and death have inspired millions of Americans, but the tribe to which she *belonged* was that of adolescent evangelicalism."[18]

In the June 14 issue of *Newsweek*, Kenneth Woodward wrote a similar piece titled, "The Making of a Martyr." "Turning martyrs to saints is something that Catholics, not Protestants, are known for. But in the world of evangelical Web sites, where pious adolescents meet like Christians in the catacombs, Cassie is the subject of countless prayers, personal testimonials and songs like 'You Went Home at Lunch time.' As budding hagiography has it, Cassie's death was part of God's plan to bring forth witnesses out of the Columbine killings who would then win others to Christ. . . . That's the message on the Cassie T-shirts."[19]

One on-line posting read: "Beyond the pain and the suffering, beyond all the accusations, blame, and questions, this one act stands out. Standing in the face of death and professing her faith in Christ knowing that it will be her last act on this earth is a testament that will live far beyond the horror and grief of last Tuesday. . . . People will ask, 'where was God? How could he have allowed this to happen?' I certainly don't pretend to be privy to God's methods, but I can say without question that God was there in Columbine High School that day. He stood with Cassie and took her into his arms . . . and I hope that with the rest of my life I can come close to attaining the faith that Cassie has and to touch the many countless lives that she does."

Another one read: "I can only pray for the strength and courage that Cassie had."

Did She or Didn't She?

During the summer the first inklings of contradictory testimony regarding Cassie's last moments began to emerge. The Bernalls already had been approached by a person from Plough Publishing, a small publishing house of the Bruderhof (a religious community with German roots, seeking to live out Christ's Sermon on the Mount) located in Farmington, Pennsylvania. At the time of her death, Cassie had been reading *Seeking Peace*, written by Christoph Arnold, a Bruderhof leader. Misty Bernall already had entertained the thought of doing a book about Cassie, and when Plough approached them, she and Brad decided that the company would be the right publisher because of their daughter's interest in Arnold's book.

"The first time we heard [about conflicting accounts] was when [Jefferson County investigators] Randy West and Kate Battan came over here to tell us that there was some doubt in their minds," said Brad. "They said this was their personal opinion and it had nothing to do with the investigation. They came over to let us know so that if, in the future, some child comes back and says, 'That's not what happened,' we'd have a heads up."

Apparently, some of the students who were near Cassie at the time of her death did not recall hearing the exchange between her and her killer. Most notable among them was Emily Wyant, who was under the table with Cassie. Immediately following the massacre, Emily was so traumatized she could not remember any details about what had happened. Several weeks into the summer, she said she did remember and indicated that Cassie's killer did not ask that question. This contradictory testimony prompted the investigators to come up with an alternative scenario—that those who had said they had heard the question posed to Cassie actually had overheard the exchange between Valeen Schnurr and the gunman. That Val survived and was able to substantiate her version of what had happened lent more credibility to this account.

Another event that produced doubt about the earlier account was when investigators took several students back into the library shortly after the shootings and asked them to recount who sat where and what they heard. When investigators asked Craig Scott where the voices came from when he heard the question posed, he pointed in the direction of Val Schnurr's location.

"When [Battan and West] came over," said Misty, "they said, 'Don't stop doing what you're doing. Don't stop doing the book. We just wanted to let you know that there are differing accounts coming out of the library.' We were told that the circumstances surrounding Cassie's death were not going to be [publicly] shared."

The Bernalls, along with Plough, immediately undertook the process of rechecking with those witnesses who had told them they had heard the exchange between Cassie and her killer.

"I called Craig Scott a couple of days after the investigators were here," said Misty, "and I said, 'Craig, it's okay if you have changed your mind. That's all right. It's okay. Just let me know right now if you think you made a mistake.' He said, 'Oh no, I still stand behind what I said in the first place.'

"We went back and rechecked. We reinterviewed people. We tried very hard to make sure that this [account] is what was said," she said.

A Plough representative, Chris Zimmerman, reinterviewed several students who were in the library during the shooting, including Joshua Lapp, Craig Scott, and Evan Todd.[20] He reinterviewed Josh on June 13, 1999, by telephone, and Josh confirmed that, despite the differing accounts that were emerging, he stood by his testimony of having heard two separate exchanges in which the gunman asked victims "Do you believe in God?" and he said he recognized the voices. He knew Cassie's voice because "I'd heard her in the halls because I'd followed her, or go the same way as her, every once in a while to class." He recognized Val Schnurr's voice because, he said, "she lives three houses down from me."

Zimmerman reinterviewed Craig Scott on June 22, 1999. During that conversation Craig said that he could not see Cassie and that his ears were ringing. "I don't remember the exact words," he said, "but I know it was dealing with God, and I know there was a yes." He said he also heard a second exchange between the shooter and a victim: "She was on the other side of the room. It was louder conversation, maybe it was because my ears were ringing." Craig expressed frustration that authorities were asserting new theories: "They can throw all this around, but I was there. Reporters can't tell me or investigators can't tell me how it went. They don't know jack. I was there. They can help somewhat to get the story together, but I heard what I heard."

On September 2, 1999, Zimmerman reinterviewed Evan Todd. He admitted to not having known Cassie prior to the shooting, and therefore could not verify her identity by means of her voice. "On April 20 I didn't know it was Cassie, but I heard a voice from a part of the room where, later, I heard was where Cassie was. She was praying out loud and they asked her if she believed in God and she said yes." Evan said that he heard another girl who had been shot on the opposite side of the library. "She was screaming 'Oh my God, oh my God'. I didn't ever hear them ask her if she believed in God."

An Expert Opinion

Zimmerman also interviewed Dee Dee McDermott, M.Ed., L.P.C., and director of the Eagle View Counseling Center in Wheat Ridge and Littleton. She worked with several library survivors and brought to light some of the delicacies of dealing with victims of trauma.

"Trauma affects every child or person differently," she said. "Some people have a great capacity for processing it as it is happening and stay what we call 'fully present.' They have a high level of recall. Others are so traumatized they do not have the capacity to process all the information. Those students would be ones who would have memory blocks. They lose pieces of time."

At the risk of sounding politically incorrect, McDermott asserted that, while there are exceptions, girls tend to process trauma more emotionally than boys and therefore are "far less able to recall specific details." Boys, she said, "have a tendency to be more present, more able to recall. They tend to be less drawn into the emotionality of it and more able to process what's happening around them."

McDermott also said that earlier testimonies are more reliable than accounts that emerge after the passage of time. As time goes on the memory fades and traumatic memories sometimes black out altogether. "The initial information from a trauma victim is generally going to be correct. I do a lot of work with sexual trauma, and when I get a call from a parent who says, 'I'm waiting with this, to let her deal with it,' I say, 'No, I need to interview her immediately so we can get the initial impact and the initial statements from her.'"

She also said it was a mistake to take the students back into the library to interview them, especially before the facility had been cleaned of blood and gore. "Trauma involves all our senses. Some people think that it will bring more back if you return to the scene. But it is highly traumatic. That's not the time to be interviewing a child," she said. Similarly, she said, these library survivors also associate the trauma with anyone in a uniform. When they can see a police officer or an FBI agent, the young people associate them with the event and "a new wave of trauma comes up, and it interferes with accuracy and them feeling safe and comfortable and just talking."

Craig Scott was sure he had heard the question put to Cassie Bernall, but then pointed in the wrong direction when asked to locate the voices. McDermott said, "If he heard what he heard, and he is standing firmly by that, I think it's incidental if he was confused. There was smoke [in the library]. It was disorienting. They were curled in the fetal position upside down, or on their backs, or looking through their legs or their knees or under their arms. It is an unfair question, and I'm sure it was frustrating for Craig. People who are interviewing these kids need to understand the dynamics of trauma, what kind of child we're dealing with, and how they're processing it. If Craig is firm on what he heard, I don't think the direction [of the voices] matters. The poor kid probably can't remember what direction he was facing."

Resting Their Case

As a result of the extensive reinterviewing by Plough and the Bernalls, they concluded there was sufficient testimony upholding the account of Cassie's confession of belief of God and chose to retain the title of the book, *She Said Yes,* and proceed. They included a disclaimer at the beginning of the book that read, "Though the precise chronology of the murderous rampage that took place at Columbine High on April 20, 1999—including the exact details of Cassie's death—may never be known, the author's description as printed in the book is based upon the reports of numerous survivors of the library (the main scene of the massacre) and takes into account their varying recollections."[21]

Lead investigator Kate Battan went public with these doubts about Cassie in September, after "five months of virtual silence," noted Dave Cullen in the article that triggered the controversy—"Inside the Columbine High Investigation: Everything you know about the Littleton killings is wrong. But the truth may be scarier than the myths."[22] Cullen asserted that "much of what was reported last spring about the motives and methods of killers Eric Harris and Dylan Klebold was untrue. . . . The sources say that many of the most notorious events from the shooting spree—repeated over and over in news reports, on TV chat shows and now a best-selling book—simply never occurred."[23]

Cullen attempted to dispel "the biggest myths" associated with the tragedy, such as who Harris and Klebold were targeting in the their rampage. While many had speculated that athletes, African-Americans and Christians had been their chief targets, Cullen asserted in the piece, based on information from investigators, that "not a scrap of evidence supports that conclusion."[24]

When it came to what happened to Cassie Bernall, Cullen wrote that "while no one would go on the record, key investigators made it clear that an alternate scenario is far more likely: The killers asked another girl, Valeen Schnurr, a similar question, then shot her, and she lived to tell about it. Schnurr's story was then apparently misattributed to Cassie."[25]

Cullen's story broke two weeks after Misty Bernall's book was released. My cover story for *Christianity Today,* entitled "'Do You Believe In God?'" also had just come out. I called Plough Publishers, and Chris Zimmerman told me that, in the course of reinterviewing the students who had been in the library, "I feel we gave the space and comfort in a setting in which they would not be traumatized. We talked to multiple survivors in the library who corroborated the encounter with Cassie. If we had any reason to question that [the encounter] took place, we never would have published the book. We stand behind the book."

When I called Steve Davis, public information officer for the Jefferson County Sheriff's department, he said that the conflicting witness statements about Cassie Bernall were "no different than any other aspect of this investigation" (though other conflicting statements didn't make headlines). Despite the media frenzy that ensued touting Battan's new theory, Davis also said, "We are not in a position to say, 'No, it didn't happen,' but there are some questions. It's not our position to tear down someone's belief of what happened in there. We will present the facts."

Newspapers and other media opened the floodgates with commentary about the demise of the so-called Columbine martyr. Cullen's piece came out on September 23. On the next day, the *Rocky Mountain News* ran a story that said "the now-famous exchange with [Cassie's] killer may not have occurred." The article recounted Emily Wyant's version of what happened to Cassie during her last moments. "She was crouched beneath a table less than two feet from Cassie Bernall when Dylan Klebold shot her. They were the only two students studying together at the table in the back of the library. Wyant told FBI investigators that she never heard Klebold ask Cassie if she believed in God. Wyant said Cassie was praying out loud after the gunmen stormed the library. 'She was saying, "Dear God. Dear God. Why is this happening? I just want to go home."' Emily wonders whether Klebold heard Cassie praying and singled her out. All of a sudden, he slammed the top of the table, said, 'Peekaboo,' and looked under the table at both girls. 'Then he looked at her, and he shot her,' Emily said."[26]

The *Denver Post* followed suit on September 25, quoting Steve Davis, who reinforced the "very strong feelings"[27] of investigators as to the doubtfulness of the martyrdom account. Cullen followed up on September 30, also citing Emily Wyant's version of what had happened. "Dylan Klebold . . . shot Cassie without exchanging a word." He added that Emily's mother "confirmed that the *Rocky Mountain News* correctly reported the details of her daughter's account."[28]

Doubt about the account as expressed in the mainstream press quickly metamorphosed into psychobabbling speculations about the faithful that fell between patronizing rationalization about the nature of belief to outright derision. Hanna Rosin, though sympathetic, boldly asserted in her piece in the *Washington Post* that Christians didn't need something to be *true* to derive religious inspiration: "In questions of death and faith, it's the power of the story that counts, the tale that helps the mind grasp the unfathomable. Compared with that comfort, the truth is a trifle."[29] Eric Zorn and Mary Schmich, in a joint column in the *Chicago Tribune*, were less magnanimous. Zorn said the Schnurr scenario didn't catch on because "it lacks the elements of persecution and death that seem to fire the imagination of the faithful." Schmich wrote that Cassie's confession was not only "unlikely, but untrue" and that it arose from a misguided desire "to give a story shape by giving it a tidy moral."[30]

Commentaries followed that chided the Christian community for embracing the "myth." Jon Carroll wrote in the *San Francisco Chronicle:* "Facts are important. We cannot understand a story if we are operating from incorrect data. . . . What Cassie Bernall said has become a symbol. It's a symbol based on a lie. There are too many lies already."[31] Ronnie Polaneczky wrote in the *Philadelphia Daily News:* "It was so easy, so comforting, to believe the most poignant, made-for-TV tale to come out of the Littleton, Colo., massacre: That Cassie Bernall was murdered for answering 'Yes' when Dylan Klebold asked if she believed in God. . . ."[32] The story was picked up by the *New York Times,* the *Los Angeles Times,* the *Boston Globe,* the *Chicago Sun-Times,* the *St. Petersburg Times,* and *People* magazine, to name a few.

Most subsequent reports presumed "the Cassie myth" to be duly debunked, though none that I was aware of, save Rosin, did any independent reporting of their own. Yet for all the opinions and commentaries, one critical fact was not reported in the wake of the controversy. That is, the ballistics report reveals that Eric Harris, not Dylan Klebold, killed Cassie Bernall. The pivotal witness who had ignited the doubt was Emily Wyant, and she had identified Klebold as Cassie's killer. No one can blame her or impugn her, given the trauma she experienced that day. But, regardless of what might have muddled her recollections, the misidentification of the killer compromises her version of events.

Time magazine published this revised account of Cassie's death in its controversial cover story of December 20, 1999: "When Harris found Cassie Bernall, he leaned down. 'Peekaboo,' he said, and killed her. His shotgun kicked, stunning him and breaking his nose. Blood streamed down his face."[33] Apart from its tacit assumption that Cassie was not asked if she believed in God, other points are worth noting about *Time's* account. Somehow, the writers had been made privy to the newly established identity of Cassie's killer, with the added pertinent details that Harris was stooping down and leaning close enough to Cassie to be struck in the nose by the kickback of the gun and to be stunned by it.

When investigators had told the Bernalls about these new details regarding Cassie's death, including the identity of the killer as Harris, they had said the information was confidential. So Brad and Misty were shocked to read the account in *Time.* "We were told [by investigators] that circumstances surrounding Cassie's death were not going to be shared," said Misty. "We have been told nothing [by the sheriff's department] regarding anyone else's death . . . and yet they have shared what they believe happened to Cassie. We thought . . . that it was a matter between the families [to decide] if we wanted to share how our child died. That's our prerogative. And that's the way it has been for everyone except Cassie." *Time* included no other descriptions of any other victims' deaths or the identity of their killers.

The Bernalls have been equally frustrated about the conflicting signals coming from the investigators in handling the controversy over Cassie's last moments. When lead investigator Kate Battan and her colleague first alerted the Bernalls to the varying accounts in the summer of 1999, they apparently didn't believe the contradictions were important enough to derail the book project. Battan told Misty not to stop writing the book. "They said this was their personal opinion and it had nothing to do with the objective of the investigation," said Brad Bernall. Yet after the Bernalls proceeded with the book, having rigorously reinvestigated eyewitness testimony that upheld the account, Battan broke "five months of virtual silence," going public about investigators' doubts within two weeks of the book's release date in September. "Somehow, their 'personal opinion' on this matter got relayed through the media as fact, when it wasn't," said Brad.

Public information officer Davis confirmed, when I asked him, that details surrounding the identity of victims' killers and the means of their deaths remain confidential. He could not explain how *Time* gained access to the information regarding Cassie's killer or why no one else's death was described in equal detail in *Time*'s article. When it came to Emily Wyant's having identified the wrong killer, he said, "Whether her account changes or proves not to be accurate—[that] happens all the time." He said Emily was not being considered a reliable witness in their investigation.

Still a Hero

Many people, including the Bernalls, have said since this controversy erupted that it doesn't matter whether Cassie said yes to her belief in God in that final moment. "The essence of Cassie wasn't her final moments," said Misty. "Cassie was a testimony to Christ's work in her life way before Columbine. And for us to focus on what happened in the library in the final moments, it's like, okay, have a controversy. But we know Cassie. She had some downs and some struggles, but Cassie said yes to God every day of her life—'Yes, I won't be popular and do what the popular kids are doing;' 'Yes, I'll follow Christ.'"

A friend from Cassie's youth group, Craig Nason, said, "A lot of people have wanted to focus on her last moments. To me, what was more important was hearing about the hard places she'd been in her life and the challenges she had overcome. The last thing we ever wanted was to make Cassie a person you couldn't relate to in some way. To us, she was just part of the group, someone we were all friends with. She wasn't the perfect little Christian. She had a lot of struggles. But she hung in there and stuck to it, despite all that she went through. That's a miracle in itself."

Whether or not Cassie said yes at gunpoint has no bearing on the example of her life and faith. As a reporter, based on my research, however, I wasn't ready to discount the testimony of her last moments. There is no denying the compelling reasons that gave rise to doubt. But there are equally compelling reasons, from a reportorial standpoint, that should cause one to pause before dismissing it as myth. The contradictoriness of conflicting testimonies does not, in and of itself, disqualify the merit of any given account. Steve Davis insisted that these differing accounts are "no different than any other aspect of this investigation." Contradictions aside, multiple independent witnesses corroborated the account of having heard Cassie being asked that question, answering it, and being shot. Also, the earliest testimony coming out of the library that day upheld, and did not contradict, the original version. One of the first people out of the library said instantly, while she was still running, "Oh my God, they asked her if she believed in God and when she said yes, they shot her." It is true that this witness did not identify that person as being Cassie Bernall. But of greater merit is that she described, not simply someone being asked "Do you believe in God?" but someone *being shot* for answering yes. That is not the scenario that unfolded for Valeen Schnurr, heroic though her encounter certainly was. She was shot *before* being asked the question, answered yes, and was left alone.

There is something to be said for the complaint of some that Christians have too quickly elevated Cassie Bernall to near-mythic status, which inevitably got translated into crass marketing opportunities. Who Cassie Bernall was, how she lived her life, and the struggles she faced every day cannot, and should not, be reduced to a slogan on a key chain, a T-shirt, or a bumper sticker. This trivialized her life and, predictably, set her up for a fall. The backlash was felt in this controversy.

So what can we ever know about Cassie Bernall's last moments? This much has not been questioned: She was shot point-blank in the head. Her killer was Eric Harris. Eric Harris had said on the prerampage videos that he wanted to shoot Christians in the head. Cassie Bernall was a Christian. She was praying out loud before Harris approached her. Harris was asking people if they believed in God based upon his hearing them utter God's name. Harris stooped down and leaned in to her before he shot her. Her hands were on her head and he rested the barrel of the gun on her ring finger (the end of it was blown off). He was close enough to be struck and stunned by the kickback of the gun. Being that close could have limited the scope of resonance of any verbal exchange that might have occurred between them.

This is what witnesses say: Craig Scott, Joshua Lapp, and Evan Todd recalled two exchanges during which a shooter asked victims if they believed in God. Craig Scott said the encounter between Val Schnurr and the gunman was "louder" than the exchange between Cassie and her killer. In Val's case, the gunman was standing, getting ready to reload when he heard her crying, "Oh my God," and asked the question. If Harris put the same question to Cassie Bernall, he did so from a stooping position and he had to have been close to her when he did it (close enough for the kickback to strike him in the nose). Joshua Lapp said Cassie paused before answering and Amanda Meyer said, "That sounds just like her. I can picture exactly what she did, because whenever she would have to give a hard answer to something, she would always turn her head and her eyes would slide a little and she would go, 'Well . . .'"

"She Deserves Some Credit . . ."

"This is what I think happened," said Brad Bernall. "The investigator thought that [the killers] walked from the front to Cassie's area, knocked on the desk, said 'Peekaboo,' and shot her. I think he may have knocked on the desk and said 'Peekaboo,' but I have not heard the 'knock-knock peekaboo' [account] from the kids who were there, so I don't know. I haven't heard that at all. I've only heard it from the investigators, and I don't know where they get it. He walked around the other side of the desk—he had to—and knelt down. Cassie had her hands over her ears or on her head—she was still able to hear—he rested the barrel of the shotgun on the right ring finger, so he had plenty of time. I believe that's when he asked her 'Do you believe in God?'—'Yes.' He pulled the trigger, killed my daughter, and because he was so close, the recoil came to his nose, broke his nose, and he was stunned. He was bleeding from the nose and he was stunned."

The day after the shooting, Cassie's brother, Chris, found on her dresser something she had written:

> Now I have given up on everything else—
> I have found it to be the only way
> to really know Christ and to experience
> the mighty power that brought
> Him back to life again,
> to find out what it really means
> to suffer and to die with Him.
>
> So, whatever it takes, I will be one who lives
> in the fresh newness of life
> of those who are alive from the dead.

A few days after Cassie died, Misty Bernall unexpectedly felt over-taken by a supernatural sense that God was in control. "I was blow-drying my hair, and all of a sudden I heard [God] say that it had to be big, because if it wasn't big, no one would have listened; and that he had been grooming Cassie all along for something like this; and that he would take care of her and take care of us.

"I remember having to stop what I was doing and sit down. I knew it wasn't from me because I was so numb—I used to wake up in the mornings and cry and walk and wonder, 'Why? How could they do this?'—so I knew it wasn't from me." Misty did not understand this strange sensation any more than she understood why it had to be Cassie, and not somebody else, whom God had chosen for this mission.

When the school community gathered for an assembly shortly after the massacre, Principal DeAngelis reminded the students about what he had said four days earlier, when he had told them to look at the people on either side and think about what life would be like without them. Amid all the trauma and grief, Amanda Meyer had forgotten about that moment and that she had been sitting next to Cassie. Hearing the principal say it again reminded her that she had looked at Cassie and had seen her sad smile.

"All of a sudden her face came back to me," she said. "It was like, she knew. She was ready to give it all up for God. It wasn't that she said one word—that wasn't the challenge for Cassie. I mean, that was hard, but probably not the hardest thing she ever did. Every day she woke up and made a commitment to God and she lived her life for God. In one moment you can say, 'Yes, I believe in God,' but that's one moment. Saying 'Yes, I believe in God' and living that out day by day is more of a challenge. That's what Cassie did. She turned her life around from where she was a few years before. I think maybe she deserves some credit for her life."

Chapter 6

Tactical Choices

Police Faced "Unbelievable Craziness"

WHEN THE JEFFERSON COUNTY Sheriff's Office released its long-awaited official report on May 15, 2000, presenting the department's version of the events of April 20, 1999, many who had followed this story, myself included, were underwhelmed. By the time of the report's release, the sheriff's office had alienated many key players in this event, including families of the murdered and injured, the school community, and the media. Before the eve of the first anniversary, lawsuits on behalf of fifteen families had been filed against the department. One, filed by the parents of Daniel Rohrbough, alleged that a sheriff's deputy—not Harris or Klebold—had fired the bullet that killed their son.

The sheriff's office had been inconsistent and, at points, seemingly disingenuous in its handling of new information as it came to light. Many families felt they had been lied to and betrayed. Members of one family, having been given new information about their student's death, were told by investigators to keep it confidential, only to hear the investigators go public with the information a short while later. As trust deteriorated, the stonewalling began and, in turn, relations between the sheriff's office and the media began to sour.

The sheriff's report was supposed to address many unanswered questions. It recounted in generalities what *happened,* though it left out many critical details. Contentions and allegations in lawsuits filed by some families appeared to fill in some of the gaps and created a disturbing scenario of what seemingly *did not happen* as this tragedy unfolded.

What the Sheriff's Report Said

According to the official report, at 11:19 A.M. on April 20, 1999, the Jefferson County Sheriff's Office Dispatch Center received its first 911 call from someone reporting an explosion in a field east of Wadsworth Boulevard. This was a diversionary bomb Eric Harris and Dylan Klebold had planted to distract officers while the boys launched their attack on their school. At the same time, students sitting outside the Columbine High School cafeteria heard one of the gunmen yell the words, "Go! Go!" followed by gunfire. Earlier that morning the gunmen had entered the school cafeteria with two duffel bags and placed them amid other backpacks under a table. The duffel bags contained twenty-pound propane tanks and "enough explosive power to kill the majority of students who soon would be arriving for 'A' lunch," the report said. The boys had rigged the timer so that it would detonate the bombs at 11:17 A.M., at which time they would be waiting in their cars, parked to the east and west of the cafeteria, poised to shoot fleeing students. The bombs didn't go off, so they improvised.

"Go! Go!" launched a forty-minute shooting spree that reflected equal parts cold calculation and random listlessness. Half the time during their rampage the shooters wandered the school looking for something or someone to shoot, seeming bored and directionless.

A Rampage Timeline

At 11:19 A.M. "the first gunshots, fired toward the west doors, kill Rachel Scott and injure Richard Castaldo," the report said.

At 11:21 A.M. a Jefferson County sheriff's deputy was dispatched to investigate the explosion east of Wadsworth Boulevard.

At 11:22 A.M. the school custodian, who had just cued up the cafeteria's surveillance tape, hit the record button and saw students looking out the windows at something happening outside. The school's resource officer, sheriff's deputy Neil Gardner, finished eating lunch in his patrol car at nearby Clement Park and received a call from the custodian, who told Gardner that he was needed at the "back lot" of the school.

At 11:23 A.M. a 911 dispatcher took a call from a Columbine student who said a girl was injured on the south lawn: "I think she's paralyzed." Deputy Gardner heard over his radio: "Female down in the south lot of Columbine High School."

At 11:24 A.M. sheriff's deputy Paul Smoker was writing a speeding ticket on West Bowles Avenue when he heard the dispatch that said a girl was down at Columbine High School. At the same time, Gardner arrived in the south parking lot, exited his vehicle, and spotted Eric Harris at the west doors of the school. Harris turned his weapon on Gardner and fired ten shots. Then his rifle jammed. Gardner returned fire with four shots at Harris, who made a sudden lurch to the right, giving Gardner the impression Harris had been hit. Harris resumed shooting at Gardner, then retreated into the school.

At 11:25 A.M. Jefferson County Sheriff's Office dispatch called all units: "Attention all units. Possible shots fired at Columbine High School. . . . One female is down." Teacher Patti Nielson, who already had encountered the gunmen in the school's upstairs hallway, dialed 911 from under the checkout desk in the school's library. The shooters were right outside the library. "Can you please hurry?" she pleaded with the dispatch officer.

At 11:26 A.M. Deputy Smoker arrived on site and received fire from Harris, who was leaning out a broken window of the doors at the west entrance. Smoker fired three rounds and Harris retreated. Patti Nielson reported to the dispatcher that smoke was coming into the library. "Oh my God, that was really close," she said. The gunmen were in the hall just outside the library doors. The dispatcher said, "We've got help on the way, ma'am." Teacher Dave Sanders, who was shepherding students out of the school, encountered the gunmen in the hallway outside the library, retreated in the opposite direction, and was shot from behind.

At 11:27 A.M. Nielson told the dispatcher the shooters were just outside the library doors. "Harris and Klebold spend almost three minutes in the library hallway randomly shooting their weapons and lighting and throwing pipe bombs," the report said.

In retrospect, some parents and others speculated that this would have been a good time for the kids in the library—by now huddled under tables—to make a break for it out the rear emergency exit. However, the dispatcher told Nielson, "We've got police officers on the scene" and "we've got to keep everyone there as calm as we can."

At 11:28 A.M. Deputy Smoker saw other deputies on school grounds near the ballfields. The dispatcher told Patti Nielson to "keep everyone low to the floor."

At 11:29 A.M. at least six deputies were on site and knew the exact location of Eric Harris and Dylan Klebold when the two walked into the school library. Nielson said to the dispatcher, "He's in the library. He's shooting at everybody."

Within three minutes of the original 911 call, "a preliminary assessment was made and a request for mutual aid was sent out."[1] That resulted in the swift and decisive descent of more than six hundred personnel from Jefferson and Arapahoe County Sheriff's Offices, the Denver and Littleton Police departments, including tactical officers with SWAT equipment, medical teams and ambulance services, and fire departments.

Once they were on site, however, swiftness and decisiveness metamorphosed into confusion and chaos. "It was unbelievable craziness," said Deputy Smoker.[2] When he had heard through the dispatcher that a girl was down, he thought it meant she had fallen, and he "didn't think much of it." Upon arrival, however, he quickly realized that, in this case, "down" meant shot through the chest and paralyzed (the reference was to Anne Marie Hochhalter), and that officers were facing the equivalent of all-out war. Exploding bombs and the sound of gunfire punctuated the wails of wounded students and the screams of others trying to flee. Several students who had been shot in the initial volley, including Anne Marie, Richard Castaldo, Lance Kirkland, Mark Taylor, and Sean Graves, were down and unable to help themselves. Rachel Scott lay dead at the top of the steps outside the school cafeteria. Dan Rohrbough lay face-down in a pool of blood at the base of the same steps.

Several things happened almost simultaneously. While the gunmen sprayed gunfire outside, students with cell phones in various parts of the school called their parents or 911. Police and tactical teams raced into the parking lot. The school's fire alarm engaged. Teachers and students who hadn't fled bolted for hiding places—in refrigerators, cupboards, closets, classrooms, and inside false ceilings. Principal Frank DeAngelis, janitors, and teachers—including Dave Sanders—rushed around the hallways directing students to safety.

The first police officers on the scene assembled a loose team of those who had responded independently from various agencies. They had not trained together, did not know one another, and had little in the way of equipment. As Harris and Klebold stalked the hallway outside the library and Patti Nielson recounted their movements to a 911 dispatcher, police officers outside were trying to figure out what to do.

Nielson's last words to the 911 dispatcher were, "They're killing kids. I need to go now."[3] She left the connection open and the dispatcher listened as the killers walked through the library taunting and shooting their victims. The killing was over in seven and a half minutes. The last person was killed at 11:35 A.M.

According to the report, the killers left the library and wandered around the hallways in the science area for several minutes. They looked through windows of classrooms and even made eye contact with students who were hiding. They tossed pipe bombs and shot randomly, sometimes into empty rooms. "Their behavior seemed directionless," the report said. The boys entered the school cafeteria at 11:44 A.M. and tried to detonate their failed bomb by shooting it. A witness heard one of them say, "Today the world is going to come to an end. Today is the day we die." They snatched drinks from water bottles left on the tables and fired a few more rounds of ammunition. They looked out the cafeteria windows and saw police, firefighters, and medical personnel gathering in greater numbers. They set off a smaller bomb that started a fire in the cafeteria, which engaged the sprinkler system. By 11:47 A.M. they had left the cafeteria and wandered into the area of the school office. The dispatcher on the other end of Patti Nielson's phone call disconnected at 11:51 A.M. "Klebold's and Harris's movements continue to be extremely random," the report noted, and at 11:56 A.M. they returned briefly to the cafeteria, "surveying the damage." They left the kitchen area at 11:59 A.M.

At 12:00 they left the cafeteria to return to the library.

At 12:05 P.M. they exchanged gunfire with police a final time from the library windows.

At 12:06 P.M. the first SWAT personnel entered the school from the east side.

At 12:08 P.M. Harris and Klebold lit a Molotov cocktail, put guns to their heads, and ended their lives near the west windows of the library, not far from the bodies of Isaiah Shoels, Matt Kechter, and Cassie Bernall.

What the Report Didn't Say

"One of the big beefs I have is why those men didn't go in there with their guns blazing as they arrived," said Cassie's father, Brad Bernall. "I was in the Navy and was prepared to shoot nuclear missiles and kill millions of people. I was there because they knew I would do it, and I knew I would do it, even knowing that I would die within one hour should it ever come to that. So I know what it means to take an oath to put your life on the line to protect others. They took a similar oath. They didn't act on it. Not one officer was hurt. And yet students and a teacher died. They should have gone in there and done their job and protected them and served the parents the way they were supposed to. The bottom line is they didn't live up to their oath."

"They were telling Patti Nielson, 'Tell those kids there is help on the way,'" said Misty Bernall. "Help was there. They were outside. We were told it was late in the afternoon before any official even entered the library. They knew that was the major source of where the conflict was. The boys shot their guns out the windows at them. They knew the boys were stationed in the library, and had they gone in there or had their sharpshooters out there, maybe Cassie wouldn't have died. Eric and Dylan had free rein to do whatever they wanted to do."

"The cops [and] the sheriffs are the guys with the bulletproof vests," said Brad. "They should have run into the school. They should have been looking through the windows. They should have shot out the windows. They should have been at the doors looking for a way to go in and shoot the guys with guns."

The Bernalls were not alone in their frustration. Brian Rohrbough said, "Jefferson County [authorities] ordered police officers to stay out of the building. The public safety officer said, 'Well, we couldn't just send the SWAT team in because what would have happened if the whole SWAT team was killed?' The management made the police officers stay out, and I'll go one further than that: The police officers [displayed] cowardice to stand behind the order."

"When [more or less] five hundred officers go to a battle zone and not one comes away with a scratch, then something's wrong," said Dale Todd.[4] "I expected dead officers, crippled officers, disfigured officers—not just children and teachers."

"I'm sure they have their explanations," said Darrell Scott, "but a lot of parents would have been grateful if there had been some wounded cops."

The Law Enforcement Perspective

"Everything I saw indicated that these teams acted as expeditiously as possible," said one officer who was on the scene but wanted to remain unidentified. "Most of these guys really are 'Boy Scouts' who want to save lives and make the world safe. But you can be sure that there has been some serious soul-searching going on since this thing."

He explained that procedure, not cowardice, broke down the rescue efforts at Columbine because the officers in charge brought the "law enforcement mentality" to the crisis. He described that as "zero casualties" and "total quality control." In other words, police are trained not to go into a volatile situation without a controlled plan of attack that will preserve the most lives.

"It's a valid strategy," said Perry Schellpheffer, an officer with the Englewood Police Department, who went in with one of the first SWAT teams. "I was in the Marines, and the Marine Corps mentality is that it is a noble thing to die for your country. You're the hero if you die saving five of your men. That's not the mentality in law enforcement. They've invested training in you, and if you die doing something irrational, you serve nobody. It's difficult to find quality people, and they don't want to waste their assets."

This "quality control" strategy meant that the law enforcement agencies that coalesced at Columbine High School had to contain the scene or secure the perimeters. That means, essentially, to keep the bad guys in and get the good guys out. There was the inner perimeter, which focused inward to contain the threat, and there was the outer perimeter, which focused outward to move the innocent away to safety. According to the model, once perimeters are secured, tactical personnel—the SWAT teams— move in to subdue the assailants. The problem in this event was that the perimeter couldn't be secured because the shooters kept moving and changing the boundaries.

The result was something that looked to the lay observer like cowardice and gross negligence. "While one murder after another was being perpetrated in the library, a dozen police officers were stationed near this exit," wrote David B. Kopel in the *Weekly Standard*. "These officers made no attempt to enter the building, walk 15 steps, and confront the murderers, who gunned down their classmates with impunity."[5] Kopel noted that an officer told him that when a Denver SWAT person tried to enter the school at that exit, he was "'ordered down' by commanders."[6]

The police at Columbine responded the way they were trained to, said the unnamed officer I spoke to, mentioned earlier. "They did as their training told them to do. They did it by the book. The problem is, the book was inadequate. The book did not cover Columbine."

"What if we would have stormed the building irrationally and killed a student other than one of the shooters?" asked Schellpheffer. "If we were indiscriminately shooting, and maybe shot another kid in a trench coat not knowing he wasn't part of it, how would that be perceived by everybody? Charging in without knowing what you're going into is an irrational act. We didn't know the circumstances—if it was ten guys with guns or five guys," he said. When he and other officers arrived on the scene, they saw so many shell casings scattered on the ground, saw so many dead and wounded, and heard so many bombs going off they didn't know what they were up against. "I thought it was a war zone," said Schellpheffer. "We're scrutinized for everything we do, so we have to be very careful."

Killing Field in Suburbia

Harris and Klebold indeed introduced warfare to Columbine High School. As Kopel noted, "Many of the SWAT officers on the scene that day were brave men who were horrified that their commanders had forbidden them to assault the killers."[7] But the law enforcement mindset prevailed and the shooters wandered around the school undeterred. Their meandering at various points suggested that the killers had been prepared for nearly any contingency—except the absence of resistance.

Columbine created a new category for SWAT teams confronted with school shootings, according to my unnamed police source. It is called "the active shooter scenario" and jettisons the "secure the perimeter" strategy in favor of swiftness, force, and the risk of casualties. Speed and surprise are crucial and officers need to be prepared to storm the school and go to the sound of the guns. "You cannot take a zero-casualties mindset into a situation like this," said the unnamed officer. "You swallow hard. Make the move. Take casualties." He concluded, "They brought a police mentality to a war situation, and lost."

Law enforcement agencies all over the country have rehearsed Columbine-like scenarios in local schools, implementing this new aggressive strategy that rescue teams on site at Columbine figured out too late.

Traffic Jam on the Airwaves

There were other complications. "One of the day's most critical challenges [was] the lack of a common radio channel police could use to talk to one another," noted an article in the *Washington Post*.[8] The officers on site had come from five jurisdictions and had formed eight tactical teams. There were not enough radio channels to accommodate the number and frequency of attempted exchanges. "Many of the 26 federal, state, and local police agencies that responded were equipped with older radio networks that made it difficult, though not impossible, to communicate with one another."[9]

Beyond stymied radio communications, students and teachers who were hiding inside the school were calling on cell phones and giving what they thought was the location of the gunmen, which kept changing. The county had thirty-two emergency 911 channels, and fifteen of them were jammed with calls about the shootings.[10] More students made their way out of the school and gave pertinent information to officers. But because of the jammed radio frequencies, the police were not able to get this information to the teams inside.

Lt. Terry Manwaring, Jefferson County's SWAT commander, arrived on the scene at about 11:38 A.M. and immediately put together an impromptu, four-man, quick-reaction team with the first officers on the scene from Jefferson County, Littleton, and Denver. With the help of four students, they sketched out a floor plan and laid out a strategy. Most of the officers did not have sufficient gear and ended up sharing guns and bulletproof vests. There was one protective shield to be shared by eleven men.

They went in shortly after noon. They found a bomb near the first entrance they tried to penetrate and so had to enter a different way. They were not aware that the cafeteria and library had been moved to the west side of the school four years earlier. So they entered along the east side, the original location. Once they were inside, in addition to experiencing general disorientation because of the massiveness of the building, the officers contended with flashing strobe lights, blaring alarms, detonating bombs, and random gunfire. There was so much noise that they couldn't distinguish a gunshot if it was twenty feet away.

"All this time you're trying not to get shot," Manwaring said. "We have no idea where the shooters are. Every time we rounded a corner, we didn't know whether it was a good guy or a bad guy."[11]

The makeshift SWAT team went from room to room, making its way by the crudely scribbled map, searching hallways, classrooms, crawl spaces, and closets. At every turn they found huddled and terrorized students, and each student had to be considered a potential suspect. They had to be frisked before they could be escorted, with their hands over their heads, out of the school. This slowed down the rescue dramatically.

From the vantage point of standard law enforcement protocol, Perry Schellpheffer said, the officers "did a pretty darn good job. They threw themselves together and went in with no information other than, 'Somebody's shooting in there. Let's go get 'em.'"

A second SWAT team entered the school around 12:20 P.M. and the third one after 1:00 P.M. Before the day was through, more than fifty officers would be combing the school.

Tending the Wounded

While law enforcement personnel were "securing the perimeter," an army of support people dealt with the damage. Firefighters and emergency medical personnel from Littleton and neighboring districts were just as consumed tending to the wounded.

John Aylward and Monte Fleming, firefighters with the Littleton Fire Department, were sitting down to an early lunch at the station when they received the call of a shooting at Columbine High School. They responded quickly, but didn't expect much would come of it. They thought it was probably a drive-by shooting. And Monte Fleming, an ex-Army medic, said he looked upon most drive-by shooters as pretty poor shots.[12]

So the firemen were unprepared for what they found upon arriving at the school. They went to the southwest corner of the school which, they had been told, was already secure. When they got there they found "a phalanx of police [with] their guns trained on the windows of the second-floor library." They saw bodies on the grass and sidewalk. In the understatement of the year, Fleming said to Aylward, "This isn't as secure as we'd like it to be."[13]

They pulled their truck as close as they could get. Aylward saw a girl down and made a break for her amid gunshots flying to and from the library windows. It was Anne Marie Hochhalter, who was paralyzed from the waist down. Aylward picked her up and carried her back to the truck.

At about the same time, police were rescuing more victims. Denver officers Capt. Vince DiManna and Lt. Pat Phelan inched toward the west entrance, seeing students down in that area. Phelan approached Rachel Scott and poised himself to lift her. "I'm getting ready to pick her up [when] her head falls to the side [and] I realize she's been shot in the head. I laid her back down."[14]

A few feet away he saw Richard Castaldo trying to wave his bullet-ridden arm. "I got up and saw he was shot in the chest. He was conscious. I was speaking to him. He appeared to be in shock. I grabbed him by the ankles and told him, 'We're getting you out of here.'" Even as the shooters were tossing a homemade grenade at them, Phelan, with the help of DiManna, managed to pull Castaldo to safety.[15]

Despite knowing Rachel Scott was gone, rescuers were haunted by the sight of her lying there with backpack still on and her hair in a pony tail. "We couldn't leave that little girl there," DiManna said.[16] They went back to her and moved her to a more secure location. The unnamed officer mentioned earlier said that this was an emotional and heroic act. "The highest value is to protect life, even if it means sacrificing a crime scene," he said. By moving her body, they compromised the crime scene, but did so, he said, "in the vain hope that maybe something could be done. They didn't want to leave her at the scene."

After moving Rachel Scott, the officers went down the concrete stairs. Monte Fleming had been attempting to get near other students who were down and had gotten as close as he could to the brick wall of the school, directly beneath the library. He came across a boy lying face down on the sidewalk and checked him for signs of life. He was cold and there was no pulse. It was Danny Rohrbough, who had been killed early in the shooting. Nearby, Sean Graves was down. The shooters stood at the library window and continued to fire. Still, Littleton paramedic Jerry Losasso pulled Graves out of harm's way to a waiting ambulance.[17] When Graves's friend Lance Kirkland saw assistance nearby, for the second time since being shot, Kirkland cried for help. Fleming heard glass shatter and a stream of shots come from the library windows. He heard Kirkland asking for help, lifted all two hundred pounds of him, and "ran under a police barrage that sounded like a howitzer going off"[18] until he reached an ambulance that was forty feet away.

When the call alerted Denver paramedics Troy Laman and Robert Montoya at 11:45 A.M. that they were needed at Columbine High School, they knew it had to be serious. They almost never left the Denver city limits. When they arrived on the scene, they started working triage. As police escorted a seemingly unending stream of students out of the school they asked, "Are you hurt? Can you walk?"[19] In time Laman and Montoya ended up at the southwest side of the school and a Denver SWAT officer, who knew Laman, said, "Troy, I need you to go in. Let's go."[20]

By this time, it was early afternoon. Laman went in through the cafeteria, which was flooded with three inches of water from the ceiling sprinklers and strangely animated by the bizarre chirping sound of ringing cell phones that had been left in backpacks. He made his way upstairs to the second level. Dave Sanders lay dying in a science room while students Aaron Hancey and Kevin Starkey tried desperately to keep him alive. Hancey had called his father on a cell phone and they stayed on the line more than two hours as his father and a police officer, on a third line, relayed first-aid instructions. At 2:00 P.M. they were told that SWAT officers were just down the hall, a couple of classrooms away. It would be nearly another hour, however, before rescuers would make their way to Sanders. Despite the briefly worded sign that had been posted in the window saying "1 bleeding to death," the outside officers were unable to get that information to the police inside the building because of the communication snafus.

At 2:38 P.M. Patrick Ireland rallied the strength to pull himself to a window. It was three hours after he had been shot twice in the head and had been fading in and out of consciousness in the library. He had use of only one side of his body, but later said he had concluded, "If I'm going to survive, I've gotta get out of here."[21] He managed to push himself to the wall under the windows and position himself so he could drop out the window. SWAT officers defied orders and approached the building (it had not been declared secure) to catch his fall. They stood atop an armored truck to catch him as he fell into their arms.

The SWAT team arrived in the science room at 2:47 P.M. They told the students and others who were tending to Sanders to put their hands on their heads and follow them out. "Someone's got to stay with Mr. Sanders," someone said. Hancey responded, "I will." An officer told Hancey that he couldn't stay and Hancey agreed to go, thinking Sanders would be taken care of. Two SWAT team members stayed with Sanders another twenty minutes waiting for paramedics. When none showed, they left him, assuming it was too late for him.

Paramedic Troy Laman showed up shortly after they had left. He said it looked as if Sanders had just drawn his last breath. He did not try to revive him. He was doing triage, which meant he had to determine who was savable and who was not. "In triage, a person who can't breathe on his own is considered dead. It's important to move on, to go past that person and find someone who can be saved."[22]

Even still, Laman couldn't move on at the moment. He was told not to leave the room until more of the building was secured. So he stayed with Sanders for several more minutes, tormented that he was not able to save him. "As paramedics, our job is to put our hands on people and take care of them. I knew there was nothing I could do for this guy. But because I was stuck in a room with him by myself for 15 minutes, I wanted to help him. I had nowhere else to go. I couldn't leave the room. I wanted to do something for him."[23]

He was finally given the go-ahead to leave. His partner, Montoya, told him by radio to move on and "find somebody to save."[24]

It was 3:22 P.M. before the first SWAT team entered the library. The low ceiling, the haze and smell of gunpowder, and the pall of death magnified the sense of stifling confinement. A layer of something gritty covered the desktops. Officers quickly came to see that the killers had generated so much firepower that gunpowder fell like rain.

Rescue workers in the library were assaulted with contradictory images. The mundane accoutrements of everyday school life stood in stark contrast to shattered windows and shards of glass all over the floor. A copy of

A Bridge Too Far displayed in a glass case; backpacks on tables; open textbooks; half-finished homework; a partially completed college application; and random notes that students had passed all lent touches of normality to the setting, as if the school day had been suspended in time. But the shell casings, the ammunition clips, the pools of blood, and the dead bodies crumpled under the desks told a different story. It was a surreal juxtaposition of images in a setting where librarians customarily shushed anyone who so much as laughed out loud. One victim was still holding a pencil. Another victim was crumpled over a desk, his computer still running. Another had a note from a friend that read, "Meet me in the library."

Troy Laman, who had left the dead Dave Sanders in the science room, made his way slowly and carefully around the library. He had been warned that backpacks, or even the bodies themselves, might be booby-trapped. He was still in the triage mode, trying to determine if anyone was alive and could be saved. If he couldn't see their faces, he touched their bodies to determine if there was life. Most of the victims were gone. But he couldn't see the face of one girl and so he touched her and turned her. It was Lisa Kreutz, and she was the last person to be taken out of the library alive.

The two killers lay amid the carnage, their ammo belts still strapped around them and their weapons beside them. Dylan Klebold wore a black shirt that bore the word "WRATH" in tall, red, block letters. Harris and Klebold each had one bare hand and a hand wearing a leather glove, which one officer said denoted a "thought-out tactical decision." Klebold's head wound did not have the purplish ring that would result from a contact wound, when the muzzle of a gun is pressed directly against the skin. This has led to some to speculate that Harris killed Klebold before taking his own life. Harris's wound had the ring and was far more traumatic.

Because the library was a crime scene, it would be more than twenty-four hours before the bodies would be removed. A police chaplain went from person to person and said a prayer of committal over each one. He did the same over the bodies of Rachel Scott and Dan Rohrbough, still outside.

The final entry of the official report that depicted the timeline of events for April 20 said: "By 4:45 p.m. the SWAT teams finished the initial search of Columbine High School, clearing the 250,000 square-foot, two-story building. The deceased, including two suspects, had been checked and pronounced dead by Dr. [Christopher] Colwell of the Denver Health Medical Center. The deadly shooting and massacre at Columbine was over."

When Cultures Collide

With visions of the JonBenet Ramsey case running through their minds, members of the Jefferson County Sheriff's Office were determined to do this right. But from the beginning some sensed that, no matter how this all shook out, there was no way they could win.

They were correct. The shaking out has been messy for Jefferson County, some of it self-inflicted. Law enforcement is a culture all its own, with its own language, rituals, norms, and mores. How the law enforcement community acts, what it does, and the way it responds is driven by its sense of mission and interpreted through the mindset of its culture. Sometimes this collides with the sensibilities of lay people, and when it does, things can and do go wrong. For all of their attempts to "do it right" with the Columbine situation, there were times when the line between what seemed right from the vantage point of law enforcement and what seemed just to citizens whose lives law enforcement intersected became blurred.

Every male who exited the school had to be frisked under the suspicion that he might be a suspect trying to escape. This approach evolved to include every student—male or female. Kids who had been terrorized and who were thinking they were living their last minutes, who had crouched in closets or remained locked inside classrooms for hours, upon rescue were ordered to lie flat on the floor with their hands behind their heads so they could be frisked. Jessica Arzola, who had hidden for more than three hours in a closet on the second floor, was frisked four times before she could leave the building. "Every wall we got to, they frisked us," she said.[25] Pastor Don Marxhausen went to the school as soon as he had heard there was trouble, and when he got close, he saw "a policeman putting a kid down with a gun, making him spread [eagle] on the ground." Even Patti Nielson, who had endured the terror of the massacre in the library and remained crumpled in a small cupboard for so long that her limbs were numb, was pulled into the hallway by SWAT personnel and ordered to put her hands behind her head so she could be frisked. To law enforcement, this is procedure. To citizens, it is part of the terror.

Evan Todd, who had been in the library and confronted by the killers, said that when he exited the school he described in detail the weapons the killers were using. He told officers that wounded students were in the library and needed to be saved. "They told me to calm down and take my frustrations elsewhere," said Todd.[26]

When Tom Klebold first learned the painful truth that his son was thought to be one of the killers, he immediately notified law enforcement through his attorney and offered to intervene. He wanted to talk to his son. He was rebuffed. One wants to ask, how could officers deny a father the chance to intervene in a life-and-death situation in the attempt to save his son? The Klebolds' and Harrises' homes were quickly taken over as crime scenes. For hours the Klebolds and the few friends who were with them were sequestered in one room of the house while officers searched. They couldn't use the bathroom without someone following them there. When they were told to leave, they were given one opportunity to put together their things—they packed a few clothes and took their bird and two cats. The Klebolds were still in shock. According to friend Judy Brown, who was with the Klebolds, Tom Klebold was saying, "This isn't happening. This is absurd. There's nothing you're going to find. Go ahead and look. I don't care. Dylan's not violent."[27]

The Past Is Prologue

Given the situation the law enforcement agencies were confronting, it is hard to begrudge them abruptness and force. But as the investigation moved into measured and reflective stages, a more complicated picture emerged regarding the Jefferson County Sheriff's Office. At one point, the Browns and the Klebolds blamed the department for what it did *not* do a year before, which, these families argued, paved the way for the Columbine incident. Eric Harris and Dylan Klebold, it turned out, were not unknown to the police.

On January 30, 1998, the two boys had been arrested for breaking into a parked van and stealing some of its contents. According to the report filed by the arresting officer, the boys were sitting in Harris's car at Deer Creek Canyon Park at about 9:30 P.M., which aroused suspicion. The park was closed to the public at sundown. The officer got out of his patrol car and walked toward Harris's car. He heard the boys making comments about some sort of metering device that had a light on it. When it lit up they said, "Cool." They were looking over other items when the officer heard Harris say, "Hey, we better put this stuff in the trunk." The officer saw the trunk unlatch, which Harris had done from the inside of the car, and when Harris got out to put the goods in the trunk, the officer made his presence known.

He asked Harris what they were doing in the park after closing and whose property they had in the car. Both boys told him they had been "messing around" near Deer Creek Canyon Road and Wadsworth when

119

they found these things stacked up neatly in the grass near a parking lot. The officer asked if he could see the items. Harris said, "Sure." The officer told the boys that he would have to call another deputy to check the parking lot to make sure no cars there had been vandalized. He said it seemed suspicious that someone would leave this property unattended in the grass, and he gave the boys one more chance to tell the truth. Harris looked at Klebold. There was a short silence. Klebold confessed that the boys had broken into a white van parked in the lot. The officer asked no more questions and took them into custody.

When the boys filled out their reports, each had a different take on how the theft had unfolded. Their own words and writing styles offer a snapshot of individual quirks and idiosyncrasies. Dylan Klebold's breezy style of writing, parenthetical commentary, and extensive use of ampersands reflects a slightly humorous but edgy nonchalance. He made a point to share an equal burden of guilt when it came to who initiated the vandalism:

> Eric & I were driving home (him driving his car), & we stopped at the parking lot thingy at Deer Creek Rd & Wadsworth. We got out & he set off a few fireworks, & then were going around smashing bottles. Then, almost at the same time, we both got the idea of breaking into this white van, which was something for an electrical (maybe) company. We hoped to get the stuff inside. I put on a snow glove, & then tried to punch thru the passenger window. I tried like 4 times & then Eric tried a couple times. We then found a rock, & I tried to break the window with that. After about 5 times, the rock broke thru, & I unlocked the door from the inside, & took electrical stuff (& other things)—(don't know exactly), & then sped off to Deer Creek open space park. We parked, & turned on the dome light to see what we had. Then, an officer saw us, got all that we had, & then went through the process. (Arresting).
>
> Dylan Klebold

Eric Harris's account included more attention to detail and a clearer demarcation between his and Klebold's respective roles in the vandalism (placing more culpability on Klebold). His version seemed fastidious and respectful:

> Me and Dylan Klebold were at a church off of Kendall and Ken Caryl with [a friend] listening to music. We then left the church (me and Dylan) and proceeded to the North West corner of Wadsworth and Deer Creek Canyon

Road. We parked in the gravel and stayed there (in my car) for a few minutes listening to a new music CD. We noticed a white van to the West and a red truck to the East of our position. We got out of my car and looked around for something to do. We found some beer bottles and we broke those for about 15 minutes. We then went back up to my car and Dylan suggested that we should steal some of the objects in the white van. At first I was very uncomfortable and questioning with the thought. I became more interested within about 5 minutes and we then decided to break the passenger window with our fists. I looked for cars and I saw a white car come from the west and pull up beside the red truck. Dylan and I waited in our car for the white car to leave, after about 5 minutes a person got out of the car and into the red truck, then both the truck and car left going westbound. We then got out of my car and I went out into the street and looked for cars as Dylan hit the window with his left fist 3 times. Then I came over and tried to hit it, one time. We decided to get a rock to use. We went North about 20 feet and Dylan found a rock big enough to have to hold in 2 hands. I went back to look for cars as Dylan broke the window on his 6th try. I then stood by my driver door and looked for cars while Dylan reached through the window and took items from the car and placed them in my back seat. After about 15 minutes (approx) Dylan opened the door twice to get more items and put them in my car. We then left the area and went to the Open Space area and parked up there. We then began to review the items and I suggested we put them (the items) into my trunk. That's when the officer confronted us.

Eric Harris

The boys were summoned to appear before Jefferson County Magistrate John A. DeVita II in District Court on March 25, 1998. They pled guilty to first-degree criminal trespass, theft, and criminal mischief. DeVita gave Klebold some unsolicited advice: "I bet you're an 'A' student if you put the brain power to paperwork," he said.[28] He was less trusting of Harris, whom he suspected had committed other petty crimes: "First time out of the box and you get caught. I don't believe it. It's a real rare occurrence when somebody gets caught the first time."[29] Their "Eddie Haskell" performances[30]— masking baneful mischievousness behind syrupy deference to authority— convinced DeVita to place them in a year-long juvenile diversion program and drop the charges in deference to community service and anger management classes. The hearing was over in less than ten minutes.

What the magistrate DeVita did not know, however, was that a few days prior to that hearing Jefferson County officers had been notified of another problem involving Eric Harris.

Several months before March 1998, Judy Brown, a friend of the Klebolds, was talking to a friend whose home had been vandalized. Judy's son Brooks had been blamed for it by Eric Harris. But Judy knew that her son had been home the evening the vandalism occurred. Brooks was the kind of person who told his mom everything, and Judy deduced from some of the things Brooks had told her that Harris likely had committed the vandalism. She called Jefferson County deputies to alert them. The deputies said they would look into it and call Harris's parents.

Apparently, word got back to Eric Harris that Judy Brown had been the source of the complaint. He threw a chunk of ice at Brooks Brown's passing car while Harris was standing at the bus stop. The ice cracked the windshield. Judy Brown was outraged. She drove to the bus stop to confront Harris and said she was going to tell his mother what had happened. As she was pulling away, Harris "grabbed onto her car screaming, his face turning red," according to an article in the *Rocky Mountain News*.[31] Kathy Harris's eyes welled with tears when Judy Brown told her about her son's behavior and vandalism.

Wayne Harris, Eric's father, called the Browns and explained that Eric had reacted that way at the bus stop out of fear. Judy Brown responded, "Your son is not afraid. Your son is terrifying. Your son is violent."[32] The elder Harris later drove his son over to the Browns and waited in the car while Eric went to the door to apologize. Eric dismissed the windshield incident as being "fun"—he said he thought the ice chunk he had thrown was a snowball. Judy Brown responded, "Eric Harris, you can pull the wool over your dad's eyes, but you're not going to pull the wool over my eyes. Stay away from my kids."[33] Harris stomped away.

Then in March, shortly before Harris and Klebold appeared in District Court, Brooks Brown told his mother that "a friend" had alerted him to an ominous threat against him on Eric Harris's Web site. He told his mother, "I can't tell you who [the friend] is, Mom, because he's afraid that Eric Harris will harm him."[34] It turned out that the friend was Dylan Klebold. Brooks Brown said that his friend Dylan was "looking out for me. That's the way he was. An extremely good kid."[35]

The Browns went to Harris's Web site and were horrified by what they saw. The postings painted a picture of a teen who possessed a hateful outlook toward nearly everybody—with anomalous glimmers of compassion for a selected few. It included, in part:

> . . . YOU KNOW WHAT I HATE!!?
> When there is a group of a—holes standing in the middle of a hallway or walkway, and they just STANDING there talking and blocking my f—ing

way!!! Get the f—— outa the way or i'll bring a friggin sawed-off shotgun to your house and blow your snotty a— head off!!

 . . . YOU KNOW WHAT I HATE!!?

When people mispronounce words! and they don't even know it too. like ofTen, or acrosT, or eXspreso, pacific (specific), or 2pAck. learn to speak correctly you morons . . .

 . . . YOU KNOW WHAT I HATE!!?

People who dont believe in personal hygiene. For the love of god and for the sake of god, CLEAN UP! . . . people with 2 inch fingernails and a whole f—ing pot full of dirt under them and raggy-a— hair or shirts stained to hell. Or people that just plain stink, and they dont do anything about it. Now, im not making fun of anyone if they cant help it, or afford it or anything like that, thats not their fault, but your some kid drivin a ford explorer and have yellow teeth, then thats just plain unhuman.

 . . . YOU KNOW WHAT I HATE!!?

People who use the same word over and over again! Like "actually", or "f— you", or "b——". Read a f—ing book or two, increase your vo-cab-u-lary ya f——ing idiots.

 . . . YOU KNOW WHAT ELSE I HATE!!?

People who THINK they are martial arts experts!

 . . . YOU KNOW WHAT I LOVE!!?

Natural SELECTION!!!!!!!!! G—d— its the best thing that ever happened to the Earth. Getting rid of all the stupid and weak orginisms [sic]. . . .

The portion that was most troubling to the Browns read:

> . . . I will rig up explosives all over a town and detonate each one of them at will after I mow down a whole f—ing area full of you snotty-a— rich mother f—ing high strung godlike attitude having worthless pieces of s— whores. i don't care if I live or die in the shootout. all I want to do is kill and injure as many of you pricks as I can, especially a few people. Like Brooks Brown.

The Browns immediately contacted the sheriff's department and handed over ten printed pages of material they had found on the Web site. The police labeled it a "suspicious incident" and on March 18, 1998 (a week before the boys' hearing before Magistrate DeVita), filed a report. In it, the officer included references to Harris's death threats against

Brooks Brown, his talk of making pipe bombs and wanting to use them to kill people, his hate-filled Web pages, and Dylan Klebold's knowledge of Harris's bomb making. The report also mentioned that the Browns had reported Harris to police earlier and thought that was why he was out to get Brooks.

Judy Brown followed up with several phone calls to the sheriff's office to inquire about what had been done about this threat. Her calls were not returned. In a matter of a few weeks, Harris removed his Web site and his threatening activity seemed to dissipate. The Browns eventually gave up.

Harris's ravings and threats, at that point, moved from a public Web site to his private journal, wherein he began to document his plans to "wage war against the human race" through an attack on Columbine.

Both boys served a year of probationary activities in a juvenile diversion program. They appeared in District Court a year after their arrest for vandalism, on February 3, 1999. Harris's termination report stated that "Eric did a very nice job on Diversion" and he "enjoy[ed]" the anger management class. It said he "fit nicely" with the counseling he received and "excelled in school." The prognosis for Harris was "good": "Eric is a very bright young man who is likely to succeed in life. He is intelligent enough to achieve lofty goals as long as he stays on task and remains motivated."

Klebold's termination report was equally glowing: "Dylan did a very nice job on Diversion." He possessed a "solid" attitude and "remained motivated." Dylan seemed to value the community service work more than anything, which the report said, he felt "was the most effective piece of Diversion." Dylan's prognosis was also "good." "Dylan is a bright young man who has a great deal of potential. If he is able to tap his potential and become self-motivated he should do well in life."

These reports were completed and the boys' records were wiped clean two months before the shooting rampage. What has come back to haunt the sheriff's office, however, is that somehow the Browns' complaint about the Web postings, filed in police records, never intersected with the police report of the boys' arrest for vandalism a few months earlier. The Web site contained enough threatening material to warrant, at the very least, a next step in following up. "What makes this more than ranting is the admission of criminal conduct coupled by probable cause to believe there were pipe bombs already built on the premises by the gun boys," said Denver defense attorney Scott Robinson in the *Rocky Mountain News*. "This is not the type of individual that the sheriff's office should have turned a blind eye to."[36] Denver attorney and legal analyst Craig Silverman said that the death threat to Brooks Brown alone would have warranted an investigation. "You cannot threaten people with death with impunity in Colorado. . . . I'm suggesting there was probably cause and certainly grounds to determine if these crimes were committed. It was a situation that cried out for an investigation.

"It is surprising," he said, "that Eric Harris' name and date of birth was not punched into a computer after the Browns' repeated complaints. It could have picked up the fact that this was a kid with a felony charge already against him in Jefferson County."[37]

Even a phone call to the Harrises about the violent Web postings might have made a difference, but his parents were never contacted by the police. The report was passed on to Columbine's deputy Neil Gardner. Sheriff John P. Stone said that reports titled "suspicious incident," as this one was, do not get the same level of attention as rapes and murders. And at the time, the Jefferson County deputies were working on more than one high-profile murder case.

To make matters worse for the Brown family, shortly after the Columbine shooting Stone publicly implicated Brooks Brown as a possible suspect. "In the days following the shooting," the *Rocky Mountain News* reported, "Stone publicly questioned Brooks Brown's relationship with the killers. He stopped short of calling Brown a suspect but said he was 'suspicious' of the teen."[38] Brooks Brown was officially cleared of any link to the incident by the sheriff's department in December 1999. As a result, the Klebold family filed suit against the Jefferson County Sheriff's Office for its failure to follow up on the Browns' complaint. "Had deputies followed through, the Klebolds contended, the parents would likely have 'become aware of dangers of which they were not aware' and that they would have stopped contact between their son and Harris," reported the *Rocky Mountain News*.[39] (The suit was later dropped.) This and other factors (discussed later) prompted the Browns to begin gathering signatures on a petition to recall Sheriff Stone.

The Tapes Don't Lie

Whatever vestige of trust existed between many of the families of the injured and murdered and the Jefferson County Sheriff's Office was put to its most severe test in December 1999. At the time, Columbine High School was making strides toward healing. In the late fall the football team captured the 5A state championship and dedicated the win to their fallen teammate, Matt Kechter, who had worn number 70 as a lineman on the varsity team. "We were coming off some positive things," said Principal Frank DeAngelis. "We had had a very good, very inspirational assembly. The football team won the championship. We had students doing well in classes. Success was happening."

Then two things derailed the healing process. First, on December 14, *Time* magazine's exclusive cover story titled "The Columbine Tapes" hit newsstands. A still photo of the killers in the cafeteria, taken from the school's surveillance camera, was on the cover. And rather than being a story about the community's positive strides toward healing, as locals had gathered from the magazine's reporters it would be, *Time*'s coverage focused on the prerampage videotapes made by Klebold and Harris. The second setback occurred on December 15 when, as a misguided prank, Florida teen Michael Ian Campbell sent an Instant Message to Columbine student Erin Walton, telling her to stay home from school the next day because he intended to "finish what [was] begun" by Harris and Klebold. The school promptly closed two days early for Christmas break. Campbell subsequently was sentenced to four months of jail time in Florida. "Everything we had worked toward on this road to recovery," said DeAngelis, "seemed to take several steps back."

Painful though they may have been, no one could begrudge the strained moments when police officers roughed up victims on the day of the incident, given what law enforcement was facing. Judy Brown's frustration that police never addressed her complaint when Harris threatened her son's life on his Web postings might have been forgotten, in time, under normal circumstances. But the cumulative effect of the hard edges and subsequent missteps of the Jefferson County Sheriff's Office ultimately created an environment in which trust eroded and hostilities emerged.

The slowness of the police response, though a tactical call, had left an impression of galling negligence as the killers moved unhindered throughout the school. This weighed heavily upon many families, some of whom continued to show good will and the desire to give the sheriff's office the benefit of the doubt. Sheriff John Stone's decision to release to *Time* the prerampage video tapes made by Harris and Klebold solidified the mistrust, magnified the hard feelings, and aroused new questions about what had motivated the killers. The community was stunned and felt betrayed both by *Time* and the sheriff, who (rightly or wrongly) they felt had been grandstanding for self-promoting purposes by giving *Time* access to the videos and posing for photographs holding the killers' guns. All this, when even the families of the murdered had not been able to view the videos.

"You Can't Understand What We Feel"

The existence of Klebold and Harris's videotapes was made public in early November, when lead investigator Kate Battan read a portion from one tape at the sentencing of Mark Manes. Harris and Klebold stated on tape that Manes sold them the TEC-DC9 Klebold used in the massacre and Philip Duran was the intermediary in the sale. Officials said they had not revealed the existence of the videotapes for fear that sympathizers of Harris and Klebold would elevate the pair to cult-hero status. "Dissemination of this information might allow them to accomplish [that] goal. And we don't want them to appear to achieve that status. So we will fight tooth and nail to prevent dissemination of those materials," said Jefferson County Deputy District Attorney Steve Jenson.[40] Once the existence of the tapes was known, however, the Jefferson County Sheriff's Office was flooded with requests from the media to view them. The department refused all requests, saying the tapes were evidence in outstanding lawsuits.

Stone's decision to grant *Time* magazine exclusive access to the videotapes was seen as an act of betrayal by just about everyone in the community, including some people in his own department, and local and national journalists were angry that their requests, submitted long before *Time*'s, had been rebuffed.

The district attorney's office was equally nonplussed: "We, in fact, were not consulted at all," said Jefferson County District Attorney Dave Thomas.[41] The school community was outraged because *Time* put the killers on the cover—as they appeared during the rampage. And this, when the school was taking the first tentative steps toward recovery.

But the people who were most deeply affected by Stone's decision were the families of the victims. *Time* published its cover story just before Christmas. "It's already put another knife in our hearts," said Rich Petrone, stepfather of Dan Rohrbough.[42] Rachel Scott's mother, Beth Nimmo, said: "This doesn't help me. Rachel didn't get to leave a goodbye tape to me. These boys got to set it up the way they wanted to and act out on it. Everyone else was a victim of what they predetermined to do. It's very disturbing, very hurtful, at a time when Christmas is hard to deal with anyway. Everywhere you look, you don't see the faces of those who are gone, but [you see] the faces of the killers, and you see them portrayed as some kind of cause."[43] Connie Michalik, mother of wounded student Richard Castaldo, said, "First they terrorize everyone and then they come back as ghosts."[44]

127

Stone seemed to recognize his mistake and sent signals that he was taking full responsibility for it. "The buck stops here," he said. But he quickly diverted some of the blame to *Time:* "I made a mistake by trusting a journalist that I thought was trustworthy, that I thought he would keep his word. . . . My mistake in this thing was not being able to properly evaluate the character and integrity of somebody I thought was a top-notch national journalist. [He] can run back to New York, and we've got to pick up the pieces."[45] These equivocations fell flat for most families. "You don't leak things like that to the media and expect it not to go anyplace," said Connie Michalik. "I guess I'm not buying their story, unless they're incredible idiots. Aren't these guys supposed to be detectives?"[46] Sam Riddle, the spokesman for the Shoels family, whose son Isaiah was the only African-American to be killed, said, "If you're talking to a reporter, it's always on the record. They insult our intelligence for the sheriff's department to say that."[47]

Time released a statement that said it had violated no agreement and that no restrictions had been given as to how the reporter would make use of the material on the tapes. Once the tapes were out, there was no turning back for Stone, who, by Colorado's Open Records Law, was forced to give other media access. When it became known a few days prior to hitting the newsstands that *Time* intended to run the story about the tapes in a special cover story, the sheriff's office invited journalists from the *Rocky Mountain News* to view the tapes right away. *Time* and the *News* had their stories on newsstands that Monday, December 13. When other media responded with outrage, Jefferson County hastily arranged another showing for journalists from forty-five other media organizations.

But before doing so, Stone invited the families to view edited portions of the tapes. The sheriff's department put together an abbreviated forty-five-minute version that included short portions from each of the tapes. One parent told me, "They said that's all we'd need to see to get a sense of what they were about."

Seeing the killers boast about their impending crimes had contradictory effects. On the one hand, it enabled some members of the community to make some sense out of what had happened. Many of the victims had not known Klebold or Harris and couldn't fathom what would have made them do something like this. Seeing them speak in cold and calculating tones about their killing filled in at least part of the picture. "It further reinforced my thoughts that they were very young and very foolish and confused young men," said Brad Bernall after viewing the edited version.[48] "I assumed that's what they'd be like," said Lance Kirkland, who was shot several times by Dylan Klebold. "It answers a lot of questions."[49]

photo by Wendy Murray Zoba

Columbine High School, Summer 1999

The "hot zone" (library windows); CHS under repair, July 1999.

Memorial

Memorial trinkets on school grounds, July 1999.

photo by Wendy Murray Zoba

Cross-maker Greg Zanis

photo by Wendy Murray Zoba

Cross Memorial, Summer 1999

Memorial crosses and the graves of Rachel Scott and Corey DePooter at Chapel Hill Memorial Garden, July 1999.

photo by Wendy Murray Zoba

Kids from St. Francis Cabrini Catholic Church, January 2000.

Cassie Bernall

Cassie Bernall with her friends.

photo by Steve Sonheim

Brad and Misty Bernall

Rachel Scott with her sisters, Dana (left) and Bethanee (middle).

Rachel Scott

photo by Wendy Murray Zoba

Rachel Scott's Grave, July 1999

photo by Steve Sonheim

Dana Scott, Rachel's sister, (left) and Lori Johnson, Rachel's youth pastor, (right).

Devon Adams

Friend of Dylan Klebold and Rachel Scott.

Craig Nason and Cassie Chance

Friends of Cassie Bernall, April 2000.

"Friend of Mine"

Jonathan and Stephen Cohen offer the final performance of their song, "Friend of Mine," at the anniversary memorial service, April 20, 2000.

Dale Todd, father of Evan Todd, said that he thought the tapes should be publicized so America could get a good look at "the kids next door." "My son said that kids are just a reflection of society, and we have a pretty sick society. Maybe we need to look deeper into the problems of our youth. Their behavior was disgusting, filthy. But these were the kids next door."[50]

For many others, seeing the killers' faces and hearing their voices only compounded their grief. The tapes contained details that showed how easy it would have been to intervene and prevent the event from happening. The boys boasted about their arsenal and provided a walk-through of Harris's bedroom, where they displayed their stash of weapons, fuses, gunpowder, and pipe bombs. "Thank God my parents don't search my room. They would have found so much s——," said Harris. He mentioned close calls, such as the time his parents found his black tackle box with pipe bombs in it (his parents removed the pipe bombs) and when a clerk from Green Mountain Guns called to tell him the ammunition clips he had ordered were in, and his father, Wayne Harris, answered the phone (he told them he hadn't ordered any clips). Klebold boasted about the time he was in his room trying on his black trench coat to see if it would conceal his shotgun, when his parents walked in. "They didn't even know it was there," he said on one tape. Don Fleming, whose daughter Kelly was killed in the library, said he was surprised to see how much weaponry Harris kept in his room. But he did not want to put blame on the parents. "They've got their hell to go through. I've got mine. It's two different hells, but it's still hell," he said.[51]

Members of another Columbine family discovered yet a different kind of hell when they realized their daughter had been named on the tapes by Harris. At one point Harris, alone and rambling in a monologue, mentioned several "b——es who never called me back." He mentioned five girls, but gave the complete name of only one. "You know who you are. Thanks, you made me feel good. Think about that for a while. . . ." This girl had met him a few years earlier at a soccer game and he had taken to her. She didn't dislike him, but had no interest in moving beyond a friendship. When he called her several times, she didn't return his calls. Her mother saw the quotes from the tape published in the newspaper and "My life changed that minute," she said. "It was just a frightful experience as far as his eyes, his demeanor. It was very scary. No feeling, no remorse, no caring in the world for what was going on. And to know he harbored this hatred for a year on somebody he didn't even know!"[52] She requested, and was granted, a temporary restraining order on the tape on which her daughter is named, for fear that someone else might pick up where Klebold and Harris had left off. On March 3, 2000, a Jefferson County district judge granted the injunction, which forbade dissemination of the tape without the girl's name being deleted.

Release of the killers' tapes brought little in the way of comfort for the Klebolds, even while the tapes vindicated their claim to have been clueless about the rage their son Dylan had felt. "Their pain can never go away," said a family friend, Nate Dykeman.[53] "But now people can see what they've been telling them the whole time is the truth." On the tapes Klebold thanked his parents for being "great parents" and for helping him find "self-awareness" and "self-reliance." "I've always loved you for that," he said. "I'm sorry I have so much rage," he said. "You can't understand what we feel, no matter how much you think you can." He imagined the remorse his parents would be feeling—"'If only we could have reached them sooner, or found this tape'"—and said, "It's what we had to do." He said, "They gave me . . . life. It's up to me what I do with it." He closed by saying, "Just know I'm going to a better place. I didn't like life too much."

Harris said, "That's it. Sorry. Good-bye."

Klebold said, "Good-bye."

Unanswered Questions

The tapes offered a chilling look at what motivated these boys, and the investigators summed it up as pure hate. When investigator Battan broke her "five months of silence" and spoke to *Salon.com* reporter Dave Cullen, she said, "'Were there things said [in the library] about jocks? Probably. About God? Probably. Was there a 'n——' comment? Probably. But that's not what it is about.'" Someone inside the investigation, whom Cullen identified as a key source, told him, "'We can tell you why they did it, because they tell us why they're going to do it. They did it because they were consumed with hate.'"

Battan reiterated as much when she discussed the contents of the official report with reporters from the *Denver Post* prior to its release: "'This was not about killing jocks or killing black people or killing Christians. It was about killing everybody.'"[54] Battan acknowledged that Harris and Klebold were heard by witnesses making remarks about God and Christianity, particularly to people who were praying out loud or saying "Oh God" out of fear. But Battan dismissed this as one of many forms of taunting the killers inflicted on their schoolmates. "The killers used religion, race or anything to belittle their victims," she said.[55]

Some parents opted to return to view the tapes in their entirety. Darrell Scott was one who did, but he stopped after viewing only one complete video. He said he couldn't stomach any more. What he saw was all he needed before rallying other parents to publicly demand Stone's resignation. On Monday, December 20, Scott stood on a platform at Trinity Christian Center (where four Columbine funerals had taken place) with several other parents of victims, flanked by the thirteen original crosses that had once stood on Rebel Hill, and called for Stone's resignation. He contended that Stone had inappropriately released the videotapes at the worst possible time and that "the whole world got to see and hear things before I did. He has wounded deeply the victims of Columbine's tragedy over and over again."[56] Tom Mauser, whose son Daniel had been killed, added, "This was more than just a simple error in judgment. Sheriff Stone broke his commitment to the victim's families. I think he's either extremely naive or extremely incompetent." Patricia DePooter, whose son Corey had died in the rampage, said, "Three strikes you're out," referring to the release of some of the hate-filled contents of Harris's Web site, the slow response of law enforcement on the day of the shooting, and release of videotapes to *Time*. Other family members present included John Tomlin, whose son John died in the library; Dale Todd, whose son Evan was injured in the library; Cindy Thourin, stepdaughter of teacher Dave Sanders, who bled to death in the science room; Rachel Scott's sister, Bethanee McCandless, and brothers Craig and Mike Scott; Larry Nimmo, Rachel's stepfather; and Rich Townsend, father of Lauren Townsend, who died in the library.[57]

But for Darrell Scott, the sense of betrayal went deeper than the means and the timing of the tapes' release. He had been told by investigators that any information relating to his daughter would be brought to his attention, and so he was shocked to hear his daughter Rachel mentioned by name on the tape he viewed. Investigators had said nothing to him about Rachel being mentioned by Eric Harris. Not only was she mentioned, she was ridiculed for her Christian beliefs. In the same segment of the video the two boys spewed a venomous and mocking tirade against Christians. Darrell Scott was so shocked that he rewound the tape, took out an audio recorder, placed it on the table, and replayed that portion of the tape to record it. He then released the contents to the public. The portion that Scott recorded included:

Klebold: "I know we're gonna have followers because we're so f—ing god-like."

Klebold: "We're not exactly human—we have human bodies but we've evolved into one step above you f—ing human s——. We actually have f—ing self-awareness."

Harris: "We need a f—ing kick start. If we have a f—ing religious war, or oil, or anything. We need to get a chain reaction going here."

Harris: "It's gonna be like Doom, man—after the bombs explode. That f—ing shotgun [he kisses the gun] straight out of Doom. Go ahead and change gun laws—how do you think we got ours?"

Harris: "Shut the f—— up, Nick, you laugh too much. And those two girls sitting next to you, they probably want you to shut up, too. Rachel and Jen and whatever."

Klebold: "Stuck up little b——es, you f—ing little Christianity, godly whores."

Harris: "Yeah, I love Jesus, I love Jesus. Shut the f— up."

Klebold: " 'What would Jesus do?' What would I do? Boosh! [he points his finger as if it were a gun at the camera].

Harris: "I would shoot you in the motherf—ing head! Go Romans— thank God they crucified that a—hole."

Both: "Go Romans! Yeah!"

Investigator Kate Battan told Scott the girl on the tape was not his daughter Rachel. She stated repeatedly and publicly that what had happened at Columbine was not "a God thing." But Darrell Scott demurred: "I won't take that at face value. She [Battan] told me that this was not a Christian thing, but all I heard on that tape was Christianity 'effing' this and 'effing' that." He said that the Rachel mentioned on the video was linked to a boy named Nick. "He is the young man [Rachel] went to prom with." The killers mocked this Rachel for her love for Jesus and made derisive references to WWJD, the popular acronym for the phrase, "What Would Jesus Do?". Rachel Scott wore a WWJD wristband. "All of that points to Rachel Scott. I've done my own investigation, and the Rachel that [Battan] is referring to is not even a Christian. My personal opinion from the beginning has been that these kids were targeted because they were Christians."

Investigators allowed that the gunmen taunted some people about God, though the official report cited only one instance—that of Val Schnurr. They resisted any serious consideration that there may have been an anti-religious element to the killers' hostilities. Darrell Scott's public disclosure of the portion of the tape that he said referenced his daughter revealed another troubling aspect of the boys' thinking. Harris specifically said he would shoot Christians in the head. In its response to the videos and the information released in the report, the sheriff's office neglected to mention that three of the thirteen who died—Rachel Scott, Cassie Bernall, and a third student whose parents did not want identified—died by gunshots to the temple at close range. All three had been known for their Christian leadership.

The official report stated that Rachel Scott died in the flurry of the first shots. It neglected to mention that she had been injured in the first volley and left on the grass crying. Eric Harris later approached her, pulled her head up by her hair, exchanged words with her (discussed in more detail in chapter 9), then shot her through the temple. The report said nothing about Cassie Bernall being shot point-blank through the temple. The same is true of the third victim, who was shot multiple times and injured at first. The killer then finished the job with a shot through the temple.

A story by Tom Foreman in *ABCNews.com,* published just before release of the investigators' report, asked, "Could [the] wounded have been saved?" Foreman wrote: "The gunmen go on to kill themselves, but even after they are dead, it takes more than three hours for the first SWAT team, slowly working its way through the school, to reach the library. By then, 10 of the students and teacher Sanders have died of their wounds."[58] If ten of the thirteen who died (not including Harris and Klebold) could have expired from their wounds because of the slowness of the rescue, as Foreman suggests, that means that only three would have died instantly.[59] Those three would have been the ones shot in the temple, who had no chance for survival. This also suggests that though thirteen *ended up* dying, three were executed, and they were well-known Christians.

I traveled to Littleton shortly after the tapes had been made public to see for myself how much antireligious vitriol existed in them. I called the sheriff's office two weeks ahead of time to set up a mutually agreeable time to view them, but they were noncommittal and told me to call when I arrived in the area. Once I was in town, I left phone messages that went unanswered for days before Kate Battan finally returned my calls on my last day. She told me that she was too busy to accommodate me that week and then asked, "What do you think you have to gain by viewing the videos anyway?"

The inappropriateness of that comment aside, I explained to her that I was interested in the killers' antireligious hostilities, given their recorded desire to shoot Christians in the head and given that three of those who died that way were indeed Christians. Battan did not disagree. She said, "You bet."[60]

Kathleen M. Heide, professor of criminology at the University of South Florida, has interviewed more than one hundred children who have been convicted of murder or attempted murder. She says that, on one level, she would not "make the leap" to suggest that the Columbine killers pursued their victims on the basis of their religious beliefs. "One could wonder where some of that hatred comes from," she adds. "When you are dealing with alienated young people, I always explore the music they are listening to. When these kids are into music that is nihilistic and shows contempt for values and institutions, that concerns me from a clinical standpoint." Such music, she says, "gives impressionable kids who are angry, alienated, or possibly clinically depressed, or who feel marginalized, an identity, a platform, and a focus for what to do with their powerlessness."

"Some of the music [the Columbine killers] were said to have listened to is anti-Christian." As for whether this influenced them to go after Christians, Heide said, "I'm not disagreeing with that, but I don't know if I would make that leap." However, she added that "if kids were killed after being asked if they believed in God, the connection is more clear and the point of religion is more significant."[61]

Eric Chester, president and founder of Generation Why and author, speaker, and youth expert in the Denver area has addressed students in high schools all over the nation since Columbine. He says, "Eric and Dylan were on a death mission and probably thought, 'Let's look for the people we hate.' Their hate knew no bounds." Chester does not think they targeted Christians, though he concedes that Christians would have been high on the list of people they hated. "The [kids] in the library were the ones who followed the rules, who did their homework during lunch. They were the salt of the earth," he says. "Eric and Dylan were probably thinking, 'Let's find the ones that are everything we're not. Let's take 'em out. Let's get as many as we can.'"[62]

The Accounting Begins

Whatever their motivation, the gunmen roamed around undaunted that day and carried their murderous plot to its bitter end. From the vantage point of law enforcement, the killers won. They may not have killed as many as they had wanted to and their plan did not unfold as they had hoped, but they picked their moment and did what they set out to do. No one, not even the police, stopped them. The subsequent lawsuits told the rest of the story.

A suit filed in April 2000 against the sheriff's department by Angela Sanders, daughter of teacher Dave Sanders, alleged that a police sharp-shooter, perched on the roof of a nearby home, had Klebold in his crosshairs, but was denied permission to fire. The suit also said that author-ities would not allow the use of battering rams, rappelling gear, or sledge-hammers that might have enabled rescuers to gain access to key locations in the school more quickly. But the delay in reaching her father, the suit alleged, was "shocking, unconscionable, and inexcusable."[63] Sanders lay dying for more than three hours before anyone reached him, despite a constant cell-phone connection that kept police informed of his condi-tion and a sign that had been posted in the window indicating that some-one was bleeding to death. Even after SWAT personnel arrived, they made no attempt to save him and sat for another twenty minutes to a half-hour while he labored near death. Medical personnel finally arrived as Sanders drew his last breath.

In addition to Sanders's suits, fourteen other families filed lawsuits against the sheriff's office in the days leading up to the first anniversary. Ten were filed in federal court, five in Jefferson County District Court. The allegations cited include wrongful death and civil rights violations, stating: (1) "the [sheriff's] department inadequately investigated the Web site maintained by Harris in which he threatened to go on a shooting spree"; (2) "although deputies traded gunfire with Harris and Klebold outside the high school, officers failed to go into the school and stop the teenagers from going inside"; and (3) "Dispatchers and 911 operators told students and teachers to stay put and that help was on the way. SWAT offi-cers didn't reach the library until four hours later."[64] The library was the last place to be secured. Patti Nielson's phone call enabled police to know exactly where the boys were and that they were killing people as they walked through the library. Many people found it galling that it took so long for before anyone entered the school generally (12:06 P.M.) and the library in particular (3:22 P.M.).

The unnamed police officer I referenced earlier said that his most dis-turbing memory of Columbine was not the image of Rachel Scott lying on the ground, or the smells of gunpowder and pall of death as he walked through the library, or even the sight of the dead bodies on the floor amid textbooks and humming computers. He was haunted most by the simple fact that there were "no dead cops." These troubled young men "hit law enforcement in the Achilles heel," he said. "We were left with a sense of helplessness and frustration that the kids were the ones who died and the killers were not stopped."

Embattled Sheriff John Stone and his undersheriff, John A. Dunaway, submitted a letter to the public with the investigators' report. The letter outlined the scope of the investigation and its conclusions. However, they ended the letter with a plaintive regret: "While this report established a record of the events of April 20, it cannot answer the most fundamental question—WHY? That is, why would two young men in the spring of their lives choose to murder faculty members and classmates? The evidence provides no definitive explanation, and the question continues to haunt us all."

Chapter 7

We Are Columbine

The Question the Killers Foisted upon Us

WHEN I RETURNED TO Littleton in January 2000, six months after my initial trip, I sensed that healing was taking place. The grief, though evident, was not as raw, and the community seemed more normalized. The families of those who had died had navigated through the first holiday season without their loved ones, and survivors had reconfigured their lives, learning to live in wheelchairs or with leg braces or with disfiguring scars or with chronic pain from bullets lodged too deep to remove. The flag memorial under the tree on school property was gone. Life at Columbine High School was on the upswing.

For most, the healing process had moved forward even if only in baby steps. Patrick Ireland, the young man who had lowered himself out the library window for all the nation to see on news video clips, had walked with the aid of a cane and leg brace on the first day of school in the Fall following the shootings. One bullet was left lodged in his brain. He had relearned basic language skills but remained partially paralyzed on his right side and walked with a list. As noted in an article in *Life* magazine: "When he gestures to emphasize a point, it is with his left hand. The right one, still partially paralyzed, stays in his lap."[1] His doctors, though encouraged by his progress, have said that the "majority of people who survive this [sort of injury] have a different life."[2]

Nicole Nowlen, who had hidden under the table with John Tomlin and had seen him get killed, still had five bullets inside her when school started, but none near vital organs. Sean Graves, among the first to be shot outside the school, had undergone several surgeries to repair damage done by the bullets that severed nerves controlling his legs. At one point his physical therapy was so painful that he vomited.[3] Mark Kintgen recovered well from buckshot wounds to the left side of his neck and head, which had special significance because his right side already was debilitated by cerebral palsy.

Mark Taylor credited God for his having survived seven gunshot wounds. He was shot in the thigh at first, and then, "Eric Harris came over to me and shot me five more times in the chest," he said.[4] The bullets penetrated his chest cavity and collapsed a lung, but missed vital organs. "I remember being in the ambulance afraid of dying. I called out to God to save me, and he answered my plea. I knew right then, I was certain that God was going to save my life."[5]

Val Schnurr survived her nine bullet wounds and embarked on a college career at the University of Northern Colorado. Lance Kirkland miraculously survived being shot in the face by Dylan Klebold but struggled with school in the aftermath.

Kacey Ruegsegger underwent three surgeries in six days to rebuild her shoulder, which was shattered when she was shot at point-blank range. A six-inch plate holds her arm bones in place and a four-inch plate keeps her shoulder intact. Her thumb has a cadaver bone and a metal plate to hold it together. She told me that she probably will never regain the full range of motion in her shoulder. And she had to learn how to write with her left hand to sign her thank-you cards. But she was thankful to return to state quarter horse competitions with her horse Big Daddy Crain, with which she had won many awards.

These were wounds on the outside. Healing of wounds on the inside, for many, was less measurable, and—on one level—more complicated. Because Columbine High School fell into the category of being a public institution, certain limits had been placed on what could be sanctioned as healing activities by the school. Notions such as "educating" kids to respect others and learning "tolerance" abounded. References to prayer, use of religious symbols, and discussions about God were not part of this conversation.

It didn't take long before the role of religion became the flashpoint of controversy. The first hint of it began with the fifteen crosses that appeared on Rebel Hill. That, however, was mostly an in-house debate among Christians as to the nature of forgiveness and the extent of the efficacy of the cross. The discussion of the role of religion in the public arena assumed a more cantankerous tone following the community memorial service five days after the massacre. Sentiments expressed in this conflict would animate a larger national debate.

Whose Service Is It?

The community memorial service took place in a shopping center parking lot near Clement Park on April 25, 1999. It had been hastily put together by local religious leaders in conjunction with the governor's office. The intention had been to include representatives from the various religious communities in the Littleton area. Speakers included Catholic Archbishop Charles Chaput of Denver, who offered the opening prayer; Rabbi Fred Greenspan, who offered the closing prayer; Colorado Governor William Owens; Jefferson County Commissioner Pat Holloway; Jefferson County School District Superintendent Jane Hammond; Littleton Mayor Pat Cronenberger; Dr. Jerry Nelson, pastor of Littleton's Southern Gables Church; Vice President Al Gore; and Franklin Graham, the son of evangelist Billy Graham. General Colin Powell and Principal Frank DeAngelis joined the others on the platform. Organizers expected a crowd of about ten thousand. More than seventy thousand showed up.

Columbine student brothers Jonathan and Stephen Cohen, strumming an acoustic guitar and singing in Dylanesque intonations, opened the service with their song "Friend of Mine," composed after the tragedy: "Can you still hear raging guns ending dreams of precious ones? In God's Son, hope will come, his red stain will take our pain. Columbine, friend of mine. Peace will come to you in time." [6]

Florists had donated twenty-five thousand bouquets of white and orange lilies, sunflowers, daisies, pink carnations, roses, which students held over their heads like banners to honor their fallen peers. A Columbine alumnus led four U.S. Air Force F-16s that flew overhead in "the missing man" formation. Christian singers Amy Grant, Michael W. Smith, and Phil Driscoll provided music. Two CHS students spoke: student body president Heather Dinkel and Amber Burgess. Amber recalled, "When I was little, in elementary school . . . I was forced to attend various Columbine activities [of my brothers]. I remember watching those students like they were superheroes. I looked up to them. But I can't even begin to tell you how much I admire all of the students and faculty that were in that building on Tuesday. . . . Coach Sanders, I love you, and I will miss you. I know that each day your memory will push me to become a better person and to live my life to its fullest." She concluded her speech by saying, "One thing that wasn't known before this tragedy is how strong our community is and that we will triumph because—*Students, help me out here*—We are Columbine! We are Columbine! We are Columbine!"[7]

Vice President Gore spoke in platitudes but not without genuine emotion: "You are not alone. The heart of America aches with you."[8] and Governor Owens read the names of the slain as thirteen white doves were released.

It was the combination of comments by Pastor Jerry Nelson and Franklin Graham that sparked controversy. Nelson offended the rabbis in attendance when he referred to some Christians imprisoned during the Holocaust who had found strength to endure through their faith in Christ. As reported in the *Washington Times*, Rabbi Stephen Foster later complained that the reference suggested that "Christians had a better chance of surviving the Holocaust" than Jews. "That's pretty offensive," he said.[9] Nelson also took the opportunity to encourage those attending to follow the example of the slain students who had given their lives to Christ. Franklin Graham, never one to mince words, spoke with evangelical fervor about the need for repentance and accepting Jesus Christ as Lord and Savior.

The final amen hardly had been uttered before dissenting voices protested the service's "evangelical" tone. "The entire community was invited to come and mourn, and then it turned into an evangelical prayer service," said Rabbi Foster. "I've had many complaints from people saying, 'Where were the Jews?' but that's not the issue. The issue was one of insensitivity to the kind of statements being made that were exclusively directed to not just Christians, but fundamental Christians." Rabbi Fred Greenspan, who offered the closing prayer, said later that the evangelical emphasis demonstrated "a pretty ignorant, narrow-minded streak of Christianity."[10]

"The consensus was that it was not inclusive to all faith communities," said the Reverend Michael Carrier, president of the Interfaith Alliance of Colorado and pastor of Calvary Presbyterian Church in Littleton.[11] "I felt like [Graham] was trying to terrorize us into heaven instead of loving us into heaven. The service was supposed to be for all the people of Colorado and the nation to find solace, not an evangelical Christian service."[12] The Reverend Don Marxhausen said that people felt "hit over the head with

Jesus."[13] He told me that the "Jesus theology" of many area evangelical churches was "so simplistic it is almost hurtful." It did not bring to bear the reflective, mysterious aspects of the faith, especially in the context of such a tragedy. Instead, he said, it offered simplistic victorious answers like, "They're with Jesus, so everything is okay."

Dick Wadhams, spokesman for Governor Owens, called these complaints "inappropriate and groundless." He said, "It is reprehensible that they would try to politicize the memorial service in the immediate aftermath of such a tragedy." The Reverend Lucia Guzman, executive director of the Colorado Council of Churches (not known for its evangelical sensibilities) noted that "the memorial service was representative of the Columbine community, which is heavily weighted toward 'what you might call evangelical or independent churches.'"[14] She added, "In no way do I feel I was excluded, but I have many rabbi colleagues who were incensed by the one-sided nature of the service. You can't put the focus on [evangelical Christianity] and then say it was inclusive of the whole community."[15]

Kevin Parker, the school volunteer who also worked for the Christian organization Young Life at Columbine, defended the service: "I think that criticism was pretty selfish, quite frankly. That memorial service was not for the rest of the country or the world. It was for the people of Littleton. Had this been a Jewish community, it would have been a more Jewish service. But this is not a Jewish community. For the most part, this should be considered a Christian community. So [the service] was reflective of our community." CHS Spanish teacher Shirley Hickman, a member of Nelson's church, said, "I've read in the media of people who complained [about the service]. I know Jerry, who spoke there, had some definite complaints. But when we were back in school, I didn't hear complaints from staff, or from kids, or from the community. I think that service represented the community. The complaints seemed to come from outside the people who were actually involved."

Other church leaders, who would number themselves among evangelicals, felt there was a kernel of truth to the criticism. Bill Oudemolen, senior pastor of Foothills Bible Church outside Littleton, said, "That service was very openly evangelistic and evangelical. It wasn't a revival meeting, but it was close. Franklin Graham stands up and invites people to put their faith in Jesus. I was comfortable with that, but some mainline denominational people were not. It was a hard-sell; it was in your face." Billy Epperhart, pastor of Trinity Christian Center, said, "I understood where the [critics] were coming from. I didn't disagree with anything that was said or represented at the service, but I might have disagreed with the timing."

Complaints about the community service captured the volatility of bringing one particular brand of religion—evangelical Christianity—into the public conversation. This inflamed evangelical and mainline people, including Jewish leaders, one against another and, said Oudemolen, "we evangelicals got very defensive." Some felt angry that people targeted only evangelicals for this kind of complaint. Would these critics sympathize if an evangelical attended a Jewish or Muslim funeral and insisted that the service not tread on his religious tenets? Others wondered if the criticism was less driven by some religious leaders feeling left out than by objections to the public expression of the Christian faith.

An Uneasy Separation

The Jefferson County School District eschewed religious expressions of any kind when it came to school-sponsored gestures of healing. This was felt most notably in the case of memorial tiles that school officials had invited members of the community to decorate as expressions of hope and healing or in memory of loved ones. The tiles, the community was told, would be placed in the hallways of the school as a permanent memorial.

At first school authorities said the tiles could not include images of anything religious, but they later changed their stance after being pressured by the community to allow religious symbols. Hundreds of memorial tiles were made, and about one hundred and sixty were put up in the hallways, many of them with Christian symbols. Authorities then did another turnaround and refused to put up new tiles with religious messages and chiseled out about eighty of those already installed. In October 1999 seven families filed suit against the Jefferson County School District through the Rutherford Institute, contending the district had violated their rights of freedom of expression. "Only religious symbols and/or religious messages were excluded," the suit read.[16]

John Whitehead, founder and president of the nonprofit civil liberties and human rights organization, the Rutherford Institute, said some of the symbols were so innocuous "you had to have the eye of the hawk to see them. When I saw the tiles, I had to look very closely to see some of the religious symbols. That's how intensely they scrutinized these."[17]

The school district, in turn, filed a motion for dismissal in November 1999. A portion of that motion said, "Had the school not imposed these limitations, the hallways might have been filled with hundreds of crosses and other indicia of religious faith, creating a setting so dominated by religious symbols that it took on the appearance of a parochial school."[18]

"They created a public forum," said Whitehead. "Once they do that, they have to be careful—they can't discriminate on the basis of content, and they did that."[19] He saw the Rutherford Institute's action as defending the freedom of religious expression in the face of the government's attempt to censor it.

This dichotomy between healing and faith in the public sector was particularly onerous to many in the school community—some church-goers, some not—because of the obvious and intense role religion had played during the massacre and in its immediate aftermath. Craig Nason, a junior at the time of the shootings, had sat huddled in the choir room not far from the library. He recalled: "Someone [from within the room] called out, 'Somebody religious better be praying right now.' They pointed to me and a couple other kids they knew were involved with Christ, and I said, 'Hey, we haven't stopped praying since second-one.' God was just giving us peace. I kept saying to myself, 'They can take my life but they can't take God away.' That's what I had to keep telling myself. That's what got me through."[20]

A photo of Jessica Holliday was taken moments after she escaped the school library and subsequently appeared in magazines and papers worldwide. She had been at a table in the library visiting with her friend, Lauren Townsend, only minutes before the killers walked in. Many had assumed, seeing her anguished image, that she was expressing grief over the loss of her friend, Lauren. Grief-stricken though she was, she said she was thinking about something else when that picture was snapped: "I was praying. I was asking, 'What just happened? Why our school? Why is everybody hurting?' I was thinking about Lauren, and I was asking 'Why? Why?' It was a moment with God."[21]

Many such moments with God were integral to the experience. Kevin Parker said that right after the shooting, "The administration of Columbine was much more open to me than ever before. Some people in the administration came up to me and said, 'Kevin, we need Young Life now more than ever.'" Teacher Shirley Hickman said that as the faculty met in the days after the tragedy to set the next course, "We opened the faculty meeting with prayer—something you don't do very often."

The Students' Voices

While some adults in the community bickered about who had the right to express what at public services and on memorial tiles, students faced each day inside the walls of Columbine High School. They walked into classrooms and scoped out the fastest escape route, saw the ghosts of lost friends they used to pass in the hallways, and broke into a cold sweat when the fire alarm sounded. I saw these young people as the conscience of the Columbine community. For all of the valued insights and opinions I had solicited and received from others in the community—mostly adults— these were the ones who had heard the gunshots that day, who had looked into the eyes of the killers, who had stepped over their fallen peers as they fled the school to escape, and who had returned to face classrooms with empty desks that friends and fellow students, or their teacher, once had occupied.

One of the first appointments I had in Littleton that January was with a group of Columbine students affiliated with Saint Francis Cabrini Catholic Church, where three of those killed—Matt Kechter, Kelly Fleming, and Dan Mauser—had attended. Their youth pastor, Jim Beckman, had warned me more than once that he wasn't sure how many kids he would be able to round up to meet with me. I sensed intense media-fatigue in a community still stinging from the *Time* magazine betrayal. I wouldn't have blamed any of them for not showing up. Walking into the church that afternoon, I expected to have to adapt my game plan and use the time to interview only Beckman.

I was shocked to find nine students waiting. We sat in a meeting area in the church, some on couches and others in folding chairs pulled up to form a circle. I sat on the floor in their midst so I could push the tape recorder in the direction of anyone speaking.

They shared with me what it had been like to return to school the fall after the shooting. Despite the community's general squeamishness about public religious expression, religion was integral to these students' stories from beginning to end. Sarah Arzola, a good friend of Rachel Scott, said the shooting had made her "afraid of everything." She said, "I'm getting better at not being so afraid of going where there's a big crowd or even just walking down the halls of my school. I always, always, pray to God that I won't be afraid, because that's something I struggle with every day."

Ben Schumann was a junior when we met. He had lost two friends: Matt Kechter, whom he had known since third grade, and Dan Mauser, whom he had known since fourth grade. "A couple of months after it happened I felt like I was to the point where I couldn't go on. I started talking to people, just trying to work through the feelings and the memories that I had. During the shooting we were sitting under the table and I just started praying; our whole table did. I don't remember even stopping, even days after that. I don't remember much else, but I remember being in constant prayer." Ben said prayer got him through the event itself and its aftermath. "My prayer life made me come to the conclusion that I should be living every day to the fullest. Everything seems a whole lot more important, because I don't know when my last day's going to be."

When the invitation went out for students and families to craft the memorial tiles, many of the youth from Saint Francis Cabrini participated. Matt Bruce, who was a sophomore in the year of the shootings and also had been a good friend of Rachel Scott, said: "I made a tile that had a religious symbol on it, and it's not up in the school. I never got it back, and I never have seen it again. It was a pretty cool tile, also. It kind of upset me that they never put it up." Sarah Arzola said she made a tile with an angel on it. "It didn't have anything else, just an angel, and it's not up. I never saw it. It discourages me." Ben Schumann added: "I put a cross with a crown of thorns on my tile, and I've looked around the school during my off hours, and I've looked at every tile, and I haven't found mine. I think it's really wrong, because that's an expression of us. Those are our tiles; they told us to put what we want on them, and they told us that they were going to put them up. And if they don't get put up, then it's kind of going back on their word."

Beyond the general indignation about their religious tiles being rejected, many of the youths believed the administration's religion-neutral stance was disingenuous. Matt said, "Religion played such a huge huge role in healing for everybody, religious or not. During the immediate days afterwards, nobody cared about church-and-state, and everybody—teachers and administration—would talk about religion." Ben said, "The thing that I don't get is, like, Sarah put an angel on her tile and they didn't put the tile up, and yet they still passed out angel pins during school. I don't understand why they can pass the pins out and they can't hang up tiles."

Religion was "part of what happened and what went on," said Matt, so he objected to the tiles having been removed. None of the students knew what had become of the religious tiles they had made. One thought "they probably threw them away." Another thought they might be "in storage somewhere." But removing the tiles, in their minds, did not erase the force and presence of religion in dealing with this tragedy.

This was made clear in the discussion about another religious symbol. Matt Bruce shared the story behind the T-shirt he was wearing. On the front it read "70 times 7," referring to the occasion in Matthew's gospel when Peter asked Jesus how many times a person should forgive a brother. Jesus answered, "Seventy times seven"[22] (Matthew 18:22). The back of the T-shirt read, "We survived, we will prevail, we have hope to carry on." Matt pointed to a small maroon cross that punctuated that slogan at the end.

"Our youth minister, Jim Beckman, had a dream about this shirt, actually," he said. "He took up a donation and made the shirt up. It became a reality. The words have special colors that are associated with them. The colors are silver, blue, and maroon, which are the colors of Columbine [silver and blue] and Chatfield [maroon, where CHS students finished the 1999 school year]. It's a powerful shirt. It's a great symbol of our faith and how we got through this. We printed up over two thousand of them and gave one to everyone in our school [when school resumed after the shooting]. There's a tiny cross on the back at the bottom. We were allowed to wear them, but we weren't allowed to hand them out on school property. We handed them out at Chatfield just outside school property."

Being allowed to wear the shirts, but having to be off school property to distribute them, was not the point of the students' confusion. Their confusion arose when the slogan—"We survived, we will prevail, we have hope to carry on"—was appropriated by the school administration as, more or less, the healing text for the occasion.

"Our principal goes to this church," added Erin Lucero, a CHS sophomore who attended Saint Francis Cabrini. "Like, when we had the assembly when we won the state football championship, he said that quote. I thought it was pretty interesting that he could say it [at an assembly] but we couldn't pass out the shirts on school property."

"He says it all the time," several kids said at once.

Matt added, "It's a really popular quote."

Erin said, "It's like, it came from this church, and he's saying it at school."

A Wounded Shepherd

When I met Principal Frank DeAngelis a day after my time with the Saint Francis Cabrini youth, I understood how he could take something that came from church, as Erin Lucero put it, and then say it at school. A man of faith and an active member of Saint Francis Cabrini, DeAngelis carried the mantle of navigator for the grieving Columbine High School community but was stripped of faith-language with which to do so. *Time,* in its December 20 cover story, included a short piece on DeAngelis, likening him to a coach: "Before he was principal, DeAngelis spent 14 years coaching football and baseball, and these days, he seems like a coach again, ready for battle."[23] Dave Cullen, in a piece he wrote for Denver's *5280* magazine, noted the same: "Two minutes into the interview, I found myself thinking of him as a coach. Not a tough-guy hell-raiser barking out orders, but a charismatic motivator inspiring fledglings toward the goal line."[24]

I saw DeAngelis as more of a pastor, or shepherd, walking the rocky hills and gullies of this tenuous sojourn with his sheep, helping them avoid the crags and hidden holes in the ground. He was a shepherd whose legs ached from the walking, but whose love for the sheep kept him, and them, moving forward.

I approached the doors of Columbine High School around 10:15 A.M. on the morning DeAngelis and I were scheduled to meet. He was tied up in a meeting, so I waited in the reception area of the front office. The sense of foreboding I had felt when I first stepped onto school property six months earlier had dissipated. The school felt *normal.*

Watching teachers come and go with student helpers, I wondered what Klebold and Harris had done in here. Had they shot through those windows that looked out over the foyer? How many bullets had landed on the floor? No one had been killed here, but I had read that the teachers' mailboxes had been knocked over. They were stacked in perfect symmetry now. The state class 5A football championship trophy stood proudly behind the reception desk, near the Columbine T-shirt displayed on the wall to promote its sales (cost: thirty dollars). Classes changed and in no time the hallways were overrun with a sea of baggy pants, backpacks, and navy blue Rebels T-shirts. Two students exchanged kisses—he wore khakis and a white baseball cap turned backward, she wore blue jeans and platform shoes. If he had been under a table in the library wearing that hat, he probably would have been shot. The killers made mention of people wearing white hats.

Nothing in the school's outward appearance betrayed that these were "halls of tragedy," as Rachel Scott prophetically called them in a journal entry. Its spit-and-polish finish and color coordination made it look as if it could be an advertisement for Martha Stewart Does High Schools. The shiny new linoleum floors in sage greens, icy blues, and country whites played well off the new purple and blue carpet. The memorial tiles lent a splash of color. They had been placed in a line that extended around the perimeter of every wall and corner in the school. Each was different but painted in varying combinations of the same hues: maroons, blues, and forest greens. There were plenty of stars, comets, planets, rainbows, flowers, geometric designs, and stick figures holding hands.

In little ways, however, the school community's vulnerability was evident. An ID card dangled around the neck of everyone. I had had to put one on, too, when I signed in. And when I wanted to wander around in the school's foyer to look at the memorial tiles, I felt as though I should ask permission to assure school personnel I was not making any false moves. From where I sat, I could see through two windows into the athletic office where Lauren Townsend's dark blue volleyball jersey, bearing number 8, was hanging on the wall.

My appointment was scheduled for around 10:30 A.M. That was about the time the wounded started to arrive. Their schedules had been adapted to accommodate physical therapy sessions or the extra time they needed to get ready. Richard Castaldo came first. He was impossible to miss with his shock of thick black hair. He wheeled himself into the main hallway, where he sat waiting for classes to change. He tilted his wheelchair against the wall and leaned his head back with his eyes closed. I wondered what he was thinking about. He used to play percussion in the school's marching band. I got up my nerve to approach him. I asked, "Are you Richard?" He looked at me and said, somewhat nervously, "Yes."

I introduced myself and asked if it would be all right if I called him later. He didn't look at me much and seemed out of sorts, damaged. "It's okay if you don't want me to," I said. He answered, "It's okay."

Anne Marie Hochhalter entered shortly after that. Her father helped her get out of their minivan and into her wheelchair, then pushed her wheelchair up to the school's front door. Paralyzed from the waist down, she had just started to regain movement in her legs in late October 1999 when her mother, Carla, walked into a pawn shop, asked to see a gun, loaded it with ammunition she had brought with her, and killed herself while the clerk was doing paperwork for the purchase. Some people said Carla Hochhalter was as much a victim of Klebold and Harris as anyone.

Frank DeAngelis finally emerged from his office about twenty minutes later than we had been scheduled to meet. He extended a firm hand and apologized for the delay. "It's been one of those days," he said.

We sat down face to face in his office. His picture ID hung around his neck with a blue and gray strap that read "We Are Columbine." I asked him how it felt to be at the center of cultural conversation. He said, "You know, if you would have given me this scenario a year ago and asked me how I would deal with it, I would say, 'I have no idea.' I'm still looking for the answers [about what] has allowed me, and the school community, the Columbine community, to get through this."

There were moments as we spoke when his eyes shone and vigor arose from his voice—"Columbine was a strong community to start with. That has enabled us to overcome this horrific event." At other times his voice wavered and he sounded tired. He pressed his fingers into his brows, or wiped his hand around his chin. "People say, 'So are you getting back to

148

some normalcy, or getting some closure?' I tell them, 'We'll never be normal again at Columbine High School.'"

He said that on the first day after the shooting he had addressed the students and the community at nearby Light of the World Catholic Church: "I said, 'I wish I could wave a magic wand and let the hurt go away. I wish I could tell you that as time goes on these scars will go away. I am going to be honest with you. The scars that we've experienced will be with us for the rest of our lives.'"

It has been a difficult road to recovery. "We start taking some steps forward," he said, "and all of a sudden an event happens which we have very little control over, and we're forced to take a giant step backwards." He was referring to such incidents as the female student receiving a threat on the Internet from a young man in Coral Gables, Florida, who said he was going to "finish the job" that Harris and Klebold had started, beginning with her. The school closed early for Christmas break because of the threat. Then in the same week, *Time* magazine published its special issue on Harris and Klebold's videotapes, prompting reporters to descend upon Columbine High School, distracting the students, who were in the midst of finals and, worse, hitting grieving parents and family members as they faced the first holiday season without their loved ones.

"That week was awful," said DeAngelis. "People are so fragile. There are people at Columbine that are tired of picking up the newspapers and reading stories about Columbine. They're tired of turning on the television sets and hearing about Columbine. It seems like every move we make is under a microscope, and we're being scrutinized and looked upon. That is as tiring as anything we're going through right now. When teachers get in their classrooms and they shut their doors, that's about as close to normalcy as they can get.

"One of the things that rejuvenated me the first semester was when I had a chance to walk out of my office and visit classes. I had an opportunity to visit every teacher's classroom at least once. I saw kids smiling. Did it make the hurt go away from last April? No. It's never going to go away."

A day didn't pass, he said, that he didn't think about April 20. "I don't care if it's a year from now or twenty years from now—I'll never forget the thirteen victims who were part of the Columbine family, [who] should be sitting in a desk or attending an extracurricular activity. They were denied that opportunity. That hurts.

"A lot of times we do not have any control over the events in our lives, and this is one of them. I could have easily have said, 'I can't handle this.' But I'm going to do the best I can to make sure this community does not fall apart. That's my biggest concern. My concern is for the parents who lost their children and the victims, the injured. But it is also important to realize that people are in different places. Some people are saying it's time to move on, and there are people saying we need more grieving time. I'm trying to convince people it's all right for them to be in different places. We need to respect where other people are. We may not necessarily be there—we may be somewhere totally opposite—but we need to respect what other people are feeling. That's important."

He rubbed his hand over his chin. "I think back to last spring, when we did an all-school assembly right before prom [the Friday before the tragedy]. I talked to students about making wise choices and shared some of my stories with them, how I lost a friend in high school to a automobile accident and [on another occasion] seeing my daughter in tears when two of her friends were killed in a car accident. I had the students close their eyes and repeat after me, 'I'm a valued member of the Columbine family. I cherish life. I promise to make wise choices each and every day of my life.' I told them to open their eyes. 'Look across and find one of your friends. What would it be like without that person?' I asked. 'I want to see each and every one of your smiling faces Monday morning.'

"The majority of the kids made wise choices that weekend. I had a student come up [the following Monday, April 19] and say, 'All our smiling faces are here, Mr. D.'"

"The first thing I did when I met with that group [of students, teachers, and parents] the next morning [after the massacre], I had them do the same thing. I said, 'I asked you last Friday to close your eyes. . . . Repeat again, 'I'm a valued member and I cherish life.' We're going to get through this."

Dave Cullen reports in his *5280* piece that more than one thousand parents, students, and teachers attended that initial assembly at Light of the World Catholic Church. Several officials from the school district spoke, and some of what they said fell flat. But when DeAngelis was introduced, "the crowd leapt to its feet as if a single body, unleashing an ecstatic roar." DeAngelis buckled, Cullen wrote, and "sobbed uncontrollably, his body shaking from head to foot. He remained hunched over for perhaps a full minute, his back to the audience, convulsions clearly visible from the back row."[25] When DeAngelis recovered, "he approached the podium without a word prepared; he just told the students what he was feeling," wrote Cullen. "He began with an apology. 'I am sorry for what happened and for what you are feeling.'"

Cullen asked DeAngelis what had gone through his mind as he sat sobbing, hunched over on the floor. "Did he feel any fear of exposing too much weakness to students looking for strength from their leader? 'No,' he says adamantly. 'That's the thing my parents always told me—don't be afraid to show your emotions. And one thing I value in people is honesty, and part of that honesty is being able to show your true feelings. I'm never embarrassed by crying in public, or showing my emotions. Because if I was, I'd be a phony, a hypocrite. That's the way I was raised.'"[26]

Like teacher Dave Sanders, Frank DeAngelis was in the hallway during the shootings April 20, shepherding kids to safety. One girl was asked by a reporter moments after she escaped the school if she had feared for her life. She said, "Not really, because the principal was with us."[27] DeAngelis wept through students' funerals and, throughout the first year after the shootings, called the parents on each deceased child's birthday. He remained haunted by the serendipity that had allowed Sanders to be shot and killed while DeAngelis escaped unharmed. The burden of trying to move forward toward healing came to rest most upon the shoulders of this wounded shepherd who was caught in the vortex of the church-state debate. He tried to steer a grieving community through this passage while being compelled to do so without the language of faith or expression of religious sensibilities. The closest he could come was to quote a slogan on a T-shirt the youth group had made, and hope that no one made an issue out of the religious implications.

"People have asked me, 'What drives people to do what Eric and Dylan did? Why do you think they did it?'" he said as our interview neared its conclusion. "I don't have the answers, I really don't. People think that I'm keeping something from them when I don't respond. I really don't have the answer. I don't know what drove them to do what they did, to have so much hate to carry out such a tragedy.

"I've been at Columbine for twenty-one years, four years as principal, but it will never be the same. A major part of me was lost on that day. At the same time, there's hope. We will always remember the students whose lives were lost. We will always remember the students who were injured. We'll never forget that as long as we live. But we survived. We will prevail. We have the hope to carry on. We are Columbine."

Is Nothing Secular?

What does the slogan "We are Columbine" mean? Who's the "we"? What does the "Columbine" mean? I saw that phrase a lot while I was there. It appeared on T-shirts, bumper stickers, and ID straps, and I couldn't get a handle on it. Nancy Gibbs had written in one of her earlier *Time* articles that Columbine opened "a sad national conversation" that "promises to be a long, hard talk." Thinking about Principal DeAngelis's burden and what it portended about that sad national conversation, however, eventually brought me to the place where I understood both the "we" and the "Columbine."

This national conversation has included, to no small degree, political discussions about how to interpret the Constitution and the place of religious liberties. It has also prompted social pundits to speculate about morality and faith. All of these have helped form a picture in my mind as to who is Columbine, and why.

The First Amendment's "establishment clause" is at the root of the church-state dilemma. It states: "Congress shall make no law respecting an establishment of religion." Those who contend that religious expression in tax-supported places violates the Constitution base their argument on this clause. Those who assert that religious expression in such venues is constitutionally protected also use this clause to make their point.

This issue, arguably, is at the heart of a paradigm shift that has been taking place in the nation. And the debate has been made more acute by what happened at Columbine High School.

In Jeffrey Rosen's essay in the *New York Times Magazine* titled, "Is Nothing Secular?"[28] the writer asserts that the wall of division between church and state is crumbling. "Whatever else it achieves, the presidential campaign of 2000 will be remembered as the time in American politics when the wall separating church and state began to collapse."[29]

Rosen argues that the "strict separationism" that dominated the nation's courts from the early 1970s to the late 1980s found its defining moment in 1971, when the Supreme Court heard *Lemon* v. *Kurtzman*. Leo Pfeffer, chief lawyer for the American Jewish Congress's Commission on Law and Social Action, whom the author calls an "uncompromising secularist," successfully argued that it was unconstitutional for "public funds to be channeled to faith-based schools and charities." *Lemon* "was a benchmark," Rosen argues in his essay. For nearly two decades subsequent to the decision, religious symbols or expressions were strictly forbidden in the public square on the same principle.

By the late 1980s, however, things had begun to change. The moral fabric of the culture was fraying, and this brought together religious groups that had been alienated from one another, namely Protestants and Catholics. Early in the twentieth century, Protestants feared that if government funds were channeled to private religious schools, Catholicism would gain an advantage because parochial schools dominated private education. Protestants resisted government assistance for religious education and defended strict separationism. But as the culture became increasingly hostile to any public religious expression, Protestants and Catholics became, to some degree, co-belligerents on many issues.

"Applying the *Lemon* test at the height of the separationist era, some lower courts interpreted the Constitution to forbid expressions of religious faith by private citizens on public property," writes Rosen. "These and other decisions that held that religion should be a completely private activity inspired an understandable backlash. For in an era when other groups in America—from gays and lesbians to ethnic minorities—were finding their voices in public, it seemed a violation of the free-speech rights of the religiously devout to forbid them to proclaim their identity in public along with everyone else."[30]

Rosen credits two developments for the paradigm shift that has subsequently taken place. The first is the population's increasing distrust of the government's ability to solve social problems. The second is the rise of litigator Michael McConnell, who has blazed a trail for equal treatment for religion.

McConnell has argued and won some critical cases that have repositioned the burden in the church-state dynamic. His first victory occurred before he ever stepped into a courtroom to argue a case. In 1981 he worked as a clerk in the Supreme Court and persuaded Justice William Brennan (whom Rosen calls a "liberal titan") to review *Widmar* v. *Vincent*. This case involved the policy of the University of Missouri at Kansas City prohibiting use of university facilities for gatherings of religious groups. The university had prevented a Bible-study group from meeting after classes and a federal district court had upheld the policy. "Once the courts had held that a public university had to allow politically subversive groups to meet," said McConnell, "it seemed crazy, like lunacy, to say that a Bible-study group couldn't meet. That just seemed like the height of anti-religious bigotry."[31]

The Supreme Court agreed, ruling eight to one in favor of the Bible study. The decision was "the first chink in the wall of separationism," Rosen writes.[32] In 1995 McConnell went before the Supreme Court to argue *Rosenberger* v. *University of Virginia*, challenging the university's refusal to allow monies from the student activities fee to go to religious journals. "Lower courts had held that a university couldn't withhold funds from a gay student newspaper because it disapproved of its message, and McConnell argued that a religious newspaper was entitled to equal treatment."[33]

The Supreme Court agreed again in a five to four vote.

Rosen believes that the Supreme Court's ruling on school vouchers will be the watershed issue that establishes the paradigm shift. In December

1999 a federal district judge in Cleveland, Ohio, struck down a voucher program that had been passed by the Ohio Legislature. "If and when the justices agree to resolve the constitutionality of vouchers," which Rosen expects will happen, "they will do so against a backdrop of decisions that have been chipping away at the wall between church and state over the past decade."[34]

So the shift, he concludes, changes the approach from not permitting any religious expression in public places to allowing equal treatment for any and all. It is a cultural signal that the American populace in general and the courts in particular are recognizing the importance of religion in people's lives and the unrelenting nature of religious allegiances. In other words, it is an acknowledgment that religious expression in public life is relevant.[35]

The Rutherford Institute's John Whitehead, who also wears the hat of cultural critic, explains it as "the sixties generation's spiritual journey coming to fruition." For thirty-five years, he says, Baby Boomers have been living in a spiritual void, eschewing religious institutions and orthodoxy. They are beginning to wake up to their spiritual longings, many embracing biblical faith more openly, paving the way for the wider culture to be more accepting. "It's different than a Bible-toting fundamentalist, Puritan-type thing," he says. "But it is authentic."

Columbine ratcheted up this cultural conversation and the paradigm shift came more into focus. In an article in the *Washington Post*, Hanna Rosin describes three amendments attached to the juvenile justice bill passed by the U.S. House of Representatives in June 1999 that she said would have been unthinkable before the Columbine school shootings:[36] the Ten Commandments Defense Act, the Freedom of Student Religious Expression amendment, and an unnamed third amendment that says religious memorials can be placed on public property without violating the Constitution. Rosin described it as "a Willy Wonka moment" for religious conservatives who finally "won the golden ticket that had eluded them." Civil libertarians cried foul: "Never before in a 24-hour period has there been such a massive attack in the U.S. House of Representatives on so many legislative fronts."[37]

The Ten Commandments Defense Act, Rosin wrote, was spearheaded by Christian activists after Judge Roy Moore, in the Alabama Circuit court, refused to remove a replica of the commandments that he had hung on the wall in his courtroom in Etowah County. Rosin wrote that Moore's feisty example did more than spur lawmakers. "Tablets have been spotted in a Lumpkin County, Georgia, courthouse; a municipal building in Ogden, Utah; a courthouse in Asheville, North Carolina; and the city hall in Manhattan, Kansas, to name a few."

The second and third amendments were "direct products of Littleton," writes Rosin. The religious expression amendment was spurred by Colorado Republican Tom Tancredo "in a moment of exasperation, when civil libertarians complained about the Christian overtones of the memorial held after the shootings." He said, "When we are desperate to strip away every degree of religiosity, we pay the price with things like Columbine. What those two young men needed was not a counselor but an exorcist." The amendment, said Rosin, "asserts that saying prayers, reading Scripture, or singing religious songs can be part of a memorial for anyone killed on school property."[38]

The third unnamed amendment, sponsored by South Carolina Republican Jim DeMint, essentially says the same thing, only applying it to a student's freedom of religious expression at school (as opposed to a public memorial service). "If we keep telling children to check their faith at the door, they won't have any basis to know right from wrong," DeMint said.[39]

All these amendments, at this writing, were locked up in the Senate, and have yet to pass scrutiny. John Whitehead didn't expect the Ten Commandments amendment to be deemed constitutional. "You can post the Ten Commandments if you do so with other historical documents, like the Magna Carta," he said. "All sorts of documents that have been pivotal in U.S. history have a lot of religious content. And you can make a good case that the Ten Commandments are the basis of criminal law in this country. But to post them alone [in a public building] is unconstitutional and the Supreme Court has a precedent right on point that says it is unconstitutional.

"The other two," he said, "are closer to being constitutionally protected."

Do We Believe in God?

I asked Frank DeAngelis during my visit what he thought would change the hearts of young people so another "Columbine" would never happen. He said, "This is my own personal opinion and not everyone agrees: Where money needs to be spent is on educating our students, teaching [them] at a young age to respect others. We need to come up with programs that teach about tolerance. Money invested like that would provide much higher dividends than some of the preventive measures that they're talking about."

But notions like tolerance and respect presuppose a moral framework that determines appropriate behavior toward others and distinguishes right from wrong. I asked him from where such a moral sensibility is derived.

He answered, "I guess the question I would ask psychologists is why did [the killers] develop their value system? I mean, at what point in their lives did they start instilling those values or believing in those values? You have kids who watch videos, you have kids that have access to the Internet, kids that listen to music. You have a thousand kids—What keeps the other 998 from *not* going out and doing what Eric and Dylan did?"

That, indeed, is the question. In the week after the shooting, Camille Paglia wrote in her column in *Salon.com*, "As an atheist, I acknowledge that religion may be socially necessary as an ethical counterweight to natural human ferocity. The primitive marauding impulse can emerge very swiftly in the alienated young."[40] She speaks as one who does not believe in God, yet her assumptions are inherently religious and can only be defended in religious terms. If humans are naturally ferocious, that vindicates and does not condemn the actions of the Columbine killers; they were only exhibiting behavior that comes naturally to humans.

Yet Paglia writes, "The totalitarian brave new world is upon us"[41] and condemns their deeds as a reflection of such. But on what basis? If ferocity is a natural human inclination, from where does she derive her sense of ethics? What explains humans who do *not* massacre their peers? Or more to the point, what explains humans who love sacrificially? Paglia appreciates the benefits of religion and its ethical counterweight, but she has already concluded that humans are naturally prone to ferocity. So, apart from something greater than that, how does one determine right from wrong?

Columbine posed a question we weren't prepared to answer and answered a question we did not ask. The unspoken subtext of Columbine, and the question it posed, is not what the killers did or did not ask their victims about God but what their deeds ask *us* about God. The question it answered that we did not ask: What does the world look like when God has been "evicted from the Big House?" as writer Richard Russo put it.[42] If what happened on April 20, 1999, is something we, as a people, cannot abide—as we seem to be concluding (even Camille Paglia says "our middle-class culture is affluent but spiritually empty"[43])—we are forced to confront the follow-up question: Do we need to invite God back into the Big House?

In a reductionist sort of way, the impulse to display the commandments in schools is an answer to that question. It is doubtful that imitation tablets hanging on a wall would have done much to deter Harris and Klebold. Based on the boys' videotapes, posting of the Ten Commandments probably would have made Harris and Klebold feel all the more giddy about desecrating those halls. Hanging kitschy Bible-story props won't solve this problem. But the sentiment is an expression of a larger truth: There is a God, and he has established a moral order, and we must find a way to make both part of the cultural conversation.

How to invite God back into the Big House is the question behind the controversy over the community memorial service. It is the question at the center of the memorial tiles controversy. It inspired the slogan on the T-shirt and undergirds the paradigm shift that is taking place in the courts. It is the question that Eric Harris and Dylan Klebold have foisted upon us. It is that "something bigger."

Frank DeAngelis wrestled with how to bring about healing in a grief-stricken community without the language of faith. He did it by co-opting slogans from a religious T-shirt. His dilemma reflects our national challenge: How do we heal a nation whose moral fabric has come apart without the language of faith? C. S. Lewis, an outspoken Christian, wrote that the practical result of an education without "objective value"—moral absolutes—"must be the destruction of the society which accepts it."[44] Friedrich Nietzsche, an outspoken atheist, said the same thing in reverse: "Morality [is] the great *antidote* against practical and theoretical nihilism."[45] Both statements imply the need for a higher law to cure the hopelessness of a morally deficient culture. Columbine has become the crucible for a larger cultural debate, not about whether Americans believe in God— numerous surveys reveal that they do—but about whether the God they believe in is *relevant*. That, in its essence, is the question Harris and Klebold put to their victims when they asked, "Do you believe in God?" even while pointing a gun to their heads. It is the question their religious taunting (and the victims' response) posed to us. It is the question, beyond being a community rallying cry, that has made us all "Columbine."

Chapter 8

Deliver Us from Evil

Whose Kingdom Is This?

WHEN I PONDER WHAT happened that day at Columbine and try to fit the pieces together, I am taken back to recollections of my first trip to Littleton two months after the shooting. I was sitting with Pastor Don Marxhausen on his back patio, eating spicy chicken wings, and we were talking about the nature of evil. He described how he had struggled during Dylan Klebold's funeral to say something to this grieving family that could impart a reason to keep going. One thing he said was, "The earth has opened up and it will be hard not fall into the pit."

The Klebolds, in burying their son, bore the full weight of a religious contradiction. On the one hand, they thought about God and his role in the universe, while on the other hand they confronted the horror of their son's crimes. How does one reconcile such pain—such evil—with the concept of a loving God? C. S. Lewis wrote: "Pain would be no problem unless, side by side with our daily experience of this painful world, we had received what we think a good assurance that ultimate reality is righteous and loving."[1] In other words, said Lewis, Christianity, with its concepts of the goodness of God and his world, "creates, rather than solves, the problem of pain."

Philosophers and religious thinkers have wrestled with this dilemma for centuries, and I won't pretend to resolve it in these pages. Nevertheless, the dynamics at Columbine offer a glimmer of possibility in regard to how one can come to terms with this apparent impossibility.

At Dylan's funeral, Marxhausen asked friends and family members to share reflections and memories about Dylan. There were plenty of tears and emotion, he said. Some said they "couldn't believe it was Dylan" who had done this, that it wasn't the Dylan they knew or remembered. Members of one family told stories about how Dylan used to come to their house and wrestle with their kids.

Tom Klebold asked, "How can this happen? We didn't even have a gun in our house. We have a BB gun to take care of woodpeckers." Sue Klebold couldn't reconcile the alleged Hitler connection. "We do seder in the house and he reads the questions," she said. The reminiscing continued for almost an hour before Pastor Marxhausen carried the rest of the service.

He read from the Psalms: "Out of the depths I cry to you, O LORD. LORD, hear my voice! Let your ears be attentive to the voice of my supplications! If you, O LORD, should mark iniquities, LORD, who could stand? But there is forgiveness with you, so that you may be revered. I wait for the LORD, my soul waits, and in his word I hope" (Ps. 130:1–5 NRSV).

His homily was based upon the episode in the life of King David when his son Absalom betrayed David and fomented a rebellion in the attempt to seize the throne. The son had grown alienated from his father, and, with his commanding look and winning personality, had gained the allegiance of many. In the decisive battle, King David's men fought fiercely and courageously and ultimately prevailed. Absalom was unceremoniously killed in the process, and when the king heard that news, all thoughts of alienation, rebellion, and betrayal evaporated. He sobbed for his lost son: "O my son Absalom! My son, my son Absalom! If only I had died instead of you—O Absalom, my son, my son!" (2 Sam. 18:33 NIV).

Pastor Marxhausen said, "Who knows why sometimes our sons and daughters do well or do wrong? Who knows why we ourselves do good and sometimes do wrong?"

He read a confession from the early church: "O God, Our heavenly Father, I confess unto thee that I have grievously sinned against thee in many ways; not only by outward transgression but also by secret thoughts and desires which I cannot fully understand, but which are all known unto thee."

That is when he said to the Klebolds. "A meteor has fallen on your house. The earth has opened up and it will be hard not to fall into the pit." He, and they, looked into the abyss. They cried out for answers and wondered where God could be in all this.

How Bad Is Bad?

If there is one word to describe what Don Marxhausen faced as he tried to comfort this grieving family, it would have to be mystery. The early church confession articulates two opposing realities with which he wrestled: On the one hand, things happen in this life that we "cannot fully understand"; on the other hand, those same things are strangely "known unto God," who allows them to happen anyway. Because Marxhausen is a pastor and conversant with spiritual matters, he has a vocabulary and point of reference with which to interpret human events, even bad ones, through the lens of a larger cosmic reality.

Part of the struggle many in our culture have faced in trying to understand what happened at Columbine is that, unlike Marxhausen, we do not possess that vocabulary or reference point. We live in a pragmatic and materialistic age, and post-Columbine, we have found ourselves pushed involuntarily into the realm of a haunting unknown—into a mystery. These are uncharted waters.

How can anyone account for what overtook those boys? Even those who do not acknowledge a higher law or a God recognized that what happened there was *truly bad*. But how bad was it? The *worst kind* of bad? Was it *evil* in its truest sense?

It has been argued that this kind of killing is not related to religious issues at all, but fits into a behavior pattern that typifies certain troubled individuals. After Columbine, the *New York Times* undertook a massive study of 100 "rampage killings" by 102 individuals that occurred since 1949, examining backgrounds and other aspects of those who perpetrated these crimes.[2] The findings are enlightening and startling, and include the following about the killers:

- The majority were white and male. Of the killers examined, eighteen were black, seven Asian, six female.
- Almost half (forty-eight) had been diagnosed with mental illness, most notably schizophrenia.
- More than half were unemployed.
- One third (thirty-three) killed themselves after committing their crimes.
- Rampages are calculated, driven by their own internal logic, and are carried out with emotional detachment; they are not the result of someone who "just snaps."

- Of the killings studied, sixty-three were committed by people who had made threats of violence before; fifty-four had specified the type of violence and the targeted victims.

- In "case after case," the study said, family members, teachers, law enforcement officers, and mental health officials missed or dismissed signs of the killer's deterioration.

- The most common triggers of a rampage were the loss of a job (forty-seven) and a divorce or breakup of a relationship (twenty-two).

- While in 1997 one-third of all homicide cases were never resolved, not one of the rampage killers examined by the *Times* got away; eighty-nine never left the scene of the crime.

- In a decade when the overall homicide rate dropped markedly, rampage killings increased markedly.

- The majority of rampage killers (81 percent) struck during the daytime.[3]

Juvenile—or "school"—rampage killers bore many of the same features but had a few additional characteristics. The study showed that while mental health problems were common among juvenile killers, the suicide rate was lower than their adult counterparts, as was the level of emotional detachment. But there was another notable distinction. Adult rampage killers tended to be loners; juvenile rampage killers often solicited and received affirmation from their peers. "Goading, sometimes even collaboration, is not uncommon among the school-age killers."[4]

This aspect of juvenile rampage killings introduces an incongruity when it comes to understanding the Columbine killings. Citing Dr. Anthony Hempel, chief forensic psychiatrist at the Vernon campus of North Texas State Hospital, the *Times* article states: "The fact that many of the adolescents were able to work with others was a strong argument that they were less likely to be mentally ill." Hempel adds, "When people pair up to commit one of these, the odds of a major mental illness go way down. Very few people who don't have a mental illness can get together and plan something with someone with a major illness."[5]

It could be argued, in the case of the Columbine killers, that Eric Harris struggled with mental illness. He was taking the drug Luvox for depression and had exhibited troubling behavior many would consider manic. But that would not account for Dylan Klebold's collaboration. He had no history of mental illness and, by all accounts, was thought to be a decent fellow by those who knew him. This forces the question: If, at least for

Dylan Klebold, mental illness did not fit the profile, then what accounted for his participation?

The *Times* study also included an in-depth look at a few killers whose stories might offer some illumination. Jamie Rouse killed two and injured one in 1995 when he opened fire at his school in Giles County, Tennessee. Prior to his deed he had stated his intentions and had given "explicit descriptions of who, where, and when [he] intended to kill."[6] Roxie Wallace walked into the bar where he had once worked in 1997 and opened fire, killing one and injuring three. "In a long prison interview," notes the *Times*, "Mr. Wallace was unable to deviate from his convoluted theory that the bar was the center of an organized-crime drug and prostitution ring with ties to . . . Satanism, President Clinton and Garrison Keillor."[7] Wayne Lo killed two and wounded four on the campus of Simon Rock College in December 1992. He said that he had received "a divine message to go to the gun store, order the ammunition with his mother's credit card, then lie and deceive and kill."[8] The *Times* notes that Lo "raged against his lawyers" because they argued in court that he was insane. He felt that his lawyers, instead, "should have investigated his victims to uncover why a heavenly power had selected them to be shot."[9]

All three of these men exhibited classic traits of rampage killers. But they also betrayed another aspect not mentioned in the *Times* report as one of the motivating factors. That is, their "homicidal rage" also carried indications of a spiritual dimension. In Jamie Rouse's high school yearbook for his senior year, he submitted this as part of his senior blurb: "I, Satan, Jamie Rouse, leave my bad memories here to my two brothers."[10] Roxie Wallace's mother said he would "talk incessantly of evil forces" and that she used to hear him "growl like a small dog or wolf."[11] Wayne Lo eventually came to see that it was not God who had told him to commit his ghastly crime, though "he remains convinced . . . that it was something outside of himself that gave him a message to do what he did. 'Perhaps . . . it was a supernatural or satanic force,' he said."[12]

Entertainment Evil vs. the Real Thing

Americans do not have a problem with the concept of evil in a generic sense. It appears on a regular basis on the movie marquee. Evil on the big screen is robust and lucrative. But it is also trivialized and tamed. It is a blip on the radar screen of an otherwise humdrum earthly existence and the humans usually win in the end by virtue of their grit and guts. A blurb in *TV Guide* recently described an upcoming program that "offered real-life examples of evil in action." "Evil in action" was evening entertainment. When supermodel Claudia Schiffer appeared as a guest on *The Tonight Show with Jay Leno* recently,[13] she came out wearing over-the-knee patent leather black boots, a tight, shiny, fire-engine red, patent-leather skirt, and a skintight black T-shirt with glittery, three-inch-high red letters that read *EVIL,* as a fashion statement.

When it comes down to it, there is no other way to explain what overtook these boys other than to call it raw evil—not the Hollywood version but the religious kind. That, in part, is why Columbine rests uneasily in so many hearts. Religion, itself, seems irrational enough to some; "religious" evil is irrational *and* creepy, and many people would rather not have this conversation. So the social discourse, instead, has focused on the disparate parts: the negative impact of computer games and violent movies, gun control, parental responsibility, and the like—things we can get our heads around.

Columbine lead investigator Kate Battan attributed a variety of motivations to the killers. Once she said they were driven by the desire for fame and retribution.[14] Later she said the rampage "was not about killing jocks or killing black people or killing Christians,"[15] but was an expression of their "philosophy" expressed on one of the prerampage videos: "That's what we do."[16] Ultimately, she and others in the sheriff's office stood behind the theory that the primary motivation was pure hate. "It was about killing everybody. They put themselves above everybody. They hated everybody,"[17] Battan said. But even she wondered, at one point, how "so much evil came out of these two teen-age boys."

Since April 20, 1999, Columbine High School has implemented several new security measures. The school has added mental health workers, another assistant principal, and another campus security advisor to the staff. A keyless entry system controls the facility. Sixteen new security cameras have been installed, and a twenty-four-hour security guard has been added to check people in and out of the building. Principal Frank DeAngelis said such measures have contributed to an increased perception of safety. But he quickly added, "I keep asking myself, would security cameras have stopped Eric and Dylan from carrying out their murderous plot? Would ID badges have stopped them? As one student very astutely pointed out, 'Eric and Dylan would have had their ID badges on as they were killing people. And cameras? Eric and Dylan would have been videotaped as they were killing people.'"

The cultural conversation has stopped short of recognizing Columbine as a manifestation of true spiritual evil because of the implications behind such a conclusion. If hell, as it were, opened up and temporarily held sway in those hallways that day, such an occurrence would mean the existence of a spiritual world, and worse, a spiritual battle. And that, to many, as I said, is irrational and creepy. Yet, in a back-handed way, acknowledging the presence of evil points the way out of this otherwise intractable set of circumstances.

If Demons Exist, So Must Angels

In an article on the movie *The Exorcist,* which Warner Bros. rereleased in the fall of 2000, John Whitehead describes how William Peter Blatty wrote the novel on which the movie is based after reading about a case of demonic possession that appeared in the *Washington Post* in 1949, his junior year in college.

> The newspaper outlined the details of a supposed demonic infestation and subsequent exorcism of a 14-year-old boy in Mount Rainier, Maryland, in 1949. "In what is perhaps one of the most remarkable experiences of its kind in recent religious history," the article began, "a fourteen-year-old Mount Rainier boy has been freed by a Catholic priest of possession by the devil."
>
> According to the *Post,* the boy's "symptoms" included the unassisted movement of his bed, mattress, a heavy armchair and assorted small objects, inexplicable scratching noises in his vicinity, and his own screaming, cursing and voicing of Latin phrases (a language he had never studied).
>
> The *Post* account made an indelible impression on the young Blatty.[18]

After reading the *Post* article, Blatty deduced that if demons existed, that would allow for the possibility of other spiritual forces, including God and life beyond the earthly existence. In Blatty's mind, writes Whitehead, "the Devil's incarnation in the Maryland boy became an apologetic for the existence of God. Whether this assumption was logical to the human mind, Blatty thought was irrelevant since 'prudent judgments do not satisfy when dealing with the supernatural; for the ultimate issue is too important; the issue is God and our hope of resurrection.'"[19]

In the movie version, a doctor who examined the possessed girl concluded that her condition was "a type of disturbance in the chemoelectrical activity of the brain." The girl, in turn, cursed and spat at him. For Blatty, the message of *The Exorcist* is that "science [is] totally inadequate in the face of religious forces."[20] A priest had to be brought in to combat spiritual force with spiritual force. In the end, the girl is delivered and the priest finds his own salvation in sacrifice.

Blatty said in a 1998 interview with Whitehead that he intended the novel to be "an 'apostolic' work . . . that would either strengthen one's faith or lead one to it."[21] He said, "If there are immaterial, intelligent forces of evil, this alone suggests the possibility of other such forces that are good. And since the demonic intelligence responds to the ritual [of exorcism] used by the Jesuits, it appears that there is God." In other words, the result suggests only one force is strong enough to confront and overcome the demonic, and that is God.

The exorcist, Father Karras, finds the girl's possession to be "the crucible of his struggle for faith, for salvation," Blatty said. For the author, *The Exorcist* "is not a horror at all. It is a supernatural detective story."[22]

Similarly, perhaps the reason gun control, violent movies, and Internet discussions have not fully answered the haunting questions behind Columbine is that sociopolitical explanations are inadequate in the face of religious forces. Prudent judgments alone do not satisfy when dealing with the supernatural. Perhaps, like *The Exorcist*, Columbine is a supernatural detective story. The clues certainly seem to be there.

Clue One: The Presence of a Malevolent Force.

Many who encountered the killers, some of whom looked into their eyes that day, said that the sense of evil was palpable. Kacey Ruegsegger, who faced them in the library, said, "There was like—I don't know if I can explain it very well—but like a spiritual battle that you could feel going on. As soon as they came in, you could feel evil in the room. You could just feel the kind of battle going on." Brittany Weeden remained hidden in the cafeteria and saw the boys when they entered after the library massacre. She said, "You could see their eyes and there was no soul or anything. There was just evil, like, pure evil." Craig Scott said, "It was somewhat demonic, just what they were saying. They were laughing."[23] Nicole Nowlen told John and Doreen Tomlin that when she was huddled under the library table with their son John and saw the legs of the killers as they approached and heard their voices, she knew "they were wicked and evil." When Valeen Schnurr spoke publicly for the first time after her ordeal in the library, she read from a paraphrase of Ephesians 6:12 in the New Testament: "We are not fighting against humans, we are fighting against forces and authorities, against rulers of darkness and spiritual powers in the heavens above." Then she said, "When I look back at the events that took place that day, I see Columbine at the mercy of a spiritual war."[24]

Ben Schumann did not come into direct contact with the killers, but he sensed something was wrong in the moments before the shooting started. "I came back to the table [in the cafeteria] and something didn't quite feel right. I kind of felt like something really bad was going to happen, but at the same time I wasn't too afraid. Then all these people came running inside saying, 'He's been shot, he's been shot!'"

"How could they have had such a lack of conscience?" asked Misty Bernall. "After the first shot was fired or the first child killed, wouldn't you wake up and go, 'What are we doing?' But they continued [shooting] and making their comments. These boys were so controlled by evil that they had no conscience." Shirley Hickman, the levelheaded Spanish teacher who had worked in an urban setting and had seen her share of school violence, said, "Every day I looked in the newspaper and there was always some new story trying to find some rationale for why this happened. They look at the video games and the media. But a lot of kids are watching those movies and not shooting people. I think it really comes down to the spiritual realm. God gave man free choice and if someone chooses to serve Satan then they are going to [exhibit] really bizarre behavior."

But what does it mean, to "choose to serve Satan"? In a culture such as ours where evil, like God, has been trivialized, it is tempting to interpret such a notion in one of two ways. The first temptation is to dismiss it as foolish, as if Satan were nothing more than the pointy-tailed, spike-headed caricature on the cans of Underwood Deviled Ham. The other temptation is to give the devil too much credit and reduce the event to being the work of Satan and his henchmen, as if Harris and Klebold were mere incidentals. The tendency of some of the local evangelical churches to emphasize the latter in the aftermath of Columbine troubled journalist Dave Cullen, as he expressed in his *Salon.com* article, "I Smell the Presence of Satan."

"The evangelicals were . . . quick to seize on the Columbine killings as evidence of Satan's work. Although most of the religious outpouring in response to the tragedy was positive, and stressed faith as a loving, healing force, some ministers deride that approach as 'Sound of Music theology,' in the words of Pastor Bill Oudemolen of Foothills Bible Church. While Oudemolen has had words of comfort for mourners in all of his sermons since the tragedy, his primary focus is on Satan. 'I smelled the presence of Satan,' he announced the Sunday after the shooting."

Cullen said later, "I was taken aback by that, because I was used to the minister being the one who emphasized taking more responsibility. I walked in [to that church] and felt like [he] was taking responsibility away from the kids. I thought we should be blaming the kids more, and here was a minister—the way I was hearing it—blaming them less and taking responsibility off of them."

Bill Oudemolen responded: "There are few people who are placing their finger on the seminal issues that bring about episodes like we saw in Wyoming with Matthew Shepard and like we saw here, and in Fort Worth, Texas. When I was standing at the corner of Pierce and Bowles near Columbine High School [right after the shooting], I had this sense that there was only one way I could explain it. I believed I *did* smell the presence of evil—not that it alleviates the blame that I would place on Harris and Klebold. I believe they made choices and were responsible. But who is the author of evil? My theological category for this is that Satan is the author of evil—a personal being, a fallen angel Lucifer, a being of light who falls in an act of rebellion and devises all these plans.

"I also believe that, as the Bible says, 'the heart is deceitful above all things and desperately wicked' and that those two boys gave place in their hearts to the devil. Ephesians 4:27 says, 'Don't give place to the devil,' or 'don't give the devil a platform or a launching pad.' Those two boys, lubricated by alcohol, as we saw on the videotapes, and spurred by hate, gave the devil a place in their hearts and acted upon what they were demonically inspired to do. Even the way that they both ended their lives in self-destruction is rooted, ultimately, in demonic activity. I think of the Gadarene demoniac in Mark's gospel[25] who was possessed by a legion of demons. He's living in a cave, he ripped all his clothes off, chains can't bind him, he's got supernatural strength, he's cutting himself. Self-destructive behavior is always rooted in demonic activity. Are the boys at fault? Yes. Is there a spiritual explanation for this? Yes. Is anybody in our culture paying attention to that? Not very many. This is not a culture that is going to turn to the theologians for answers."

But those who have addressed the issue in societal terms have done so only on the surface. Their answers have not stemmed from the most haunting questions. Theologian N. T. Wright offers a measured approach for helping the average person understand this seemingly irrational topic: "'The Satan', 'the Evil One', is not equal and opposite to God; but 'he' or 'it' is a potent force, opposed to God's good creation, and particularly to the human beings whom God wishes to put in authority over his world." Wright, like Bill Oudemolen, says evil finds expression when humans open themselves up to its influence and thus "give authority to forces of destruction and malevolence."[26] Evil is "real and powerful," he says, and humans are its valid secondary agents. "As we each grapple with our own testing and temptation," he writes, ". . . we are caught up into something bigger than ourselves."[27] In other words, at certain points humans make choices that open the door to malevolent visitors, and, given enough elbow room, the visitors start running the show.

After her death, Cassie Bernall's parents found a passage underlined in a book she had been reading, *Discipleship: Living for Christ in the Daily Grind,* by Heinrich Arnold: "Modern man . . . does not see that there is a power of good and a power of evil quite apart from him, and that the course of life depends on the power to which he opens his heart."[28] Eric Harris and Dylan Klebold "opened their hearts" to that power in stages and lost themselves in the process. Don Marxhausen called it "radical asunderment," or disconnectedness. "If we are created in the image of God, we're created to have relationships. Wholeness is connectedness; evil would be the opposite—relationships broken apart. In one sense, the final word of sanity before the shooting started was when the boys told a friend of theirs [in the school parking lot], 'Go away and don't come back.' From that point on it was chaos and evil. Fingers and arms were shot off of people they knew. That had to be the total destruction of connectedness."

Marxhausen explained his theory about evil as it played out in the lives of Eric and Dylan. "First part: Rage built up over the years of being different and outcast and shamed. Second part: These kids hid their anxiety; their parents were not privy to it. Number three: Evil occurred incrementally. Fourth part: [They] got a plan." All four parts of Marxhausen's theory of evil depend upon human instrumentality. These boys made small choices that ultimately engaged bigger forces. Once "the plan," as Marxhausen called it, was put into motion, those forces took charge, which would explain why Brittany Weeden said there was no soul in their eyes. Eric Harris and Dylan Klebold, as Marxhausen put it, "crossed over" and "got lost."

Clue Two: The Presence of a Benevolent Force.

This then introduces another clue into the supernatural detective story. According to author Blatty's logic, if there are malevolent religious forces, this allows for the possibility of the existence of benevolent ones. If there are demons, there could be angels. And indeed, witnesses who mentioned the overpowering sense of evil in the presence of the killers made equal reference to a similar sense of the presence of God and his angels. Kacey Ruegsegger, who had huddled under a study carrel as the killers approached, said: "I felt, like, God's presence—or [maybe it was] just angels—with me and in the room." Brittany Weeden, who saw the killers when they entered the cafeteria, said, "It felt like angels were around us. And the bombs [they had planted in the cafeteria] didn't go off. It was like the angels must have been around them so they wouldn't have gone off. They [the killers] came down and it was just evil, but angels had to be there for us to be alive." Craig Scott felt an inexplicable sense of God's closeness to his situation: "I asked God to give me courage and take away my fear. As soon as I prayed that, I stabilized. I was probably one of the most stabilized kids there. Then I felt like God told me to get out of there and he did. He said, 'Get out.'"[29]

Ben Schumann said, "From all the ammunition and the bombs that they had, there should [have been] twenty times the amount of people killed than there were. God, like, he did kind of stop them, in a way, because if he hadn't been there, there would have been so many more people killed." One student said he felt like "angels [were] all around us" because three students who were right behind him got shot.[30] Another said: "We were so protected and so comforted through it all."[31]

Surprisingly, despite the trauma and horror of what happened that day, many attested that it actually galvanized their faith in God and their belief in his goodness. Amber Rosetta, a freshman that year, said, "Even while I was praying, I came to a point where I knew that I wasn't afraid to die. In the midst of everything that was going on, I had peace with God. It wasn't so much that [I thought] the shooters weren't going to touch me or shoot me or that I wasn't going to die. It was more like I felt safe, like . . . there was nothing they could do that could touch me spiritually." Sarah Arzola said, "In the midst of everything I lost hope in a lot of things, but God wasn't one of them. I always thought that it would be hard to stay close to God and still love God if something like this were to happen to you, because that's what people have told me. But it wasn't so for me."

Blatty's logic offers a kind of map to help us navigate the mystery of what happened at Columbine. The starting point is to recognize the manifestation of a malevolent power, or evil. This, in turn, opens up the possibility of the existence of a benevolent power, which allows for the existence of God. In *The Exorcist*, based upon a real-life case of demon possession, the malevolent force responded to only one thing: God's power summoned in the name of Jesus Christ. When applying this "logic" to Columbine, the same could be said. It is evident that evil was active and that God and his angels were similarly active in thwarting its force and facilitating aid and protection. This, in turn, points to the third clue in the spiritual detective story.

Clue Three: God Was in Control.

Many testified that God never abdicated control at Columbine. When pieces of the picture slowly came into focus after the event, a striking confluence of remarkable prerampage moments suggested that, before the first shot was fired, God had been preparing these young people for their encounters with destiny. Matt Bruce recalled, "Just a week or two before April 20, we had a prayer meeting at our church. And we were talking about how things were getting on our nerves and how all these people were bugging us and how a bunch of petty things were bringing us down. And Jim [Beckman, the youth pastor] had everybody close their eyes and he walked out of the room. Then he walked back in, pretending he was pushing something really heavy. He got into the room and said, 'This is a coffin'—*this was before the twentieth*—'Would that issue really matter if that person that you are angry at or that you're having trouble with were dead right now?' It hit home and we realized that, in comparison to life or death, the petty things that we go through really don't matter. Then shortly after that, a bunch of people that we might have been having trouble with could actually have died."

Ben Schumann added: "A monsignor came to church a month or two before the shooting. And during his homily, he's like, 'We're in the midst of a great spiritual war. And a lot of you guys will be called to be martyrs.' The thing that sticks out in my mind mostly is that he was walking around the pews and was saying, 'Now, imagine someone came storming in here with a gun right now and held it to your head and asked you if you believed in God, would you be able to say yes?' I didn't think much of it at the time. I was kind of like, 'Wow, that'd be crazy.' Then, two weeks after the shooting, I was talking to my mom and she was like, 'Don't you remember what the priest said?' I was like, 'Whoa.' It was freaky, but it was definitely a wake-up call."

Despite her personal loss, Misty Bernall was convinced that God had been in control throughout the event: "I think that God allowed so much of it to happen and then said, 'That's enough.' So many more of our kids could have died."

But this revisits the conundrum mentioned earlier: If God could say "enough" at any point, why didn't he say "enough" before any of the lives were lost? Misty just as easily could have asked, "If God allowed only so much, why did that little bit have to include the death of my daughter?"

In my reflections with Don Marxhausen about the nature of evil, he said, "The book of Job doesn't give any answers as to why evil happens. It's like trying to make sense out of nonsense." He cited the Old Testament book of Job because it depicts the philosophical struggles that arise when evil plays out in the human arena under the watchful eye of a loving God. Marxhausen was right when he said Job does not explain why "evil happens." But it does offer a paradigm that shows the way through the experience for those who have come to see both evil and God in this event. Job helps the reader who believes in God remain "a person of faith"—as Marxhausen put it—in a world filled with pain and unanswered questions.

A Revolution in Knowing God

At the beginning of the book of Job, the reader finds a dialogue between God and Satan during which Satan levels the charge that Job's faith is not sincere but is self-serving, since he has never been truly put to the test. "Yes, Job fears God, but not without good reason!" Satan says. "You have always protected him and his home and his property from harm. You have made him prosperous in everything he does. Look how rich he is! But take away everything he has, and he will surely curse you to your face!" (Job 1: 9–11 NLT).

God, on the other hand, maintains that Job loves and serves him with a pure heart, and he pronounces Job blameless. Satan challenges God to remove the hedge of protection and then watch Job curse God. God meets the challenge. Through tragedy and calamity, he allows Satan to remove all of Job's blessings, including his children and many earthly possessions. Then God permits Satan to afflict Job's body, leaving him the picture of misery with crusting sores sitting on top of an ash heap. Job still does not curse God, and so proves God correct.

If the story had ended there, the moral would have been that God was right! But the story did not end there. It moved forward to include visits from three so-called friends of Job (and later a fourth). At first they sat speechless with him for seven days and nights out of respect for his grief. But their religiosity got the better of them, and they started to preach. They introduced the religious logic of the day into Job's tragic situation and put him on the defensive.

They operated out of the assumption that human suffering must be linked to preceding bad behavior. Jesus' own disciples thousands of years later embraced this line of thinking when, seeing a man who had been born blind, they asked Jesus, "Why was this man born blind? Was it as result of his own sins or those of his parents?" Job's friends concluded similarly that Job must have committed a great sin to have brought on such calamity. They urged him to identify it, repent, and plead for God's forgiveness.

Job responded, "Honest words are painful, but what do your criticisms amount to? Stop assuming my guilt, for I am righteous. Don't be so unjust.

Do you think I am lying? Don't I know the difference between right and wrong?" (Job 6:25, 29–30 NLT).

Job's response was more than an expression of personal indignation. It introduced a revolutionary understanding about God. The assumption of the day saw God's interaction with people as being almost mathematical: good living merited his blessing; bad living incurred his wrath. Job insisted to his friends that, in spite of his suffering, he was a righteous man and had not violated his relationship with God. This introduced an unheard of juxtaposition of two contradictory realities: one, that life's events do not always conform to the logic of cause and effect; and two, God was still God and he reigned in his heaven. For all of Job's suffering, he never concluded that God was capricious. For all of his confusion and even anger toward God, Job never challenged the Almighty's prerogatives.

Still, he groped for answers and, on other points, demanded an explanation from God. This highlights a second radical departure from the wisdom of the day regarding how one relates to God. Though Job did not call into question God's power, he did shake his fist at what he perceived to be God's nature. In chapter after chapter, Job complained about God's sense of justice and besmirched God's benevolence; William Safire calls the book of Job a "daring manifesto."[32] But even this ranting, in a backhanded way, reflected a departure from the conventional understanding of how God related to his people. Job presented his complaint directly to God, which—rather than drive a wedge between them—established new levels of intimacy and security. Rather than assume God was aloof and far off, as would have been the typical religious view of the day, Job assumed God was near, interactive, and intimately acquainted with the situation at hand, tormenting though it was. Job approached God boldly and questioned him unstintingly, as a good friend who trusts another enough to be the bearer of bad news. Job never doubted that God was near enough to hear and generous enough to endure this reproach. (God eventually put some sobering questions to Job that effectively ended the discussion, but that is another conversation.)

A glimmer of insight partway through his ordeal ultimately allowed Job to come to terms with his circumstances, introducing a third revolutionary concept. Job said, "But as for me, I know that my Redeemer lives, and that he will stand upon the earth at last. And after my body has decayed, yet in my body I will see God!" (Job 19:25–26 NLT). This new idea also brought resolution to Job's otherwise intractable problem.

Up to this point there had been nothing in the book of Job to suggest any hope of a robust afterlife beyond the traditional Jewish conception of Sheol—a shadowy existence cut off from God and community.[33] This passage introduces a new paradigm. Whether Job expected to see God *after death* is difficult to determine because of corruption of the original text.[34] But Old Testament professor John E. Hartley, chairman of the Department of Biblical Studies at the Graduate School of Theology, Azusa Pacific University, points out in his commentary on Job that, whether before or after death, Job's confession is "built upon the same logic . . . of redemption that stands as the premise of the New Testament doctrine of resurrection." In other words, Job expressed a revolutionary trust that his redeemer-vindicator would, in the end, come to his defense and make all wrongs right. The term redeemer is an intentional allusion, says Hartley, to the qualities of deliverance and love that are associated with God. Job is essentially saying that he believes in God's goodness and justice, even if that justice is left in God's hands and deferred until the end ("at last"). He trusts his redeemer (God) whom he sees as being greater than Job's circumstances. Job "makes an unconditional affirmation about God's commitment to him against all circumstantial evidence to the contrary," writes Hartley. "Only by pure faith can a person believe in God's justice amidst suffering, assured within his heart that out of his sorrow God will restore his honor."[35] Job understood and expressed through this remarkable confession that there was something more to this picture than what his eye could see from within the constraints of his tortured circumstances.

Job did not have the benefit of seeing that larger narrative playing out with him at its center; he could not view his world from the top down, the way God and Satan did, but only from the bottom up, from the limited vantage point of humanity. Even so, in clarifying glimpses, Job came to terms with these circumstances and maintained his belief in God through this radical redefinition of how to relate to him. He understood that God remained in control of his universe even while the circumstances of Job's life did not conform to the logic of cause and effect; he assumed that God was near and interactive and could be brought directly into the situation at hand; and he concluded that God's vision and purpose were bigger than events in the human arena and that God would not only have the final word but also execute perfect justice.

At the end of the book of Job, God rebuked Job's so-called friends. "You have not been right in what you said about me, as my servant Job was," he said. Then he told Job to pray for them. "My servant Job will pray for you and I will accept his prayer on your behalf" (Job 42:7–9 NLT). So Job prayed for his tormentors.

God restored Job's fortunes, perhaps as a symbolic foretaste of the resurrected life of fullness and resolution that Job had seen in glimpses. "He also gave him seven more sons and three more daughters. . . . In all the land there were no other women as lovely as the daughters of Job" (Job 42:13, 15 NLT). This revolutionary book concludes: "Job lived . . . to see four generations of his children and grandchildren. Then he died, an old man who had lived a long, good life" (Job 42:16–17 NLT).

God had put Job to the test. Job never understood the backdrop of his trials—that his life had been a crucible for resolving a disagreement between God and his antagonist, the devil. In his testing, one could say, a meteor fell on Job's house. He stood the test and emerged "a person of faith."

Heaven's Response to Evil

N. T. Wright asks, "What, then, is evil, and how are we delivered from it?" The way to understand it, he says, is to look at it the way Jesus saw it. He recognized the reality and power of evil. It was not something to trivialize, as if it didn't exist; and it was not something to wallow in, giving it more deference and influence that it deserves. Wright says Jesus took the power of evil seriously, and we ought to also, not gloating self-righteously, as if we were impervious to its assaults.

Jesus confronted evil with what Wright calls "the power of the kingdom announcement."[36] That means that Jesus understood evil as a spiritual force that could be met only with a more powerful spiritual force. That is why he taught his disciples to pray, "Deliver us from evil"—recognizing that "when he prayed it himself *the answer was 'No',*" notes Wright. Jesus prayed that prayer, using different words, in the garden of Gethsemane the night before he was crucified: "'Father, if you are willing, please take this cup of suffering away from me." The gospel writer Luke said that "he was in such agony of spirit that his sweat fell to the ground like great drops of blood" (Luke 22: 42, NLT). He would be the one, notes Wright, "who *was* led to the Testing [and] who was *not* delivered from Evil."

We've already examined, in chapter three, how on the cross Jesus bore the full force of evil and God's condemnation of it. So, on one level, at this dark impasse, Jesus surrendered. Yet after all was said and done in those unforgiving moments on the cross, God turned the tables and restored his Son to his rightful place of authority by raising him from the dead a few days later. It was as if God shook a fist at the Evil One and said, "Even at its worst, your dark forces are not more powerful than I." Jesus, in teaching his disciples to pray this way, wanted his followers to recognize evil as being real but also to see "the reality of his victory over it."[37]

Wright concludes, "The rest of us are therefore commanded to pray that we may be delivered from the power of Evil. And we can pray that prayer with confidence precisely because Jesus has met that power and has defeated it once and for all." Job anticipated that when he proclaimed that his redeemer-vindicator (a foreshadowing of Jesus) would stand upon the earth "at last." If it is true, that means evil at its worst is not stronger than the power of God to overcome it. Which means that, even at Columbine High School on April 20, 1999, for all the chaos, horror, and evil that was unleashed that day, God did not abdicate control and did not leave himself without a testimony. He will be the ultimate victor.

Chapter 9

Rachel's Vision

The Promise to See God

I AM SITTING ON THE grass wondering where You are. My mouth is dry. The playground is empty, like it is meant for a purpose that no one understands. The carousels stand motionless, the swings without rhythm. It is a pretty day. The sun is meant to fill us with good things and there is no one to receive it.

Do You see me? Have You come to me and I did not see You? Am I blind? What do You want? Do You want me?

The sun is coming up behind the trees.

"Do you see the sun?"

I see it.

"No, you don't. It is obscured by the trees. You see the trees."

I see the sun.

"You see the light from the sun, so you know it is there. But you don't see the sun. You see the trees. That is how you have known Me. You saw part of Me, so you knew I was there. But you didn't see Me."

The sun is rising. It gives life to the leaves and spirit to the wind. The trees can't contain it. The sun is above the trees.

"Now you see clearly. Now you see the sun. And now you are going to see Me clearly."

This is my rendering of an event described to me by Lori Johnson, Rachel Scott's small group leader and youth pastor. Lori said that immediately following this experience in the park, Rachel ran up to her and described it to her in detail. It occurred about a year before she was killed. As Lori told it to me, Rachel took a walk at a playground early in the morning to watch the sunrise because she was discouraged.

In addition to walks in the park, she sometimes worked through these hard stretches by writing in her journals. On March 1, 1998, she wrote: "Dear God, Sometimes when I'm craving your Spirit, nothing happens. I stand there with my hands stretched towards heaven crying out Your name—and nothing. Is it because I have not been keeping my quiet times? Is there sin in my life that's keeping me from you? What can I do? Why have I been able to keep faith like a child until now. Why do I have to question Your existence?"[1]

Rachel grew up the third child of five in a preacher's home. Darrell and Beth Scott had moved from a church-planting situation in Salt Lake City to the Denver area in the late 1970s to start another church. They were soon joined by Darrell's brother Larry, and his wife Mary, and together the families laid the foundation for the Word and Praise Fellowship. During the next ten years, these families worked side by side and even sometimes lived side by side in apartments or basements of facilities they rented for the church.

It would have been easy for Rachel to have gotten lost in the shuffle, the third of three sisters, followed by two brothers, and squeezed in between her two cousins, Jeff (a year older) and Sarah (a year younger). Amid the constant activity of siblings and cousins along with the demands of life as a pastor's kid in a new church, Rachel found creative ways to define herself and managed to set her own course.

The youngsters from both Scott families grew up with church woven into the fabric of their lives. They helped their parents clean and refurbish the storefront property secured for services and they passed notes while sitting in the pews during worship. (The kids still have some of the notes.)

"Those were good growing up years for our kids and Darrell's kids," said Larry Scott.

But Rachel's young life soon would be beset by one of many contradictions that would define and challenge her understanding of the world. In 1988, when Rachel was seven, her father left the family and the church. The divorce of her parents fractured this young family and confused her perceptions of God. To make matters worse, Rachel's mother, Beth, had known life only as a pastor's wife and stay-at-home mom, and was forced to take menial work to keep food on the table. This began a long season of turmoil and hardship for the family, with Rachel in the center of it.

Rachel became particularly close to her cousins, Jeff and Sarah, and frequented their home as a stable refuge. Sarah and Rachel used to play house, go roller skating, and "were into Barbies big time," said Sarah. They shared a love of dramatics and worked together at Trinity Christian Center as drama leaders in the youth program. She and Sarah designed a T-shirt for the youth group that said: "I'm a God-loving, Jesus-freaking, Satan-bashing, World-changing Christian." They used to make so much racket singing karaoke for hours on end at the cousins' house that Larry would have to find respite someplace else. "It would get on my nerves, you know, as a man," he said. The girls wrote songs and recorded tapes to send to youth group friends who had gone off to college. They made frequent contributions to church talent shows "doing Carman [songs] and break-dancing for Jesus," Mary said.

Rachel's relationship with her cousin Jeff was more subdued and reflective. For years they had shared a "floating journal," passed back and forth every three or four days, in which they shared their deepest thoughts. "We balanced each other out," Jeff said. Rachel went through phases when she wondered why people didn't accept her or why she was so distant from her father. Jeff went through phases when he wasn't sure if he believed in God or if he wanted to finish school. "We shared a lot of problems together. She was the strongest of all of us," he said.

The evening before the day she died, Rachel stopped by to give Jeff his history book. (They had shared a locker since sixth grade.) "She got grounded for her grades being bad," said Jeff, "so we didn't get to go out that night." Rachel picked up their shared journal and told him, "I have a lot to write in it." It was in her backpack the day she was killed.

The contradictions in Rachel's life bore down on her as the hard edges of adolescence played out in her teen years. She came of age struggling with her father's absence, to the point that "she started going after boys," Jeff said. "She struggled with temptation, guy affection. We always talked about boyfriend and girlfriend stuff and shared our temptations," he said. "We watched out for each other." Her freshman and sophomore years in high school were a particularly "confusing time" for Rachel, according to Sarah. Jeff added, "We all went through a time of partying and smoking—doing what teens do."

Rachel felt self-conscious about the shape of her nose and felt sure the boy she wanted to ask to the prom would never say yes. (He did.) At the same time, she possessed an irrepressible flair for the outrageous and felt comfortable performing imaginative dramatic interpretations in front of audiences. She wore goofy hats, Dr. Suess or Gilligan hats among her favorites. At the prom she wore sunglasses that made her look like a movie star.

Zach Johnston remembered her as a "warm, caring, and funny" person. In his Web posting he described the day he and Rachel, as lab partners, had dissected a baby pig: "[Rachel] was really scared and shaking when they put the pig down in the dissection tray. So I tied two strings to the pig's arms and made it dance around and sing songs. She thought it was really funny and soon started cutting this poor dead pig apart in all kinds of strange ways."

At the same time, Rachel also wrestled with how God fit into her life. Beyond the challenges of adolescence, she possessed deep inner thoughts and impulses that perplexed and tormented her—and at the same time filled her with longing. The journal entry of March 1, 1998, continued, "I don't understand. I want to feel you in my heart, mind, and soul in life. I want heads to turn in the halls when I walk by. I want them to stare at me, watching and wanting the light you put in me. I want to overflow my cup with your Spirit. I want so much from you."

She sensed that God had given her a special mission, which thrilled her. But it also vexed her. Her longings took on an unshakable dark side, and she suffered bouts of morose imaginings. She also developed stomach problems and, at times, thought she was going to die. On March 7, 1998, she wrote, "God, I have this terrible sharp dull pain in my stomach. I don't know if it's a spiritual feeling, if the Enemy is attacking or if it's just sickness. Whatever it is, I just ask for Your healing. If it's a spiritual feeling, I ask you to bless it. If it's the Enemy, I ask you to bind it. If it's just sickness, I ask you to heal it."

The walk at the playground early that morning was her attempt to come to terms with her longing for God, her fear that he might be unreachable, and a desire to know what her place was in his plan. That is when she "heard his voice." Her relationship with God took on new meaning that day. It was when her world began to change. Jeff noticed a dramatic change in her attitude toward partying. "All of a sudden, one time she totally popped out of that phase," he said. Her vision of God on the playground that morning marked the beginning of the last year of her life.

A Year of Contradictions

Rachel made some decisions after that experience. She resolved to live boldly and without apology in her stand for God and to abandon the "party scene" that she and some friends had pursued. She paid a price for such a stand when some of these friends abandoned her. One time when she walked into the girls' lavatory at school, they were there and laughed at her and walked out. On another occasion, she sat down with them in the school cafeteria and they moved someplace else.

On April 20, 1998—a year to the day before she died—she wrote in her journal:

> It's like I have a heavy heart and this burden upon my back and I don't know what it is. There is something in me that makes me want to cry and I don't know what it is. Things have definitely changed. Last week was so hard. Besides missing Breakthrough [youth group] I lost all my friends at school. Now that I have begun to walk my talk they make fun of me. I don't even know what I have done. I don't really have to say anything and they turn me away. But you know what? It's worth it to me. I am not going to apologize for speaking the name of Jesus. I'm not going to justify my faith to them and I'm not going to hide the light God has put in me. If I have to sacrifice everything, I will. I will take it. If my friends have to become my enemies for me to be with my best friend Jesus, then that's fine with me.

A few weeks later, near the end of Rachel's sophomore year, she wrote in her journal dated May 2, 1998, "This will be my last year, Lord. I've gotten what I can. Thank you."

Some noticed that her last year was a time when she came into her own and seemed more peaceful and happy than she had ever been. "She became clear on some things and became secure in her relationship with God and who he made her to be," said her aunt, Mary Scott. "She was more peaceful and confident when she spoke." Rachel's last year, Mary said, was like "wet cement that finally got firm."

By this time Rachel and her older sister Dana, then twenty-two, had grown closer than at any other time of their lives. This was largely due to their belonging to the same youth group, Breakthrough, in which they each served as a small-group leader of a cell group. "I got to watch her go down to the altar and cry and pray with people. I got to watch her worship God," said Dana. "Nobody else in my family did, because we all went to different churches."

Dana recalled that many of the conversations she shared with Rachel during this time possessed an undercurrent of resignation. "Sometimes we would talk about getting old, and it was like she didn't believe she was going to live to be very old. Or we would talk about wedding stuff, and she would not really respond to that. It was like she didn't really think that she would get married, but I don't think she had any clue why. It was something she just sort of felt."

Her cousin Jeff had similar recollections. "She'd always talk to me and Sarah about how she was going to die. I remember lying in my bed thinking, 'Why would she say that?'"

During this final year of her life, Rachel stopped in a rainstorm to hold an umbrella over a young man who was changing a flat tire. She told a handicapped young man at school, who was largely ignored, that one day she would take him to a movie. She befriended a young woman whose Goth appearance had been off-putting to most everyone else. Nearly every Columbine student I interviewed told me he or she had been a friend of Rachel Scott. It seemed as if everyone whose lives she touched, even remotely, came away feeling like Rachel was a friend.

But even after so many things had come together for her, the contradictions did not dissipate. Dark thoughts plagued her and she seemed preoccupied with her own mortality. A few days before she died, Rachel wrote:

> I'm drowning
> In my own lake of despair
> I'm choking
> My hand wrapped around my neck;
> I'm dying
> Quickly my soul leaves, slowly my body withers.
> It isn't suicide,
> I consider it homicide.
> The world you have created has led to my death.[2]

Two weeks before she died, Rachel performed the romantic lead role in the school's spring play, written, directed, and produced by students and called *Smoke in the Room*. It debuted April 2. "She was perfect," said Devon Adams, who also was in the play. "The kid who wrote it knew from the beginning that he wanted [the lead] to be Rachel because it fit her perfectly. She had to wear totally whacked out clothes, change hair style and color [to purple]. Rachel was willing to do everything."

A week before the shootings, she and Dana had gotten into an argument before Rachel left to spend the night at a friend's house. As Dana was getting ready for bed, the phone rang. "It was Rachel," said Dana. "She called to say, 'I'm sorry.'"

Dana apologized too. "Then, I don't know why," said Dana, "but I felt impressed to tell her that I loved her. So I said, 'Well, I love you.' She said, 'I love you, too.' And we hung up. After we hung up I sat on my bed for a while and thought that I couldn't think of the last time I had told her that.

"That was a God-given moment. When I look back on it now, it would have tormented me to think that I couldn't remember the last time I told Rachel that I loved her."

Rachel and her father, Darrell, shared a similar God-given moment that week before she died. A spontaneous conversation evolved into a serious heart-to-heart when Rachel shared with her father some of the pain and frustrations she had felt while growing up. It gave him the opportunity to ask for her forgiveness and to restore the relationship. It was an intense and intimate conversation that enabled both of them to break through the heartache from the past and step into a new beginning.

The God Problem

Among Rachel's last utterances on Earth were the words, "Bye, sweetie," spoken to a passing acquaintance moments before the shooting started. She was among the first to be shot that day, though she was not killed in the first volley. According to her sister Dana, she had been shot in the leg and side as she sat at the top of the concrete steps outside the school cafeteria and talked with Richard Castaldo. Both students were leveled with multiple gunshot wounds. He lay paralyzed and pretended to be dead. She was on the ground crying. Witnesses told Dana that the gunmen went down the concrete steps and shot other people. "They came back up and they were going into the school," said Dana. "Rachel was there. She was crying. And that's when they confronted her with the question, 'Do you believe in God?' She said 'Yes,' and they took a gun to her temple and killed her. She was shot three times; first in the leg, arm, and side, then she was killed after that question."

One wonders why her killer, Eric Harris, went back to Rachel Scott as she lay on the ground crying. None of the others they had shot in that opening fusillade outside the cafeteria lay dead from their wounds, save Danny Rohrbough. Harris evidently felt no compunction over returning to any of them to finish them off. He went back only to Rachel. He pulled her head up by the ponytail and said something to her. I called Richard Castaldo after we met in January and asked him what Harris said to Rachel before he shot her. He told me, "I don't remember any of that. I don't have any recollection. I was probably not really conscious at the time, either."

I spoke with Richard's mother, Connie Michalik, the following spring. She said that shortly after the shooting, once Richard was conscious and could speak (only in a whisper), the first thing he said was, "Is Rachel okay?" His mother told him that Rachel hadn't made it. Then, despite his weakened condition, Richard began to speak in fragments with great earnestness. Connie bent close to him. "I had my ear right next to his mouth so I could hear what he was saying. He said they were being mean to her and teasing her about God. He could hear her crying. He said he heard 'God' several times in a taunting sarcastic tone. He said that they wanted her to say something and kept asking her questions. Then a gun went off."

Other witnesses concurred that Rachel's killer said something to her before he shot her through the head. Some accounts say that he asked her if she believed in God and that Rachel said, "You know I do." Connie Michalik said that would have been consistent with "what they were saying to a lot of other kids."

Eric Harris had a God problem. He seemed hell-bent on defying anyone he heard utter God's name. "God? Do you believe in God?" And if there was anyone he knew who loved God, it was Rachel Scott. She had performed pantomimes that carried religious themes and had spoken to him and Dylan Klebold about faith in God. Rachel Scott had befriended those boys.

Harris could have walked past her on his way into the building that day. He had walked past all the other students who lay bleeding in the grass. But he returned to Rachel and lifted her head by her hair and asked her a question and shot her in the head. Why?

When, during her junior year, Rachel had performed a pantomime called "Who Nailed Him There?" about the man who put the nails in Jesus' hands and feet to secure him to the cross, the background music cut out midway through her performance. She continued without the music. When the music finally came back on, it picked up where she was in the routine. Dylan Klebold was the sound technician that day and some have speculated that he might have purposefully sabotaged her performance. But Devon Adams, who was a friend of Rachel and Dylan, was in the sound booth with him when it happened. She said Dylan rescued Rachel's performance. "He was freakin' out," she said. "He's going, 'Stupid tape!' Rachel kept going, and he tried his best to get it back up. It was just a bad tape. He got it to work better than it had been. He adjusted the levels a little bit and it came out okay." Devon said Rachel was "a wreck" after that performance but that she thanked Dylan for fixing the tape. "That was the only time I ever saw her cry," she said.

As Rachel lay dead outside the school, her brother Craig was bantering in the library with his friends Isaiah Shoels and Matt Kechter when

Patti Nielson ran in and told them all to get under the tables. "My first reaction was that it was a senior prank and that those were paintball guns," said Craig. "Me and Matt got under the desk. It still didn't seem real to us. It seemed like a dream or something. That's when we heard Eric and Dylan coming into the school. Finally reality hit that it was for real.

"As soon as they came in, they were shooting kids. He shot Isaiah with a shotgun. The gunmen did ask two different people if they believed in God."[3]

Craig prayed to God and asked him to take away his fear. Then, when the moment was right, he was sure he heard God tell him, "Get out." He rallied the library survivors and led the way out, stopping to help Kacey Ruegsegger on his way. Then, once they had been led to safety, he gathered a small contingent and asked which of them still had brothers and sisters in the school. "I asked them if they had any brothers or sisters in the school and they said, 'yeah.' And I said, 'I'm going to pray for your brothers and sisters.' All these people I was praying for, [about] thirty minutes later their brothers and sisters were showing up.

"I said, 'See, I told you. I told you prayer works. I told you your sister was going to come out of this.' They thanked me and kept praying for my sister.[4] And I kept praying for my sister. When I didn't see her, something told me something wasn't right with Rachel."[5]

Even Rachel's death was riddled with contradictions. She died at the hands of social outcasts she had tried to befriend. Her brother, in the epicenter of the massacre, emerged untouched while she, in open air where there was freedom to run, lost her life in the opening shots. "Rachel should be alive and Craig should be dead," said Darrell Scott. "She was outside the building. Craig was in the killing room." Craig prayed for the siblings of his friends, proclaiming that prayer worked as these brothers and sisters appeared shortly thereafter. But his own sister was the one sibling who did not make it out that day.

Teen Martyrs?

Rachel's small-group leader and youth pastor, Lori Johnson, said that immediately after the shooting the members of Rachel's cell group were shocked, but at the same time, they rallied and took charge. Some believed that Rachel's death had bequeathed them a mantle. "They were struck with the sense that there was a reason why it was allowed to happen here, that it could have happened anywhere in any city or to anyone.

They saw it was a time to take a stand for God," she said. "A lot of adults were stunned and couldn't do anything. It was the high school students, the young people in the cell group, who stood up and said, 'This is a time to be a witness.'"

These young people saw Rachel as a martyr who had taken a stand for her beliefs in the face of death. The account of Rachel's confession of faith at gunpoint had a galvanizing effect on the faith of her peers. "To think that someone seventeen years old was among the ranks of the martyrs, like the Apostle Paul, was amazing," said Lori Johnson. "But then to watch kids in my cell group boldly take a stand—people who would have been too scared to go up and talk to someone—was also amazing." These teens and others answered the call Pastor Bruce Porter issued when he said at Rachel's funeral: "Rachel carried a torch—a torch of truth, a torch of compassion, a torch of love, a torch of the good news of Jesus Christ her Lord, of whom she was not ashamed even in her hour of death. I want to lay a challenge before each and every one of you young people here today: The torch has fallen from Rachel's hand. Who will pick it up again? Who will pick up the torch again?"[6] During the funeral, hundreds of young people rose from their seats to answer that call. Hundreds more sent Porter notes and messages in the days that followed, telling him that young people in churches had established clubs and Bible studies to pick up the torch Rachel dropped. "Rachel would want us to go on and make an impact," the kids in Rachel's small group concluded. "God wants us to do that too."

Bill Oudemolen, pastor of Foothills Bible Church, said that Columbine "ironically, brought some health to our youth ministry and to the kids themselves in terms of their willingness to stand for Christ. It is fairly widely assumed among our youth that there were kids who were standing for Christ in the midst of that tragedy. That there are people who are paying a price for their faith in our community has become an inspiration."

Some questioned whether it was overstating the case to label as teen martyrs those who died at Columbine after being asked if they believed in God. J. Bottum wrote in *First Things,* referring to Cassie Bernall's death, "Fearing that her death will help right-wing preachers whip up the 'absurd' belief that Christians are a threatened minority in America when 'the real martyrs today are in China and Sudan,' one prominent Protestant commentator denied in the second week after the murder that Cassie Bernall had suffered anything that could properly be called martyrdom. She wasn't killed by any agency of a government aiming to suppress her religion, but merely by insane criminals aiming at thrills."[7]

Some wondered if Christians too anxiously seized upon the term "martyr" and owned the Columbine victims as such. As martyrdoms go, the way of death for Rachel and Cassie, awful as it was, did not reach the same level of systematic torture that accompanied the "sacred ordeals" of some martyrs of the third and fourth centuries at the hands of Diocletian and his lot.[8] The church historian Eusebius (c. A.D. 260–339) wrote: "I myself saw some of these mass executions by decapitation or fire, a slaughter that dulled the murderous ax until it wore out and broke in pieces, while executioners grew so tired they had to work in shifts."[9] "Some were killed with an ax, as in Arabia, or had their legs broken, as in Cappadocia," he wrote. Others were hung upside down over a slow fire (Mesopotamia); were mutilated and butchered (Alexandria); or roasted on hot grid irons (Antioch).[10]

There is no arguing that the deaths of the Columbine Christians did not arise from a state-ordained, barbaric "perpetual war" against believers such as marked these early centuries. Neither did their deaths evoke the drama and nobility associated with some of the more notable martyrdoms, such as that of the young Roman patron Perpetua, who was arrested and killed in A.D. 203. She said yes, as the students did, when asked if she was a Christian, but her confession was viewed as a betrayal of the state. When the day of execution arrived, Perpetua and three fellow Christians, including her maidservant Felicity, "marched from the prison to the amphitheater joyfully as if they were going to heaven."[11]

"The crowd was horrified when they saw that one was a delicate young girl and the other was a woman fresh from child birth with the milk still dripping from her breasts."[12] The women were brought back to have their nakedness covered with unbelted tunics. The animals in the arena tossed Perpetua so she fell on her back and threw Felicity to the ground, but did not inflict death on either. The executioners decided to expedite things by use of the sword and, according to eyewitnesses, the martyrs "took the sword in silence." But Perpetua's executioner botched it, missing her neck and piercing through to her collar bone. She recoiled in pain, but quickly gathered herself and "took the trembling hand of the young gladiator and guided it to her throat." A witness concluded, "It was as though so great a woman, feared as she was by the unclean spirit, could not be dispatched unless she herself was willing."[13]

The girls at Columbine who died making confessions of faith did not have the opportunity to exhibit such prescience. Rachel was writhing in the grass, having been shot several times already, and Cassie was praying to God, begging him to let her go back home to her family. But, as writer Bottum argues in his *First Things* essay, the circumstances surrounding their deaths do not diminish the force of their testimonies. In fact, he argues that the particulars of their last moments make the case for their being authentic martyrs. "She [referring to Cassie, though the same could be said of Rachel] had no time to calculate the probabilities; she simply had a gun put to her head and the question of her faith posed in the context of life and death . . . a sudden rolling of life to a single point and an instantaneous fulfillment of Christ's promise in Matthew 10:32 [KJV]: 'Whosoever therefore shall confess me before men, him will I confess also before my Father.' This is an image to move a child to enormous heroism and sacrifice."[14]

Bottum describes how the prayer circles that spontaneously gathered in Clement Park in the immediate aftermath of the shooting kept enlarging until what had started as a circle of three or four became a cumbersome crowd. Those on the outer edges could only raise an arm in the direction of the one praying. "The praying crowds seemed to have no special desire to hear politicians come to town and demand gun control, or television commentators denounce pornography on the Internet and violence in popular music and the failure of public schools. . . . The mourners wanted instead to hear the stories of teenage girls with guns to their heads being asked to deny the Lord."[15]

The etymology of the word martyr, from the Greek word *martus*, meant witness in the legal sense. The gospels used the term this way numerous times (i.e.: "many false witnesses spoke against him," Mark 14:56 NLT). By the end of the New Testament (in the book of Revelation, written in about A.D. 90), the term already had taken on the meaning of blood witness for those who died for their faith: "And when the Lamb broke the fifth seal, I saw under the altar the souls of all who had been martyred for the word of God and for being faithful in their witness" (Rev. 6:9 NLT). By the third century, the church father Origen had provided a definition that became widely accepted: a martyr—or witness—is "one who of his own free choice chooses to die for the sake of religion."[16] Herbert Lockyer, author of the book *Last Words of Saints and Sinners*, more recently described martyrs as those who "sealed their testimony with their heart's blood."[17]

The mantle of being a blood witness in early Christianity carried such force and left such a testimony that it took on an aura of a divine gift and privilege. Many actually sought it out. Over the centuries martyrs and their relics (hair, bones, items of clothing) often were venerated after their deaths and thought to possess supernatural powers. (Key chains were not the first attempt to commodify holy living.)

A Christian hymn echoes the refrain, "There is power in the blood," referring to Jesus Christ's sacrifice on the cross. But the same could be said of the blood of the martyrs, not in a salvific sense, but in a testimonial one. And that power becomes even more acute and inspiring when it emanates from the blood of fellow high-schoolers. These testimonies were magnified in the hearts and minds of students, not because the girls carried a spiritual glow that made them seem destined for beatification, but for exactly the opposite reason. They were *normal* teens—Rachel had smoked and paced the floor prior to asking a boy to attend the prom; Cassie had struggled with her weight and felt like "a loser" because she wasn't asked to the prom. It was their normalcy that crowned their deaths with such force. It seared the consciences of their fellow students and awakened two impulses that otherwise had evaded them. First, in shattering the common teenage myth of immortality, their deaths introduced a newfound sense of urgency that there may not be a tomorrow. Second, their willingness to die proclaiming a higher allegiance instead of lying to save their lives punched home the promise of eternity—that choices we make on earth make an impact after death. This introduced a new possibility into the jaded world many teens inhabit—a world in which no gratification is withheld, except something worth dying for. These girls "sealed their testimony with their heart's blood."

Lori Johnson said that Rachel's death drove her peers to think about life in new terms. "You don't know if you have tomorrow," she said. "When something like this happens, we had this awareness that all of a sudden you could be faced with eternity. You think about that. It was a wake-up call to all of us. We asked ourselves . . . what are we doing wasting our time? We need to be reaching people."

A Longing Generation

These sudden, intense glimpses of the fleeting aspect of life and something greater to live for in eternity captured a longing in this generation that, even before Columbine, already was beginning to emerge.

Generational writers William Strauss and Neil Howe[18] say today's Millennial teens are destined to become the next civic-minded generation, cut from a cloth similar to that of the World War II generation. Millennials are coming of age in an era when there is a notable absence of heroes for young people to emulate. Strauss asserts that this vacuum will rally today's teens to answer the call to heroism and emerge as the next heroes. "We are looking for heroes and they will find that path. They themselves will clean up youth culture."[19]

Since Columbine, this longing has translated into a heightened desire to know God. In the aftermath of the shootings, churches in the Littleton area saw an immediate swelling of their attendance numbers[20] and youth group attendance, also, reflected a precipitous increase. Some of that has leveled off, but nearly every youth program in the area has registered and sustained increased numbers. And this trend has moved beyond Littleton. "Today, some young people are rebelling in a whole new way—by seeking religion," Lisa Miller wrote in the *Wall Street Journal.* "Ministers and rabbis say they are seeing an increasing number of teens walking into houses of worship without their parents, looking for an intense experience, a close encounter with a higher power."[21]

A recent study conducted by the Barna Research Group revealed that while "teens continue to be more broadly involved in church-based activities than are adults" and that their active participation "far exceeds the participation level among adults," their motivation for doing so is derived more from "relational opportunities" than a desire to be connected to a church.[22] A recent Gallup poll concurred: "Most young Americans believe it is very important that life be meaningful and have a purpose," noted George Gallup. "Yet a high percentage of these same people believe that most churches and synagogues today are not effective in helping people find meaning in life."[23] George Barna concluded: "Most teens are desperately striving to determine a valid and compelling purpose for life" and they "will give the Church a chance," but, he said, "the Church must earn the time and attention of teens—and that means becoming a provider of value."[24]

Newsweek's recent cover package "What Teens Believe"[25] highlights the fact that while 78 percent of teens say religion is important, only half said they attended services regularly. "Many describe themselves as spiritual rather than religious."[26] Churches having the greatest impact on this generation are those churches that are bold enough to redefine the approach to God and worship in terms that resonate with the peculiarities of this new breed. For many, that has meant things like the revival of "the ancient practices exploring Gregorian chants, cabals, the Latin mass. . . . Youth group volleyball and pizza parties are out; ceremonies and candles are in."[27] They want "hard-core" religious expression, which means that many teens prefer a mission trip to El Salvador over a Wednesday night burger bash.

Approaches to worship that seem to connect most effectively are those that require something of the worshiper and remove "the holy" from the realm of being simply another consumer option. They counter the passivity of being entertained with interactivity of worship that demands initiative and response. The lulling aspect of the media environment is met with tactile expressions of worship; its isolation, with intimacy; its distorted worldviews, with a view toward eternity.[28]

The wild success of the book *Jesus Freaks,* written by members of the Christian rock group dc Talk, suggests that the martyr narrative is striking a chord with today's youth. The book, written for teens, highlights the martyrdoms of people from every corner of the globe throughout Christian history, beginning with the early deacon Stephen and continuing through Cassie Bernall. My son, Ben (then seventeen) had been reading the book when he came bounding into my bedroom one time after attending youth group and announced, "When I die, I want you to play the Supertones' song 'Heaven'[29] at my memorial service." My heart skipped a few beats and my blood ran cold. Then I said, "Okay." I realized I was confronting a new paradigm for how young people interpret their allegiance to God. This was a post-Columbine conversation.

My son Jon (then sixteen) also had been reading the book. He was particularly struck by the testimony of an eighteen-year-old Russian named Ivan who served in the Soviet military in 1970. Authorities attempting to make him renounce his Christian faith forced Ivan to stand in subzero temperatures wearing his summer uniform for twelve nights. "A lark threatened with death for singing would still continue to sing. She cannot renounce her nature. Neither can we Christians," Ivan said to his tormentors. The torture tactics intensified and in 1972 Ivan wrote to his parents, "You will not see me anymore." When the Soviets returned Ivan's body to his parents, it was obvious he had been stabbed six times around the heart, wounded on his head and around his mouth, and been beaten from head to feet. Ivan "died with difficulty," his commander told the family. "He fought death, but he died a Christian."[30]

The book of martyrs was named after dc Talk's hit song that asks the question: "What would people think when they hear that I'm a Jesus Freak? What will people do if they find that it's true? I don't really care if they label me a Jesus Freak 'cause there ain't no disguising the truth."

"I looked up the word freak," said band member Toby McKeehan, who wrote the song with Mark Heimermann. "It said 'an ardent enthusiast.' Then, when I began to read these stories [about martyrs], I realized that being a Jesus Freak is deeper than being an ardent enthusiast. These are the ultimate Jesus Freaks—the people who are willing to die for their faith. When you look at the killings at Wedgewood [Baptist Church, Fort Worth, Texas, September 1999] and Columbine, I believe that people are going to have to start counting the cost of saying 'I'm a Christian' because it could cost you something. I talked to a kid yesterday who told me that on his first day of school as a freshman, a kid walked up to him and said, 'I'm going to kick your a—, 'cause you're part of the God squad.' This generation is into extremes. There are extreme sports and Hollywood is into throwing extremes at us. People that are into darkness are extreme about their darkness. They're not toying in it."

These extremes are showing themselves in matters of faith. There is a new willingness to put it all on the line for God—even life, if necessary—as exemplified by Rachel and Cassie. Conversely, a more vociferous brand of hostility toward Christians also seems to be emerging, as was demonstrated by Eric Harris and Dylan Klebold. My son told me that, as he walked out of school recently and was just off school property, he saw a classmate don a T-shirt that read "Christian Killer."

"I believe that Christians will live up to those extremes because that is what the culture calls for," said dc Talk's McKeehan. "Believers need to be just as potent."

"At youth group, we're really starting to understand the urgency of telling people they have to decide, that they can't stand on the fence," said my son Ben. "We realize through things like Columbine that we might not be here tomorrow, or they might not. We had better say what we've got to say now."

The Columbine tragedy became a defining moment for this generation. It heightened the sense of the fleetingness of life and so lent it a feeling of urgency. And it brought a moment of clarity to the religious quest that so many teens have undertaken. At Columbine, teens got a picture of a faith worth dying for.

"This tragedy was a wound to open up the hearts of the kids in this country," said Darrell Scott. "I believe they're going to see a movement of God that our generation never saw." *Newsweek*'s study says the same thing. The "unsung story of today's teenagers may be how religious or spiritual they are," the article notes. And, quoting Conrad Cherry, director of the Center for Study of Religion and American Culture at Indiana University-Purdue University Indianapolis, the story goes so far as to say, "We're witnessing a new revival of religion." [31]

The Next Generation of Heroes

Some of the youths from Saint Francis Cabrini Catholic church feared that when history looks back on this period, it would mark them as "the generation of the shootings." "Our generation has gone through so many shootings—not just Columbine, like, all the other ones that happened, too," said Erin Lucero. "But we shine through." Sarah Schumann added, "A lot of people think that this generation is bad [because of these shootings]. But if you look back, so many teens have a relationship with God. It shows people that, yeah, something really bad happened, but it also shows that teens can be great and that we do have relationships with God."

Rather than create a picture of desperation among teens, these young people would like to think that the picture that emerged from Columbine is one of heroism and renewed faith in God. "I said I thought we might be thought of as the 'generation of the shootings,'" said Matt Bruce, "but I think our generation will be remembered as the generation of the faith. Our generation is extremely faithful, and we will be remembered for overcoming these tragedies and for making the world an awesome place.

"The devil played a big part in this—the shooters asked people if they believed in God, and that gives you a clue. The devil tried to bring us down. And, obviously, he didn't succeed. If you think about it, it's kind of funny that the devil suffered. If you ask somebody if they believe in God and then they say yes and then you kill them, that's like a huge testimony to your faith; it's the last thing you do on this earth. It's humiliating to the devil that that happened. His goal obviously was to kill a lot of people and to have us lose our hope in God. The opposite happened."

Sarah Arzola said, "At first, when we were hearing person after person that died, one thing that most of them had in common is that they were Christians. And I just thought, 'God didn't take anybody that wasn't ready to go.' And that gave me some peace."

A new intensity about matters of faith has emerged in this up-and-coming generation since Columbine. A girl in Cassie Bernall's youth group said Cassie's death raised the bar for today's youth in living up to what it means to be a Christian. Valeen Schnurr said, "So many battles took place that day—the battle between good and evil, my personal battle with the fight to stay alive after being shot numerous times, also the fight to stand for what I believe, even if it meant to die for it."[32]

Jeremiah Neitz embodied this same boldness when Larry Gene Ashbrook walked into the sanctuary of Wedgewood Baptist Church in Fort Worth, Texas, September 15, 1999, and killed seven people (wounding seven more). They had gathered for a See You At the Pole Rally, and when the shooting started, kids were diving under pews and running in every direction to get out of the line of fire. Youth pastor Adam Hammond, covered in the blood of one of the slain, was huddled under the pew where Neitz was sitting and tugged at Neitz's leg to get him to take cover. Neitz, then nineteen, didn't move. He stayed in the pew, praying, with his face in his hands. "I was just praying to God to let this end," he said. "He [Ashbrook] kept saying that Christianity was b.s. So I stood up and told him, 'Sir, what you need is Jesus Christ.'" Ashbrook pointed the gun at Neitz and shouted curses at him.

"I held my hands up to my side and said, 'Sir, you can shoot me if you want. But I know where I'm going. I'm going to heaven. What about you?'"

Ashbrook pointed the gun at his own head and killed himself.[33]

I saw this new spiritual intensity among youth myself one day last spring, when I sat with my husband in a circle of teens we would be leading on a mission trip to Ecuador. My husband had just read a brief account of the martyrdom in 1956 of five missionaries who tried to reach a tribe in Ecuador for Christ. The missionaries were armed but did not wield their weapons to defend themselves against the tribesmen's spears. The testimony of their martyrdom eventually won the tribespeople to faith in the God whom the missionaries loved enough to die for. Our team would be going to the place where these missionaries had lived before they were martyred. After reading the account, our meeting concluded in prayer. But I didn't feel like praying. In fact, I had other things on my mind. I felt empty, and old, and tired. I sat dutifully, in any case, and kept my head down expecting that it wouldn't take long for everyone's prayers to be exhausted. I don't remember much of what these young people prayed. But I do recall wondering when they were going to stop. I heard things like, "Put down our pride, Lord. Let this trip not be about us, but about you." And, "Let your glory show through, no matter what it might mean for us." And "May our lives live out the gospel, just like the martyrs whose lives changed the hearts of that tribe." And, "It is awesome to think, Father, that the power you demonstrated in changing their hearts is the same power you have given us access to."

This went on for some time, and then my heart began to quicken. Soon, I felt that I, too, had to pray. I don't remember what I said, but I remember being moved and elevated by the young people's boldness and their faith.

Not long after that, I found these reflections on my son's desk:

Here is a feeble human's attempt to describe an inscrutable God;
How dare I use the name?
The shadow of God is so bright I am
Blinded.
What is this creation that hates you?
This creation that flees from its Creator?

Why don't you lay your mighty hand of justice on us?

You descend into darkness, rejected by many.
Lord, why do you love the enemy?
But who is this? Dare I say his name?
Jesus.
More humble than all others.
You were mocked, whipped, your skin torn like leather
God, I treat you as an inanimate object.
What grief, you sweat blood.
A crown of thorns pressed into your skull
Your beautiful face, smashed, torn.
What great glory being mutilated.
You went from the highest to the lowest
For me.

My life, as small as it is, is yours
completely. I apologize for
how short it is.

When God impressed on Rachel that day at the park that she would see him clearly, she probably didn't think her death would be the spark to ignite the hearts of her peers and enable *them* to see God more clearly. And when she wrote in her journal, "I want you to overflow my cup," she probably didn't imagine that cup would spill over with her blood, transforming for a new generation what it means to say you believe in God.

Chapter 10

God in the Storm

Coming to Terms with Fifteen Losses

I RETURNED TO LITTLETON during the week of April 20, 2000, for the one-year anniversary of the Columbine tragedy. I don't know what I was expecting, but it wasn't the constant juxtaposition of the numbers fifteen and thirteen. Nearly every conversation I had, whether an official interview or a casual chat, drew a line of demarcation between fifteen and thirteen crosses, or trees, or whatever. The cross controversy was alive and wasn't going away.

One evening I attended a public meeting sponsored by the planning committee for a community memorial. There was no discussion of numbers here; the planners stood irrevocably in the thirteen camp. But I met three men at that meeting who registered their unsolicited opinions about the cross debate. Two were friends of Greg Zanis, the carpenter from Illinois who had made the original crosses. One told me that Greg was planning to return to Colorado on April 19 to erect the crosses in Clement Park for the anniversary. This friend was indignant that Zanis at first had been told the crosses could be placed only on the northeast corner of the park, which had been designated a "First Amendment zone" ("I thought the whole country was a

First Amendment zone," he said). But what really got his goat was the letter he had just received from Robert Easton, executive director of the Foothills Park and Recreation District, requesting that Zanis not bring the crosses at all. They would "create controversy and discomfort," the letter said. This friend reiterated that he didn't understand how crosses would create any controversy, especially because so many of those to be memorialized were Christians. He said, "People might have a problem with fifteen," but emphasized that Zanis had no intention of adding two more to the original thirteen. This friend added, however, that he felt sorry that the grieving families of the killers had to be left out of everything all the time. "They were victims, too."

Then Zanis's other friend approached, equally nonplussed about the park manager's request. He said that he could understand using a strong-arming tactic if Zanis had threatened to put up fifteen, which he hadn't done. Then, as an aside, this friend said that he believed there should be some acknowledgment of the loss of the two boys. "They were under our charge and we failed them. We lost them."

As I left that meeting, the cross controversy came up a third time when a reporter from the *Rocky Mountain News* approached me and, thinking I was a member of the community, asked why I had made the effort to come out. When it came to light that I was a journalist from Illinois and had personal contact with the "guy who made the crosses," this reporter said, "Next time you see him will you thank him for me for putting up the fifteen? They were victims too—victims at their own hands, but still victims."

How Much Room at the Cross?

The fifteen/thirteen debate came up again when I met with seventeen-year-old Devon Adams, who was completing her junior year at Columbine. She had been a good friend of Dylan Klebold and was part of a small circle of CHS students who had met regularly since May 1999 to work through the tragedy by writing poetry.[1] Because of her friendship with Klebold, it had been difficult for her to express her grief through the standard avenues, such as school assemblies or memorial tiles.

Devon wrote a poem called "A Blessing" in which she struggled to reconcile two Dylans. There was the kind and playful Dylan she remembered, who used to bounce balls off her head in the swimming pool and who wore a goofy Hawaiian shirt to her "murder mystery" sixteenth birthday party, playing Les Baggs the Tourist. Then there was the other Dylan—

the one who hid semiautomatic weapons under his trench coat and laughed after calling Isaiah Shoels a racial epithet.

As part of her grieving process, Devon planted a tree and wrote about it in the poem excerpted here:

> May this living memory
> Grow as tall as you
> And taller
> To heaven, to the angels, to God herself
>
> May the roots grow to Hell
> And bridge the gap
> Bring together love and hate
> Create absolute understanding.[2]

Her longing for absolute understanding was a prayer everyone in the community seemed to utter at some point, but it was a longing that for many remained unmet. Devon's frustration was real: In all of the community-sponsored healing events, two names never came up. To most people, there was only that one Dylan, the evil one. "There are people who won't accept that he was a friend to people, that he was nice, smart, gentle. Some won't hear about it," she said.

Still, Devon did not cling to sentimental remembrances of her lost friend, as if to absolve him of his crimes. She was in math class when the shooting started and escaped quickly without encountering the killers. She reached safety and was listening to news reports that included descriptions of the killers, but no names. "I knew immediately that it was Eric, and when I heard the description of the other boy, I knew it had to be Dylan," she said. Devon returned to the school and went to police to identify her friend as one of the killers.

"I have never tried to defend Dylan, ever. There's nothing to defend. What he did was wrong and I can never make excuses or defend that," she said. "The boys had to be punished. They did something terribly wrong and they hurt so many people," she said. But Devon felt frustrated that the people of one church condemned Eric and Dylan to hell but "were never willing to talk about it." That is, she felt that church—and others—seemed unwilling to talk about the *other* Dylan and Eric, the human beings. She said, "I felt sorry for any kid who knew them in that church. It was harsh."

This was when she brought up the cross controversy. "Those [two] crosses were in no way there to glorify them. They were there as a memorial for their friends. They were our friends, and we're allowed to mourn too. By ripping down those crosses, people were saying that we weren't allowed to mourn. According to the Bible, Christ died on the cross for all sins," said Devon. She felt that destroying the two crosses implied that Christ died for all sins—except Eric's and Dylan's.

A Line in the Sand

Then there was my meeting with Columbine senior Craig Nason and Cassie Chance, a senior at another local high school. Both were eighteen and active in the youth program at West Bowles Community Church; both had known Cassie Bernall; and both were intimately connected to an ordeal that helped to define the terms of the fifteen/thirteen debate.

In the fall of 1999 the church's youth group decided to set up a memorial to honor the families of those who had died at Columbine. "We have a prayer garden in the back of the church," said Cassie, "and our youth pastor, Dave [McPherson], was talking about planting trees there. He was grappling with whether to plant fifteen or thirteen. He knew by planting fifteen there would be no support from anywhere. He didn't even know how the congregation would take it."

Earlier that fall, before the plan had been acted upon, Brian and Lisa Rohrbough had attended West Bowles and heard McPherson announce the intention to create a memorial garden. At the time, he spoke of including fifteen rocks. Outraged at the notion of fifteen anything, Rohrbough met with church leaders before they acted. He said that the church leaders, "promised us they wouldn't do anything to honor [the two killers] and nothing with the number fifteen. You can't honor murderers. They're getting enough fame."[3]

The plan to establish a memorial garden moved forward. Since the trees were meant to express sympathy and solidarity for the grieving families, people began to wonder what this meant for the families of the killers. According to West Bowles pastor George Kirsten, despite the previous conversation with Rohrbough, he said, "We began to think, 'Do you exclude the two families? What do you say to them?' This is not a memorial. We are simply remembering the 15 families."[4]

Before the issue had been completely settled in their minds, the nursery called to say that the trees were in and needed to be delivered by a certain date. "Dave hadn't specified numbers," said Cassie Chance. "He said, 'Just bring them over.'" The nursery delivered fifteen trees.

This caused the members of the youth group to pause, not wanting to offend anyone. But in the end they decided to go forward and plant all fifteen. "We thought it through," said Craig. "What's been overlooked here has been that the Harris and the Klebold families have been put out. Whether or not they should have done more is up for anyone to say. Who is a perfect parent? I know my parents didn't know a lot of what I used to do. The point is, these families were just as much in need of prayer, if not more. They've lost their sons to start, and then they have to deal with knowing their sons were responsible for something so horrible that's just killed this community. This is not to memorialize what [the killers] have done, or to say, 'It's okay—you're victims,' or whatever. But the Klebolds and Harrises need our prayers."

Approximately fifty picketers showed up on Sunday morning, September 26, 1999, carrying signs that read "Unrepentant murderers honored here" and "No peace for the wicked." With the media looking on, Al Velasquez (father of murdered student Kyle Velasquez) and Rich Petrone (stepfather of Danny Rohrbough), using Brian Rohrbough's tools, went onto church property while people worshiped inside and sawed down the two trees that stood at the pinnacle of the semicircle. Petrone said, "I was getting all my anger out on that tree. It felt good."[5]

George Kirsten expressed regret about the pain the trees had caused these families and said he understood why Rohrbough felt such anger. Despite the previous conversation they had shared about not doing anything involving the number fifteen, the church had neglected to contact Rohrbough when it moved forward with the decision. "This is where we dropped the ball," said Kirsten.[6]

"The hard part was, these were hurting people," said Craig Nason. "They'd lost people, too, and we knew that. But this was to create peace for them. Some people said, 'Why did you do it?' Well, because we think it's important to make a stand on something like this. This is for their benefit, and if they think coming here and cutting those trees down is going to help them, that's sad. It makes you realize that the two families that did this are still hurting. They have not made any peace with this, and we need to pray more for them."

Craig Nason had gone to Rebel Hill when the fifteen crosses first went up, and he recognized the role the two crosses had played in the community's response to the event. "Part of the healing process for some was writing [on the crosses] to Eric and Dylan," he said. Many of the notes on their crosses included comments like, "How could you have done this?" But he had noticed that as many people wrote, "I'm sorry that I didn't know what hurt you had."

"I saw so much of that written on those crosses," said Craig. "Then it turned into this crazy thing that we were trying to memorialize Eric and

Dylan and trying to make what they did look like it was okay. It got taken to a different place."

That place has been a netherworld of random impulses of justice and mercy, as if they floated around this conversation and occasionally collided, but never achieved a balance and interplay. Those who wanted to include fifteen crosses were tagged as libertarians who extended unconditional mercy without lending weight to the gravity of these crimes or the need for justice. Those who wanted to exclude the boys by dismissing anything with the number fifteen seemed to stand on the side of justice without consideration of mitigating factors that might elicit mercy.

"The easy thing to do is to say that Eric and Dylan were just a couple of psychos and that it was all them," said Craig. "But there are a lot of kids like them who might not shoot their schools but who have the same hurt inside, who have been rejected." Craig was trying to get across that, though the killers acted upon it wrongly, their pain was legitimate and part of the responsibility rested upon the community that had allowed these boys' tormentors to run roughshod over them with impunity.

"There's a difference between forgiveness and saying what they did was okay," said Craig Nason. "That's where people lose us."

Beyond taking away a vehicle for the grief of friends of the boys, tearing down the crosses had diminished the community's opportunity to reflect on its role in the tragedy. Instead, the act had drawn a line in the sand and established an artificial wall between justice and mercy. Those in favor of fifteen were forced into a position they weren't claiming, making it appear they wanted to extend mercy without justice, as if guilt didn't matter. Those on the other side seemed to stake out a position of advocating justice without mercy. "People are like, 'What they did was horrible,' and I'm like, 'Yeah, no doubt,'" said Craig. "All I know is that before I even knew it was Eric and Dylan, when I was in the choir room [during the rampage], I was praying, 'God, be with whoever is doing this. Be with them, God. They don't know what they are doing.' Jesus was on the cross saying, 'Forgive them; they don't know what they are doing.' It's a tragedy. Those two are gone. But it's wrong to say that only thirteen were lost that day. I mean, thirteen were victims, but two were truly lost. Somewhere along the line, we lost those guys."

April 20, 2000

As far as the community-sponsored anniversary events were concerned, the number fifteen didn't come up. It was as if the two killers and their families had not existed.

April 20 was the last full day of my trip, and the sky was as blue as I had seen it. Clement Park was overtaken by communications trucks with satellite dishes and abuzz with media people jockeying cameras and microphones and talking on cell phones. Rick Kaufman, spokesman for Jefferson County Schools, was to hold a press conference at 10:00 A.M., and by 9:30 the media horde, myself included, had started to gather on the hillside where he was scheduled to appear. That was where I found Greg Zanis, the cross maker, who had arrived the previous evening with a Christian motorcycle club as escort. He hadn't seen Easton's letter requesting that he not bring the crosses to the park and he didn't want to know about it when I brought it up. The crosses were still in his truck. He didn't plan to set them up until after the press conference. He was milling around with the aim of recruiting students to carry the crosses once he was ready.

Kaufman appeared, though it was a trick getting his microphone stand to stabilize on the sloping hillside. I was knocked in the head by a media microphone on a boom (without receiving an apology) and was asked by a cameraman to move to the right.

Kaufman spoke in subdued tones. He said that a private school assembly was under way for CHS students as he spoke and that the mood was "somber and reflective." The questions started flowing.

"How many students were attending?"

About one thousand students had come to school that day for the assembly, with five hundred to six hundred parents attending a separate assembly in a different part of the school.

"Have there been any threats to Columbine today?"

There have been no threats, he said.

"What about bomb-sniffing dogs?"

No bomb-sniffing dogs.

"What kinds of things were being said at the assembly?"

Staff members reflected on the past year and each person who died was represented by a spokesperson.

"Can you tell us what the emotions are like for the students today?"

It is a difficult day, he said. There is a lot of crying and hugging.

"There are more of you [media] than there are of us," he said. He asked us to give the kids the space they needed.

I asked, "Has there been any contact with the families of the killers, or any attempt to include them in any way?"

No, he said, there had been no contact with the families of the killers.

"We are Columbine" did not apply in the case of the Harrises and Klebolds. They had not made any public appearances or granted interviews (not for a lack of interested parties) and had rarely issued statements during the first year.[7] They did, however, release public apologies in the local newspapers a week before the first anniversary. "We loved our son dearly, and search our souls daily for some glimmer of a reason why he would have done such a horrible thing,"[8] wrote the Harrises. "There are no words to convey how sorry we are for the pain that has been brought upon the community as a result of our son's actions," wrote the Klebolds. "The pain of others compounds our own as we struggle to live a life without the son we cherished."[9]

The local papers, in the meantime, ran human interest stories about the other families of the slain and the injured in the week leading up to the anniversary. Much of the coverage indicated that they were inching forward in their recovery. The organization HOPE (Healing of People Everywhere), spearheaded by victims' families to raise funds for a new library, had become a constructive outlet for many. By the first anniversary, it had raised nearly two-thirds of the $3.1 million needed to transform the present library into a glassed atrium and build a new library facility. By early May 2000, the drive reached that goal, and the atrium was unveiled in August.

At the same time, each family had a different story to tell and had set its own course for getting through this. Michael and Vonda Shoels, step-father and mother of Isaiah Shoels, had moved to Houston to give their family the chance to start over. Tom and Linda Mauser, parents of Daniel, took different paths: Linda kept a low profile, choosing instead to pre-pare to adopt a baby girl from China; Tom became known nationally as an advocate for stricter gun control through SAFE Colorado (Sane Alter-natives to the Firearms Epidemic), the organization he launched with oth-ers from the community. Al Velasquez daily wore a shirt and baseball cap bearing Kyle's name; his wife, Phyllis, wrote in her journal a lot. One entry read, "There are times life feels familiar. Most times, I wander in a foreign landscape searching for the familiar."[10] Linda Sanders traveled to the MGM Grand Hotel in Las Vegas in February, where her husband Dave Sanders had proposed to her. There she accepted the ESPN Arthur Ashe Courage Award on behalf of her deceased husband. Dave Sanders's daughter from a previous marriage, Angela, barely made it through her speech at the event, until she looked up and saw National Basketball Association super-star Michael Jordan smile and wink at her. "I knew that his dad had been killed, too. I fed off his strength," she said.[11] Joe and Ann Kechter laughed and cried hearing stories they had never heard about their son from his many friends and cherished the championship ring Matt would have received for playing lineman on the school's state-championship football team in his junior year. Don and Dee Fleming planted forget-me-nots and columbines in "Kelly's garden," a special plot in their backyard dedicated to the memory of their daughter. Lauren Townsend's mother, Dawn Anna, assumed the role of spokesperson for HOPE and thought about Lauren when the wind blew: "Lauren wrote once about God being in the wind. . . . There are times when the wind is blowing and I turn my back to the wind and pretend it's Lauren putting her arms around me."[12] Corey DePooter's parents, Patricia and Neal, said their son "would have told us to move on. He would not like us moping around." They got involved with the Marine Corps Toys for Tots program.[13]

The Rohrboughs and Petrones, families of slain student Dan Rohrbough's father and mother, were embroiled in legal battles. Still, they reflected on the happy memories of their son. Sue Petrone reclaimed the two concrete slabs from the sidewalk where Danny had died and placed them in a corner of her yard. She perched a porch swing on it and planted pansies and columbines around it. "It's hard to describe, but it means a lot to me to have it here. It's very calming," she said.[14] Brian Rohrbough liked to think about the time Dan had left for Kansas with his grandfather. When Brian arrived a few days later and opened the front door, he found Dan smiling from ear to ear in a spot where he had waited all day for his dad. "I envision a time when that happens again," he said.[15]

Darrell Scott spent the first year on the road, speaking and reading from Rachel's journals at youth rallies, frequently accompanied by Greg Zanis and the original thirteen crosses. Darrell remarried in February but barely missed a beat on his speaking tour under the auspices of his newly formed organization, The Columbine Redemption. Beth Nimmo, Rachel Scott's mom, stayed close to home, giving special care to her son, Craig, whose healing process had been more jagged. Her thoughts returned to her daughter most frequently in the mornings, when Rachel used to come into the bathroom and snatch her mom's makeup. Since the February after the shooting, Beth had undertaken a special ministry to her neighbor Kelly Grizzell, whose daughter, Stephanie Hart, was murdered with her boyfriend, Nick Kunzelman, in the Subway sandwich shop on Valentine's Day. Stephanie had made a cake for Beth in the shape of one of Rachel's famous hats after Rachel died.

Brad and Misty Bernall and their son, Chris, spent the one-year anniversary dedicating the Cassie Bernall Home for Children in Las Lajas, Honduras. Misty's book *She Said Yes* sold nearly half a million copies and won a Christopher Award[16] in February 2000. Chris was active in the same youth group Cassie had once enjoyed at West Bowles Community. "She was my sister, but she really belonged to God," he said. "He put her in our family for us to learn for a while. I think I'm at peace with that."[17]

By the one-year anniversary, John and Doreen Tomlin felt their lives had reached a kind of normalcy, "but not the same kind of normal," said John.[18] Doreen wrote in a public letter: "We desperately miss our John . . . Some days, the pain of losing him seems unbearable, but then we look to our Lord and gain immeasurable comfort, knowing that he has John with him." Her husband John said, "For the families of the children who did this, we will be praying for them. We feel no hatred against them."[19]

This was one of the few references made to those other families during the anniversary events. While healing was taking place in small steps in the lives of many, much of the Columbine community remained torn up, rife with discord, and targeting blame. Lawsuits abounded, and some laid blame on the Harrises and Klebolds for not having done enough to prevent the tragedy. The Shoels, who filed a $250 million lawsuit against the families, were not moved by their publicized letters of apology: "Why didn't they have better control over their child? . . . Now they want to seek our forgiveness. Ain't that pitiful."[20]

Power in the Crosses

After Rick Kaufman's news conference, I was curious to see if Robert Easton's dire predictions that the presence of crosses would cause controversy and discomfort would come true. I made my way to the northeast corner and the "First Amendment zone" and passed some Goth students along the way. They had all manner of piercings and tattoos in places that looked like it had to hurt. I asked if they were from Columbine and they said, "No."

"You ditching school?"

"My mom said I could," one girl said.

I found Zanis and his contingent in the free-speech zone, where the Traveling Led Nerds, fifty feet away, already had undertaken the exercise of their First Amendment rights in the form of a drum-beating bongo celebration. He was rustling up students to carry the crosses from a shelter to the sidewalk, where thirteen stands were set in place, and he was grateful when the Goth kids showed up. They were pleased to fill out the remaining need for cross bearers.

I wouldn't have called it "systematic" when the students started putting up the crosses. The beams were long and unwieldy, and the dangling ribbons, rosaries, and laminated poetry complicated matters. Some of the young people could barely carry the crosses, let alone lift and center them and turn them so the names faced the same direction. The media people were no help. They snapped pictures and filmed the whole thing in all of its inglorious awkwardness. Some of the names on the crosses pointed west, others pointed east. I tried to tell Greg that maybe he should have someone turn some of the crosses around so the names all faced the same direction—for the sake of pictures. But he's hard of hearing and didn't get it.

Once the thirteen crosses were in, uniformly or no, Greg announced that he wanted to form a circle to pray over each cross and invited anyone who was so inclined to join in. At first only four or five gathered with him, holding hands and bowing heads while Greg prayed. His prayers were short and heartfelt. He prayed for the families represented by each cross and said something about each victim. "John Tomlin always kept a Bible in his truck," he said. Kelly Fleming "was such a beautiful girl." The "last words Isaiah Shoels heard were words of hate," he said. It was all he could do to keep from breaking into tears right there on the sidewalk. "It's hard to do this," he said. "I am honored to use my hands to make these crosses."

The circle grew wider with each prayer, and by the time he reached the end of the line, at Danny Rohrbough's cross, twenty or more people had joined the circle, including the Goth kids. Zanis prayed, "I know I have caused this family a lot of pain. I hope that they can find it in their hearts to forgive me." Then he invited others to pray: "Is anybody in the circle brave enough to speak?" Someone said, "It's wonderful that we're praying. I think we owe a prayer for the other two who died. We need to create a circle of prayer for them." She was crying. Then another person prayed, "None of us is the same person since this happened. Some are struggling more than others with this. None of the victims would want them to continue in their suffering." More than one prayer went up for the Harris and Klebold families, and I did not miss the irony that these prayers spontaneously arose from the circle around the cross of Dan Rohrbough, whose family had been the most proactive about disowning "anything related to the number fifteen." Someone else prayed: "I want to thank God how he's turned this into a good thing. Rachel and Cassie gave their lives for God. In a culture of death, life is a precious gift." Then the Goth girl prayed, the one I had passed earlier. She said, "I want to pray for all the families, especially the family of Rachel Scott."

When the prayers were exhausted, Zanis said, "Go hug somebody you don't know. Show them you love them." The media people maneuvered themselves accordingly, and I went to the Goth girl who had prayed for the Scott family. I asked her if she had known Rachel. She said, "Yes, but I don't want to talk about it." I decided then to remove my bright red press pass for the remainder of the day.

The memorial service was soon to begin, and I followed the stream of people headed toward the amphitheater. A pack of students carrying balloons and flowers gathered at the top of Rebel Hill. The atmosphere seemed almost festive.

The inner section of the amphitheater closest to the stage had been cordoned off for CHS students and their parents. Other than members of the designated media pool, journalists were consigned to the outer edges with the other onlookers not related to the school. An older man sat next to an opening to the student section. Opening my notebook and showing him my press pass, I asked, "Is there someplace special where the media are supposed to go?" He said, "Well, you're supposed to have a gold star, but go ahead."

I found myself in the unlikely situation of looking for a seat on the hillside a few rows back from the stage in the midst of a throng of CHS students and their parents. I wore the T-shirt that the Saint Francis Cabrini kids had given me—the same shirt their youth pastor, Jim Beckman, had thought up with the slogan that Frank DeAngelis had co-opted: "We survived. We will prevail. We have hope to carry on." I fit right in with the others there. I looked like a Columbine mom.

The girl in front me wore a WWJD bracelet and the guy next to her wore a baseball hat backward. "We Are Columbine" T-shirts abounded, and I saw a lot of "Never Forget" Columbine pins and signs that read "A Time to Remember; a Time to Hope"—the theme of the day. The students seemed glad to have a day off and the sunshine lifted everyone's spirits.

The mood quickly changed, however, after the national anthem, when Steve and Jonathan Cohen took the platform to sing "Friend of Mine," the song they composed and sang the year before at the first community memorial. The crowd greeted them with rousing applause, shouts, and whoops. Steve (a senior the year of the shooting) quelled them and said, "I'd like to let you guys know this is the final time we'll be doing this song. From the beginning the purpose of this song was just to glorify God and to serve you guys."

So they sang. It sounded homespun, but it changed the mood. It took people back. When they sang the words, "Columbine, flower bloom, tenderly I sing to you," a hush descended. When they sang, "Do you still hear raging guns? Ending dreams of precious ones?" tears fell. Mine did, too. It struck me that this was practically the first moment of my one-year sojourn in which I wasn't sitting at somebody else's kitchen table, or in someone's living room, or across a pastor's desk, or on the floor with a group of students listening to *their* stories. This was my moment to come to terms with this event. My notebook, camera, and press pass were tucked away in my backpack and I didn't try to stop the tears. I looked like a Columbine mom. No one knew I was a journalist.

Jim Beckman—the youth pastor from Saint Francis Cabrini—offered the opening prayer. He prayed that we might see the victories of these modern times in spite of the violence of Columbine. Crime was down "to pre-1970 levels"; teen pregnancy was down 7.5 percent since 1974; sexual activity among teens had been declining for three straight years; abortions were down 15 percent since 1990; the divorce rate was down 19 percent since 1981, and 76 percent of Americans favored faith-based solutions to today's problems. I hadn't heard such demographic recitations articulated in prayer before, but it was refreshing to hear some good news. "The tide is turning," he said, "and I believe it is our young people that are fighting the hardest. It is our young people that are the heroes and it is their faith that is an inspiration to us all."

He closed with a quote from Billy Graham: "'The hope that each of us has is not in who governs us or what laws are passed or what great things we do as a nation. Our hope is in the power of God working through the hearts of people.' That is where our hope is in this country. That is where our hope is in this life. Jesus Christ, be our hope."

Principal Frank DeAngelis received a standing ovation when he rose to the microphone. Impassioned as always, he didn't try to hide his own tears. Devon Adams told me that at the preprom assembly this year he seemed more subdued than usual. He didn't quote anyone famous in his speech: "We're all going, 'Oh, quote Aristotle—come on! Quote Plato!'" she said. I suppose it was a good sign on this day when he quoted a famous author: "Ernest Hemingway wrote, 'The world breaks everyone, and then we are stronger in broken places.'"

"Our scars will remain with us forever," DeAngelis said. "Together we will recover the strength and hope to carry on."

United Methodist clergywoman, Lucia Guzman, read the names of each of the slain. She recalled being in Central America during the turbulent 1980s, when guerrilla fighting and death squads dominated, and the village would gather on the hillside in the evenings to call roll. "There were those who were missing—fathers, mothers, children, grandchildren—and the village would gather, not knowing whether these were dead or simply lost. They read the names of everyone who was a member of that community, and if that one was missing, it was the community who said, 'Present.'" She invited the Columbine community to do the same and asked the audience to stand while she read the names.

"Cassie Bernall."

The crowd responded, "*PRESENT.*"

"Steven Curnow."

"PRESENT."

"Corey DePooter."

"PRESENT."

"Kelly Fleming."

"PRESENT . . ."

And on it went, down the list of thirteen names read aloud and publicly recognized and punctuated by the single toll of a bell.

Patti Nielson delivered the most riveting speech of the day. "At this exact time one year ago, I was curled up in a cupboard in a back room of the library. Please forgive me for taking you back to that day. But you need to know where I was in order to understand my story," she said. Then she asked, "Have you ever wondered what thoughts would go through your head at the moment of your death?"

She recounted what she was doing and thinking as the gunmen were killing people in the library. "I was praying for the children who were being shot and for the children who were shooting them," she said. She thanked God that her children were not with her. "I prayed that help would arrive soon, and I asked God to forgive me of my sins before I died."

As time went on, and she moved to the cupboard in the back room of the library, she thought about her loved ones—her husband and parents, sisters, nieces and nephews, and friends. But more so than these, her thoughts centered around her three young children. "I worried about them being raised without a mother. I worried about them grieving without me there to comfort them."

However, another thought tormented her even more. "I knew my family would grieve, but I did not want the circumstances of my death to make them bitter and angry. I did not want my children to grow up consumed by anger or absorbed in self-pity. I just wanted them to be happy, whether I was there or not.

"I don't know why I survived," she said. "But I can't help wondering, could these have been the last thoughts of one of those who died in that same place on that same day? Could they, too, have wanted desperately to tell their families and friends that same thing?

"For me," she said in closing, "I want today to mark the day that I let go the anger, allowed myself the peace that comes from acceptance and forgiveness and gave myself permission to be happy again. That is what I would have wanted for my family. That is what I wish for all of you."

The service wound down with several cliché-filled speeches. I noticed cynical smirks and rolling eyeballs on the faces of students when the board of education president, Jon DeStefano, said, "You have given new meaning to the term 'school spirit'" and "you have won our nation's heart." Music teacher Lee Andres got the prize for most animated moment with his comment: "One thing I learned is that the media is untrustworthy." (Sustained applause.) "A lot that was said about Columbine in the media was inaccurate at best and lies at the worst." (Hoots, howls, whoops, and sustained applause.) By this point the standing ovations were tiresome, and one CHS dad to my right groaned, "Now we gotta sit down again."

The only hint of the otherwise neglected theme of "fifteen of anything" attended the speeches of Columbine seniors Sergio Gonzales and Matt Varney, and this only in a back-handed way. Gonzales said, "We need to reevaluate who we are as a community and who we are as people. . . . We share a joke about another person with our friend because, it's just a joke, right? It means nothing. But it does mean something to the person that is being insulted and teased. Do you know that person? Have you taken the time to know who they are inside? If you look around, you'll see many faces, and many times we neglect to realize how precious they are, how astounding they are." Varney echoed the thought: "How can we make this loss meaningful? By simple acts of kindness. . . . Students, while walking through the halls of your school, never underestimate the importance of a simple 'hi' to those you do not know very well. It can make that person's day. It all begins with simple acts of kindness." No names were mentioned, but the subtext of Sergio and Matt's plea was clear: When it came to people on the fringe, it was time to start showing everyone those nice things— such as kindness and tolerance—that were not shown in the cases of Eric Harris and Dylan Klebold.

When the service ended, I thought about making my way to the platform to greet Jim Beckman and Frank DeAngelis, but that would have put me back in the category of a journalist, and that wasn't where I wanted to be at the moment. They were shaking hands and giving hugs to people, and I could see that this was their moment to be with their community, and I wasn't part of that picture. I left the barricaded area and tried to get my bearings. Students lingered, many chatting into microphones held dutifully by the media horde. I walked to the free-speech zone in search of Greg Zanis to say good-bye. A few persevering Traveling Led Nerds beat away on their drums and invited me to join them. I passed, but affirmed their exuberance. Greg was hugging a woman who had been crying at one of his crosses. Contrary to Easton's foreboding, the crosses were a success and gave passing visitors an opportunity to reflect, cry, or say a prayer. I hung around for a few minutes, hoping to catch Zanis in a moment when he wasn't ministering, but the one chance I had evaporated when a passerby looked twice at the model Zanis had displayed of a thirteen-story cross memorial he wanted to build. I walked to my car. He'd never miss me.

I was ready to go home. But I had one final stop to make before bringing this one-year pilgrimage to its conclusion.

God in the Storm

Rachel's headstone had butterflies on it. Her father had told me that Rachel loved butterflies—"She always wore them in her hair and had them on her bed and everywhere," he said. "No one knew that except family and friends." The cemetery memorial garden, with Rachel's and Corey's graves and thirteen memorial crosses, had been greatly spruced up since I had been there in July. Headstones, a brick walkway, and four black marble benches had been added.

But it was too much to hope for the solitude I had enjoyed in July. There was no end to people coming and going during the few minutes I took to pay my respects. Two Columbine guys pulled up in a white car with the names of the thirteen written in white shoe polish on the car windows; Kyle, Kelly, and Lauren appeared on the left passenger side. The visitors stopped in front of every cross. At John Tomlin's, one fellow put his hand on the shoulder of the other.

I noticed a man sitting alone on the bench next to mine. He was beefy and tanned, and had a thick neck, the haircut of a Marine, thighs like tree trunks, and sunglasses that looked like the kind Tom Cruise would wear. I thought he must be a cop, but I had no way of knowing without intruding. He sat, his elbows on his thighs, looking at the crosses. He sniffled now and then, and I finally decided he was crying. I wondered what his connection was to these kids, though it wasn't as if one needed a connection to cry in front of those crosses. Some of the families had filed lawsuits against the Jefferson County Sheriff's Office alleging that SWAT officers had wanted to storm the school to subdue the shooters but were forbidden to do so by the sheriff's commanders. Maybe this man was one of the ones who had wanted to go in. Maybe he was crying because those crosses should have represented other lives lost to this madness.

An older man stood behind me, over the grave of Rachel Scott. He had flowing white hair and a gentle face with age lines that looked as though they had crept onto the wrong face, making him older than he was supposed to be. He looked up at the sky and curled his lip. Sometimes he put his hands on his face. He was crying and didn't try to hide it. I thought

210

Rachel might have done one of her well-known random acts of kindness for him and won him over. She had a way of doing that with people.

A young couple pulled up in a car and stood next to the older man at Rachel's grave. The girl was in front of her boyfriend. She held her head low and the breeze tousled her curly black locks. The boy stood behind her, his arms circling her waist, as though he were holding her up. He rested his head on her shoulder.

People had left all kinds of new gadgets and do-dads at Rachel's grave—fresh flowers, teddy bears, balloons, cards and notes, ceramic angels, pinwheels. The epitaph under her name read, "She was the 'joy' of our lives." Corey DePooter's grave, next to hers, sported a similar new collection. The family of Steven Curnow had left red roses with a note that said something to the effect that they have gotten to know his family this year, and wish they could have known him. "You seemed like a really great kid."

I returned to the unmarked grave—which had been confirmed to me as Dylan's grave—and sat under a nearby tree. Of course, there were no flowers or pinwheels or angels anywhere near this grave. The grass had grown up, so it looked as though a grave didn't exist. But it did. Six feet down was a body, and no matter how hard people tried to forget that fact, it wasn't going to change that reality.

My thoughts returned to my first trip to Littleton, when emotions here were still raw and the grief so overwhelming. When I had returned home from that visit, two of my sons were nearly out the door on a trip of their own—to Colorado, ironically—for a wilderness adventure with their youth group.

They were gone for ten days, and I didn't remember much about it other than being afflicted with morbid thoughts about them dying, cold and alone, on their solo (a night and a day on their own), or their feet slipping on the face of a cliff, or their raft overturning in the rapids and carrying them down the river. Such perverse musings didn't dissipate even after their safe return. I found myself looking at their healthy, robust bodies and listening to their chatter, and thinking, *What if this is the last moment I stand in their bodily presence?* Ben would say things to Jon like, "You shoulda heard me lay the smack down in a conversation about why Superman is better than Batman." *What if I never heard "You shoulda heard me lay the smack down" from those lips again?*

My tortured mental state reached a crisis when the youth group sponsored a parents' night after the trip. Both of my sons had been asked to give a brief talk about their experiences, but Jon took more than his share of time. He described how the trip "really helped me understand the fear of God." He had been lying on the floor of the bus one night trying to sleep when a thunderstorm descended—"not like the thunderstorms here in Illinois. It was, like, nonstop lightning." He looked out the bus window and saw the power of the storm and he felt overcome by God's "awesomeness." He said he heard God speak to him in the storm, and the parents in the pews, myself included, were on the edge of our seats wondering what God said. I already had a lump in my throat. Then Jon told us what he heard God say: "I could smash you like an ant."

The congregation laughed out loud. I did, too. *That* was Jon's transcendent moment with God on the floor of the bus in the grip of a storm— *I could smash you like an ant?*

The youth pastor decided to pass up the message he had prepared because so many teens, my son chief among them, couldn't stop talking about Colorado. The evening ended with singing led by the students and their worship leader, a young man the kids called "Rejoice Boy." He went to the platform with guitar in hand, and two or three other musicians followed. Rejoice Boy said, "Everybody stand up. Let's praise God."

We obeyed. The youth-group kids stood as a bundle of T-shirts, shaved heads, dreadlocks, random piercings, and blue nail polish in the middle section of the sanctuary—against the improbable backdrop of refined molding, satin banners, and brass candelabras. Rejoice Boy bobbed up and down keeping time. He told us to take the pink insert from our bulletins and follow the words. Then he closed his eyes and played and sang.

I hadn't heard the song before, but the youth group knew it well and carried us. Their voices rose and sounded like one, except for the female voices that brought in the harmony. They sang, heads up, eyes closed, some with raised hands and their voices carrying what their hearts could not contain.

"Over all the earth You reign on high." I found the harmony and sang with the girls. In my heart I said, *Yes, Lord, you do reign.*

"Every mountain, stream, every sunset sky. . . . But my one request, Lord, my only aim is that you'd reign in me again." *I've lost myself in this story, Lord. Reign in me again.*

Rejoice Boy took us to the second verse. I was trying not to let tears fall, though it wasn't easy and getting harder.

"Lord, reign in me, reign in Your power. . . ." *I can honestly say that is my prayer, Lord. Reign in me, in all my weakness and confusion and exhaustion.*

"Over all my dreams, in my darkest hour. . . ." *What? I can't sing that.* I didn't sing it. *I don't want You to reign over my dreams; I don't want to think about "darkest hours." I have seen what that looks like in the faces of the Columbine parents. You reigned over their dreams and those dreams were shattered. I don't give you my dreams. I don't want you reigning over my darkest hour.*

212

Rejoice Boy sang, "You are the Lord of all I am . . . Over every thought, over every word."

I quit singing. The tears wouldn't stop.

The young people sang, "May my life reflect the beauty of my Lord. . . ." *Beauty? What beauty? Children lying dead on the floor of their high school?*

" 'Cause you mean more to me than any earthly thing. . . ." *I cannot sing those words.*

Rejoice Boy took us back to the chorus, "Lord, reign in me, reign in Your power, over all my dreams, in my darkest hour," and I cried in my heart, *You could smash me like an ant!*

I looked up. The singing youth wore their Wilderness T-shirts that read: "Do Not Fear What They Fear."

The song echoed in the sanctuary. "You are the Lord of all I am, won't you reign in me again . . . ?"[21]

"You Cannot Run from It"

Zach Johnston concluded his extensive Web posting, cited so often here, with this: "I had a dream of me being in the library. I thought to myself, 'My god, I'm going to die without a chance!'" In his dream, the killer pointed a gun at his forehead and Zach grabbed it. "Did I succeed in stopping him? Or did I perish? I keep thinking about how this could have been a possibility." Zach ended his posting: "Go ahead, blame the guns, the lack of metal detectors, the parents, the video games, the other students, the lack of religion in the schools, or whatever you fancy. But what happens when people who are not logical exist in our world? *This.* You cannot run from it."

That was exactly the feeling I had when I encountered the words to that song: You cannot run from it. I realized that even if every corner of our dark culture were swept clean, if every gun law was passed and enforced, if all parents knew exactly where their teens were at 11:00 P.M., there would always be something to fear that we couldn't outrun. Circumstances befall us in life that, like the trials of Job, have nothing to do with our goodness or badness, or how much control we think we wield. The Columbine mothers lamented, "All I did was send my kid off to school that day." Something will always remind us, as author John Updike has put it, "If this physical world is all, then it is a closed hell in which we are confined . . . like prisoners in chains, condemned to watch other prisoners being slain."[22]

In an essay in the *New Yorker,* Updike described how he had heard God through a thunderstorm, too. The storm had seemed as turbulent as the one my son encountered, but evoked a different response. At the time, Updike was in a hotel in Florence, Italy, near the great domed cathedral called the Duomo. He tossed in his bed with insomnia, feeling "fearful and adrift."

"While I watched, the rain intensified, rattling on tile roofs near and far; . . . I was not alone in the universe. The rippling rods of rain drove down upon the vertical beam of light at the base of the giant dome as if to demolish it; but the bulb, its pillar of light, the hulking old cathedral crouched like a stoic mute dragon, the thick tiles and gurgling gutters around me all could withstand the soaking, the thunder, the shuddering flashes of light. I was filled with a glad sense of exterior activity. God was at work—at ease, even. . . . All of this felt like a transaction, a rescue."

In the one storm, my son saw God as mighty and awesome and it elicited a sense of fear. In the other storm, Updike saw those very aspects of God's nature as proffering safety, comfort, and assurance.

I eventually sang the words to that song. It felt like a dagger going into my heart. And then it felt like a release, like a rescue. What was killing me was also saving me, as though I was being broken and finding strength in that broken place. Jon told me later that when he heard God say, "I could smash you like an ant," it didn't so much inspire fear that God might do it as bring into focus how frail humans are in the light of who God is. "It made me realize that there's no excuse for not doing what God wants me to do; that I shouldn't even be questioning God," he said. That God "could smash me like an ant" doesn't mean he's inclined to, but that his ways are higher than my ways, and I can't negotiate the terms.

That is why, at its heart, Columbine is a story about God—because it is a story about storms. It is about fearing that God will send us a storm that will smash us like an ant, and it is about searching for him there and then finding him. It is about being rescued from our fears.

The Only Thing Big Enough

As I sat near those graves during my last hours in Colorado and looked at the thirteen crosses of Columbine, I wondered how there could ever be enough flowers, pinwheels, and Jesus poems to compensate for this loss. There will never be enough blame. Brian Rohrbough had called the cross "a dangerous symbol." I had come to see that it *is* dangerous, not because it was used to memorialize murderers but because it is the only symbol that can bear the burden of doing so. Just as there never could be enough teddy bears or places to lay blame, there could be no end to the blood that would have to be shed to atone for this and all evils of this world. That is why God transferred that burden to his Son and his blood. The cross is the only symbol that depicts the price God paid to compensate for evil that seemingly knows no bounds. It is the picture of perfect justice. And that is why—regardless of the emotional aspects of the crosses at Littleton—theologically speaking, there have to be fifteen crosses.

The sixteenth-century reformer Martin Luther said, "Justice and mercy kiss at the cross." As the guilt, resting on God's Son, remits the justice we crave, it also delivers us from the justice we deserve. If we searched our hearts, we'd likely admit that, at the moment of death, we would probably pray something like Patti Nielson had when she thought she was about to be killed: "God, forgive me of my sins before I die." Even Job, the most righteous of men, recognized when he responded to God's challenge from a whirlwind that "I am nothing—how could I ever find the answers? I will put my hand over my mouth in silence."[23] So, as much as the cross is the picture of God's justice, it is also the picture of his mercy.

I understand why people put up only thirteen crosses. But from the vantage point of eternity, somewhere, somehow the number fifteen has to be reckoned with in all this. And it might as well be with the image of the cross, because whether on the side of justice or the side of mercy, that is where we all eventually meet, relinquishing our terms.

A dog had barked incessantly from a nearby residence during my reflections under that tree at the cemetery. I was annoyed: *Why don't they shut that dog up? Don't they realize people are mourning here?* But it was a rude reminder that life marches on. I packed my notebooks, film cartridges, and cassette tapes, walked to my car and took a final look at the thirteen crosses. I thought about heaven. C. S. Lewis wrote: "I think earth, if chosen instead of Heaven, will turn out to have been, all along, only a region in Hell: and earth, if put second to Heaven, to have been from the beginning a part of Heaven itself."[24]

I couldn't wait to get home. I wanted to taste the grilled ham-and-cheese sandwiches my husband makes and listen to my sons imitating Homer Simpson or celebrating accomplishments on the pommel horse or updating me on the latest movie worth seeing. I wanted to ride my bike and plant impatiens in my patio and watch the sun's rays stream through my window. Dave Sanders and the students who died at Columbine had taught me that normalcy is a foretaste of heaven. And heaven is nearer than you think.

Notes

Chapter 1

1. Nancy Gibbs, ". . . In Sorrow and Disbelief," *Time*, 3 May 1999, p. 25.
2. Ford Fessesden, "They Threaten, Seethe and Unhinge, Then Kill in Quantity," *New York Times*, 9 April 2000, p. 20. This was the first of a four-part special series the *Times* ran on the results of its own investigation of one hundred rampage attacks over the past fifty years.
3. Ibid., p. 1.
4. Nancy Gibbs, "Noon in the Garden of Good and Evil," *Time*, 17 May 1999, p. 54.
5. Kevin Simpson, "Cross-Bearer Gets Cold Reception," DenverPost.com, 20 November 1999. www.denverpost.com/news/shot1120a.htm.
6. Staff and wire reports, "Churches Grow After Tragedy," DenverPost.com, 17 July 1999. www.denverpost.com/news/shot0717.htm.
7. Columbine High School is not in Littleton. Littleton is in Arapahoe County and has its own school district. Columbine High School, like much of the southwest metropolitan Denver area, has been designated a Littleton mailing address.

Chapter 2

1. Michelle Oetter, "The John Tomlin I Knew," *Rachel's Journal*, January 2000, p. 17. This magazine is now out of print.
2. www.everwonder.com/david/rebldomakr. This site contains material that may be offensive to some. Please note: This is not Zach Johnston's Web site. The original site where I found this posting no longer exists.
3. www.rockymountainnews.com/shooting/report/columbinereport/pages/suspects_text.htm.
4. Mark Obmascik, "Through the Eyes of Survivors," *DenverPost.com*, 13 June 1999, p. 3. www.denverpost.com/news/shot0613a.htm.
5. Ibid., p. 1.
6. Lisa Levitt Ryckman and Mike Anton, "Mundane Gave Way to Madness," *InsideDenver.com*, 25 April 1999, pp.4–5. www.insidedenver.com/shooting/0425xsho1.shtml.
7. The testimonies of Seth Houy and Crystal Woodham were recorded on a video presentation made by the youth group of West Bowles Community Church, which Cassie Bernall had attended, shortly after the shooting.

8. Obmascik, "Survivors," p. 7.

9. According to Valeen Schnurr, she was shot before, not after, she was asked, "Do you believe in God?"

10. Lisa Levitt Ryckman, "The Girl in the Picture," *InsideDenver.com*, 27 June 1999, p. 2. www.insidedenver.com/shooting/0627/jess1.shtml.

11. Obmascik, "Survivors," p. 9.

12. Ibid., p. 8.

13. Nancy Gibbs, ". . . in Sorrow and Disbelief," *Time*, 3 May 1999, 31.

14. Woody Paige, "Library Survivor Breaks Silence," *DenverPost.com*, 12 June 1999. www.denverpost.com/news/shot0612.htm. The following several paragraphs recounting Nielson's ordeal are taken from this article.

15. The killers had actually returned to the library to kill themselves around noon.

16. Dick Foster, "Mourners Recall Respectful Teen," *InsideDenver.com*, 24 April 1999, p. 1. www.insidedenver.com/shooting/0424funr2.shtml.

17. Charles Spurgeon, *Morning and Evening* (Grand Rapids: Zondervan, 1955, 1976), pp. 224–225.

Chapter 3

1. April Washington, "Carpenter Removes Crosses He Had Erected for the Dead," *RockyMountainNews.com*, 3 May 1999, p. 1. www.insidedenver.com/shooting/0503cros7.shtml.

2. Joel Patenaude, "Way of the Cross," *Aurora Beacon News*, 19–25 May 1999, sec. A, p. 4.

3. C. S. Lewis, *Mere Christianity* (New York: MacMillan, 1943), p. 58.

4. Ibid., p. 57.

5. N. T. Wright, *The Lord & His Prayer*, (Grand Rapids: Eerdmans, 1996), p. 69. Wright credits this analogy to Albert Schweitzer.

6. Ibid., p. 68.

7. Ibid., pp. 71–72.

Chapter 4

1. Pam Belluck and Jodi Wilgoren, "Caring Parents, No Answers, In Columbine Killers' Past," *New York Times*, 29 June 1999, sec. A, p. 16.

2. Lynn Bartels and Carla Crowder, "Fatal Friendship," *InsideDenver.com*, 22 August 1999. www.insidedenver.com/shooting/0822fatal.shtml.

3. Kevin Simpson and Jason Blevins, "Mystery How Team Players Became Loners," *DenverPost.com*, 23 April 1999, p. 1. www.denverpost.com/news/shot0423d.htm.

4. Bartels and Crowder, "Fatal," p. 4.

5. Belluck and Wilgoren, "Caring," sec. A, p. 16.

6. Ibid.

7. Ibid.

8. Eric Pooley, "Portrait of a Deadly Bond," *Time*, 10 May 1999, 30.

9. Simpson and Blevins, "Mystery," p. 1.

10. Pooley, "Portrait," p. 30.

11. A study in the *American Journal of Psychiatry* states that "this drug can induce mania in some patients when it is given in normal doses," September 1991, p. 1264.

12. Michael Wolff, "Why Your Kids Know More About the Future Than You Do," *New York,* 17 May 1999, p. 30.

13. Spoken at the 1998 Princeton Lectures on Youth, Church, and Culture; published as "Youth Between Late Modernity and Postmodernity," in *Growing Up Postmodern: Imitating Christ in the Age of 'Whatever',* (Princeton: Institute for Youth Ministry, Princeton Theological Seminary, 1999), p. 33.

14. In his essay "How 'I' Moved Heaven and Earth," *New York Times Magazine,* 17 October 1999, p. 87, Richard Russo asserts that the entire twentieth century could be called the "Me Millennium." He writes: "Indeed the long historical view suggests that the 'Me Decade' of the 1970s was little more than a particularly virulent manifestation of a 600-year philosophical trend. We're living at the tag end of the 'Me Millennium.'" This chapter highlights the "virulent manifestations" of this trend as they played out in the last decades of the 1900s.

15. 6 April 1966.

16. Susan Littwin, *The Postponed Generation* (New York: William Morrow, 1986), pp. 19, 22.

17. Also duly noted by Wolff, "Why Your Kids," p. 30.

18. This term was coined by authors William Strauss and Neil Howe in their book *Generations* (New York: William Morrow, 1991).

19. Ibid., pp. 321–326. Between 1960 and 1980, when these people were being born, the percentage of mothers with children under five who entered the workforce, full- or part-time, increased from 20 to 47 percent. The number of latchkey kids doubled in the 1970s. Parents of Gen Xers were twice as likely to get divorced than their forbears. Generation X has been the most aborted and the most incarcerated generation in American history.

20. Andrew Guy Jr. and Janet Bingham, "Minorities Are Columbine, Too," *Denver-Post.com,* 25 July 1999, p. 2. www.denverpost.com/news/shot0725.htm.

21. Taken from the school's Web page.

22. Wolff, "Why Your Kids," p. 30.

23. Denby, in "Buried Alive," *The New Yorker,* 15 July 1996, writes, "The media have become three-dimensional, inescapable, omnivorous, and self-referring—a closed system that seems, for many of the kids, to answer all their questions," p. 51. He writes elsewhere in the article, "How do you control what they breathe?" p. 49.

24. Roberto Rivera, "Nothing, Nihilism, and Videotape," *AFA Journal* (February 2000): 19. The work by Thomas Hibbs that Rivera cites is *Shows About Nothing: Nihilism in Popular Culture from The Exorcist to Seinfeld,* (Dallas: Spence Publishing, 1999).

25. Rivera, "Nothing," p. 19.

26. Geoffrey Cowley, "Why Children Turn Violent," *Newsweek,* 6 April 1998, p. 25.

27. Rivera, "Nothing," p. 19.

28. Kristen Go, "Web Sites Worship Teen Killers," *DenverPost.com,* 14 December 1999, p. 1. www.denverpost.com/news/news1214h.htm.

29. Wendy Murray Zoba, "Tough Love Saved Cassie," *Christianity Today,* 4 October 1999, p. 43.

30. Denby, "Buried," p. 51.

31. Sharon Begley, "Why the Young Kill," *Newsweek,* 3 May 1999, p. 34.

32. Peter Applebome, "No Room for Children in a World of Little Adults," *New York Times,* 10 May 1998, sec. 4, p. 1.

33. Bruce Orwell, "Cut the Cute Stuff: Kids Flock to Adult Flicks," *Wall Street Journal,* 29 August 1997, sec. B, p. 6.

34. Carrie Stetler, "Girls Find Comfort in Teen Magazines," *Religion News Service,* 10 June 1996, p. 11.

35. Peggy Orenstein, "One Hundred Years of Adolescence," *New York Times Book Review,* 5 October 1997, p. 25.

36. Ron Stodghill II, "Where'd You Learn *That?*" *Time,* 15 June 1998, p. 52.

37. Ibid., p. 54.

38. Ibid.

39. Anne Jarrell, "The Face of Teenage Sex Grows Younger," *New York Times,* 3 April 2000, sec. B, p. 1.

40. Ibid., sec. B, p. 8.

41. Stephen S. Hall, "The Bully in the Mirror," *New York Times Magazine,* 22 August 1999.

42. Ibid., p. 33.

43. Ibid., p. 35.

44. Ibid., p. 33.

45. Ibid., p. 32.

46. Adrian Nicole LeBlanc, "The Outsiders," *New York Times Magazine,* 22 August 1999, p. 38.

47. Ibid., pp. 38–39.

48. Jeff Brazil, "Play Dough," *American Demographics,* December 1999, p. 59.

49. Ibid., p. 58. The author notes that "allowance" is used broadly to include money given as a weekly sum, for doing chores, and general handouts. Researcher Jay Zagorsky was shocked when he studied the results of a 1997 U.S. Department of Labor-sponsored survey. His results confirmed that figure.

50. Ibid.

51. Dale Russakoff, "Birth of a New Boom," *Washington Post National Weekly Edition,* 28 September 1998, p. 6

52. Brazil, "Play Dough," p. 59.

53. Ibid.

54. Stacey Schultz, "Talk to Kids About Drugs? Parents Just Don't Do It," *U.S. News and World Report,* 7 February 2000, p. 56.

55. Mike A. Males, "Five Myths, and Why Adults Believe They Are True," *New York Times,* 29 April 1998, p. 9.

56. Stodghill, "Where'd," p. 57.

57. Patricia Hersch, *A Tribe Apart* (New York: Ballantine, 1998), p. 19.

58. Ibid., pp. 18, 20.

59. Cowley, "Why Children," p. 25.

60. Schultz, "Talk," p. 57.

61. Richard Rodriguez, "Growing Up Fast," *U.S. News and World Report,* 7 April 1997, p. 67.

62. Ibid., p. 62.

63. Led by Paul Vitz; the report from the Council on Families is called "The Course of True Love."

64. Martin Marty, "Youth Between Later Modernity and Postmodernity," *Growing Up Postmodern: Imitating Christ in the Age of 'Whatever'* (Princeton: Institute for Youth Ministry, Princeton Theological Seminary, 1999), pp. 35–36.

65. Lewis H. Lapham, "In the Garden of Tabloid Delight," *Harpers,* August 1997, p. 43.

66. David Denby, "Buried Alive," *New Yorker,* 15 July 1996, p. 48.

67. 17 October 1999.

68. Ibid., pp. 87, 89. Russo also writes: "The millennium has also suggested that it is easier to evict God from the Big House than it is to find a new tenant, someone to collect the rent from the rest of us who have for so long dwelt in the servants quarters."

69. Elissa Haney, "Lessons in Violence," *Infoplease.com,* www.infoplease.com/spot/ schoolviolence1.html and Richard Lacayo, "Toward the Root of the Evil," *Time,* 6 April 1998, pp. 38–39

70. Gordon Witkin, Mike Tharp, Joannie M. Schrof, Thomas Toch, and Christy Scattarella, "Again," *U.S. News and World Report,* 1 June 1998, p. 16.

71. Cowley, p. 24.

72. Ibid.

73. Sharon Begley, "Why the Young Kill," *Newsweek,* 3 May 1999, p. 35.

74. Lacayo, "Toward," p. 38.

75. C. S. Lewis, *The Abolition of Man* (New York: MacMillan, 1947), p. 29.

76. Ibid., pp. 33, 34, 39.

77. Russo, *New York Times Magazine,* 17 October 1999, p. 88.

Chapter 5

1. Misty Bernall, *She Said Yes* (Farmington: Plough, 1999), p. 72–73.

2. Ibid., p. 63.

3. Ibid., pp. 97–98.

4. Matt Labash, "'Do You Believe In God?' 'Yes.'," *Weekly Standard,* 10 May 1999, p. 21.

5. The explosion the Bernalls heard was a bomb that detonated in the southwest parking lot of the school at 10:36 P.M.

6. Mark Obmascik, "Bloodbath leaves 15 dead, 28 hurt," *DenverPost.com,* 21 April 1999, p. 1. www.denverpost.com/news/shot0420a.htm.

7. Julian Prodis Sulek and Tracy Seipel, "Death, in a Flash—and a Whim," *The San Jose Mercury News Online,* 21 April 1999, p. 3.www.mercurycenter.com/nation/shooting/ reconstruct.htm.

8. Lisa Levitt Ryckman and Mike Anton, "Mundane Gave Way to Madness," *Inside-Denver.com,* 25 April 1999, p. 6. www.insidedenver.com/shooting/0425xsho1.shtml

9. Rebecca Jones, "Girl Did Not Forsake God," *InsideDenver.com,* 27 April, p. 2. www.insidedenver.com/shooting/0427val1.shtml. Mark Schnurr, Valeen's father, told me that this report was inaccurate and that he called Rebecca Jones to alert her to it. She does not recall that conversation.

10. Nancy Gibbs, ". . . In Sorrow and Disbelief," *Time,* 3 May 1999, pp. 25, 30.

11. Matthew Heimer, "Adding Up the Facts," *Brill's Content,* July/August 1999, p. 73.

12. Labash, "'Do You," pp. 21–22.

13. J. Bottum, "A Martyr Is Born," *Weekly Standard,* 10 May 1999, p. 12.

14. Dave Cullen, "I Smell the Presence of Satan," *Salon.com,* 15 May 1999, p. 2. www.salon.com/news/feature/1999/05/15/evangelicals/index.html.

15. Nancy Gibbs, "Noon in the Garden of Good and Evil," *Time,* 17 May 1999, p. 54.

16. Woody Paige, "Library Survivor Breaks Silence," *DenverPost.com,* 12 June 1999, p. 4. www.denverpost.com/news/shot0612.htm.

17. Mark Obmascik, "Through the Eyes of Survivors," *DenverPost.com,* 13 June 1999, pp. 8–9. www.denverpost.com/news/shot0613a.htm.

18. David Van Biema, "A Surge of Teen Spirit," *Time*, 31 May 1999, p. 58.

19. Kenneth L. Woodward, "The Making of a Martyr," *Newsweek*, 14 June 1999, p. 64.

20. These interviews and the one that follows with Dee Dee McDermott were documented by Plough in a report titled, "Excerpts from the Background Material and Selected News Stories Recounting the Dialogue Between Cassie Bernall and her Killer on April 20, 1999," used here with permission from Plough.

21. Bernall, *She Said Yes*, "From the Publisher," a note before the table of contents.

22. *Salon.com*, 23 September 1999. www.salon.com/news/feature/1999/09/23/columbine/.

23. Dave Cullen, "Inside the Columbine High Investigation," pp. 1.1,2.

24. Ibid., p. 2.1.

25. Ibid., p. 2.2.

26. Dan Luzadder and Katie Kerwin McCrimmon, "Accounts Differ on Question to Bernall," *InsideDenver.com*, 24 September 1999, p. 2. www.rockymountainnews.com/shooting/0924cass1.shtml.

27. Susan Besze Wallace, "Faith in Cassie's Last Words Wavers," *DenverPost.com*, 25 September 1999, p. 1. www.denverpost.com/news/shot0925.htm.

28. Dave Cullen, "Who Said 'Yes'?" *Salon.com*, 30 September 1999, p. 2.1. www.salon.com/news/feature/1999/09/30/bernall/index.html.

29. Hanna Rosin, "Columbine Miracle: A Matter of Belief," *Washington Post*, 14 October 1999, sec. C, p. 1.

30. Mary Schmich and Eric Zorn, "Saintly Legend May Live Long Past Columbine Facts," *Chicago Tribune*, 20 October 1999, sec. 2, p. 1.

31. Jon Carroll, "She Didn't Say Anything," *San Francisco Chronicle* online edition, 4 October 1999, p. 1.

32. Ronnie Polaneczky, "The Truth About Cassie," *Philadelphia Daily News*, online version, 4 October 1999, p. 1–2.

33. Nancy Gibbs and Timothy Roche, "The Columbine Tapes," *Time*, 20 December 1999, p. 48.

Chapter 6

1. According to a posting on the Jefferson County Sheriff's Office Web site, www.jeffcosheriff.com/columbine.htm.

2. Steve Myers, "'It was unbelievable craziness,'" *InsideDenver.com*, 28 April 1999, p. 1. www.rockymountainnews.com/shooting/0428paul3.shtml.

3. Woody Paige, "Library Survivor Breaks Silence," *Denver Post Online*, 12 June 1999. www.denverpost.com/news/shot0612.htm.

4. In *Time* magazine, 20 December 1999, p. 48.

5. David B. Kopel, "What If We Had Taken Columbine Seriously?" *Weekly Standard*, 24 April/1 May 2000, p. 20.

6. Ibid.

7. Ibid., p. 21.

8. Barbara Vobejda, Cheryl W. Thompson, and David B. Ottaway, "Response in Littleton Was Swift but Unsure," *WashingtonPost.com*, 12 May 1999, sec. A, p. 1. www.washingtonpost.com/wp-srv/nat...m/juvmurders/stories/littleton051297.htm.

9. Peter G. Chronis, "Columbine Chaos Spurs Radio Upgrades," *Denver Post Online*, 8 November 1999, p. 1. www.denverpost.com/news/news1108d.htm.

10. Vobejda, "Response," sec. A, p. 1.

11. Ibid.

12. Lisa Levitt Ryckman and Mike Anton, "Mundane Gave Way to Madness," *Inside-Denver.com*, 25 April 1999, p. 2. www.rockymountainnews.com/shooting/0425xsho1.shtml.

13. Ibid., p. 6.

14. Mark Obmascik, "Through the Eyes of Survivors," *Denver Post Online*, 13 June 1999, pp. 8–9.

15. Ibid., p. 11.

16. Ibid.

17. Ibid.

18. Ryckman and Anton, "Mundane," p. 7.

19. Ibid.

20. Ibid.

21. Gerard Wright, "The Comeback Kid," *Life*, January 2000, p. 48.

22. Ryckman and Anton, "Mundane," p. 8.

23. Ibid.

24. Ibid.

25. Vobejda, "Response," p. 6.

26. Nancy Gibbs and Timothy Roche, "The Columbine Tapes," *Time*, 20 December 1999, p. 49.

27. Lynn Bartels, " 'It's Dylan' Starts Spiral of Misery," *InsideDenver.com*, 29 April 1999, p. 2. www.rockymountainnews.com/shooting/0429tell2.shtml.

28. Mike Anton and Lisa Levitt Ryckman, "In Hindsight, Signs to Killings Obvious," *InsideDenver.com*, 2 May 1999, p. 3. www.rockymountainnews.com/shooting/0502why10.shtml.

29. Ibid.

30. Eric Pooley, "Portrait of a Deadly Bond," *Time*, 10 May 1999, p. 31.

31. Lynn Bartels and Carla Crowder, "Fatal Friendship," *RockyMountainNews.com*, 22 August, 1999, p. 15. www.rockymountainnews.com/shooting/0822fata1.shtml.

32. Ibid.

33. Ibid.

34. Ibid.

35. Anton and Ryckman, "In Hindsight," p. 3.

36. Sue Lindsay, "Harris Complaint 'Cried Out' for Probe," *InsideDenver.com*, 10 May 1999, pp. 1–2. www.rockymountainnews.com/shooting1051prob3.shtml.

37. Ibid., pp. 2–3.

38. Charles Able, "Couple Seeks To Recall Sheriff," *InsideDenver.com*, 3 February 2000, p. 2. www.rockymountainnews.com/shooting/0203reca1.shtml.

39. Kevin Vaughan, "Klebold Family Plans to Sue Jeffco," *InsideDenver.com*, 16 October 1999, p. 2. www.rockymountainnews.com/shooting/1016fami1.shtml.

40. Howard Pankratz, "Police Reveal Killers' Videos," *Denver Post Online*, 11 November 1999, p. 1. www.denverpost.com/news/shot1111.htm.

41. Marilyn Robinson and Peter G. Chronis, "Sheriff's Office Criticized for Leaking Tapes," *Denver Post Online*, 14 December 1999, p. 1. www.denverpost.com/news/news1214a.htm.

42. Kevin Simpson, "Victim's Families Feel Victimized Again by Release, Excuses," *Denver Post Online*, 14 December 1999, p. 1. www.denverpost.com/news/news1214f.htm.

43. Ibid.

44. Ibid., p. 2.

45. Charles Able and Kevin Vaughan, "Sheriff: 'The buck stops here'," *InsideDenver.com*, 15 December 1999, p. 1. www.rockymountainnews.com/shooting/1215ston1.shtml.

46. Simpson, "Victimized Again," p. 1.

47. Ibid., p. 3.

48. Carlos Illescas, "Viewing Brings Pain, Some Answers," *Denver Post Online,* 14 December, 1999, pp.1–2. www.denverpost.com/news/news1214i.htm.

49. Simpson, "Victimized Again," p. 2.

50. Illescas, "Some Answers," p. 2.

51. Lynn Bartels, "'They've Got Their Hell . . . I've Got Mine,'" *InsideDenver.com,* 15 December 1999, p. 3. www.rockymountainnews.com/shooting/1215room2.shtml.

52. Peggy Lowe, "Family of Girl Harris Named Lives in Fear of Tapes' Release," *Denver Post Online,* 21 December 1999, p. 2. www.denverpost.com/news/shot1221b.htm.

53. Trent Selbert, "Painful Vindication for Klebolds," *Denver Post Online,* 14 December 1999, p. 1. www.denverpost.com/news/news1214g.htm.

54. Peggy Lowe, "Facts Clarify But Can't Justify Killers' Acts," *Denver Post Online,* 12 March 2000, p. 3. www.denverpost.com/news/shot0312c.htm.

55. Ibid.

56. Peggy Lowe, "Victims Call for Stone's Job," *Denver Post Online,* 21 December 1999, p. 1. www.denverpost.com/news/shot1221a.htm.

57. Ibid., pp. 1–2. All of the information about who was in attendance at this gathering came from this article.

58. Tom Foreman, "Columbine, By the Minute," *ABCNews.com,* 2 May 2000, p. 2. www.abcnews.go.com/sections/us/dailynews/columbine_foreman000502.html.

59. Until the ballistics reports and autopsies are made public, a definitive determination cannot be made as to who might have survived their wounds had rescue been immediate.

60. This conversation took place on 13 January 2000. I left Littleton without seeing the videos. My subsequent persistent attempts to gain access were derailed when lawsuits were filed to keep the videos under wraps.

61. Phone interview, 21 February 2000.

62. Ibid.

63. Howard Pankratz, "Police Passed Up Shot at Klebold, One Lawsuit Says," *Denver Post,* 20 April 2000, sec. A, p. 14.

64. Ibid.

Chapter 7

1. Gerard Wright, "The Comeback Kid," *Life,* January 2000, p. 50.

2. "Small Steps," *People,* 30 August 1999, p. 54.

3. Ibid., p. 56.

4. Andy Vuong, "Wounded Student Back from the Brink," *Denver Post Online,* 27 January 2000, p. 1. www.denverpost.com/news/shot0127.htm.

5. John C. Ensslin, "Columbine Victim: Faith Saved My Life," *InsideDenver.com,* 27 January 2000, p. 1. www.rockymountainnews.com/shooting/0127tay14.shtml.

6. Lyrics and music by Jonathan and Stephen Cohen.

7. Excerpted from www.disastercenter.com/Student.html, pp. 4, 5.

8. "'You Are Not Alone': Nation Mourns with Littleton," *CNN.com,* 25 April 1999, p. 1. www.cnn.com/us/9904/25/shooting.memorial/.

9. Foster's remarks were made to the Denver Interfaith Clergy Alliance, covered by Valerie Richardson, "Evangelical Tone of Memorial Spurs Backlash," *Washington Times,* 30 April 1999. I got the article through *FreeRepublic.com* at www.freerepublic.com/forum/a372c874112ae.htm, p. 2.

10. Ibid.

11. Ibid., p. 1.

12. Virginia Culver, "Sunday Event Offended Some," *Denver Post Online,* 29 April 1999, p. 1. www.denverpost.com/news/shot0429h.htm.

13. Dave Cullen, "'I Smell the Presence of Satan,'" *Salon.com,* 15 May 1999, p. 1.3. www.salon.com/news/feature/1999/05/15/evangelicals/index.html.

14. Richardson, "Evangelical," p. 2.

15. Ibid.

16. Steve Rabey, "Videos of Hate," *Christianity Today,* 7 February 2000, p. 21.

17. Phone interview, 14 March 2000.

18. Rabey, "Videos," p. 21.

19. Dave Cullen, "Rutherford Institute Sues Columbine Officials," *Salon.com,* 7 October 1999, p. 2.1. www.salon.com/news/feature/1999/10/07/columbine/index.html.

20. Cassie Bernall's youth group video.

21. Lisa Levitt Ryckman, "The Girl in the Picture," *Inside Denver.com,* 27 June 1999, p. 6. www.rockymountainnews.com/shooting/0627jess1.shtml.

22. Some translations render it "seventy-seven times," but the meaning is the same.

23. "Could He Have Done More?" *Time,* 20 December 1999, p. 48.

24. David Cullen, "The Principal," *5280* online version, August/September 1999, p. 3. www.5280pub.com/library/0899/principal.html.

25. Ibid., p. 2.

26. Ibid., pp. 1, 2

27. Ibid.

28. Jeffery Rosen, "Is Nothing Secular?" *New York Times Magazine,* 30 January 2000.

29. Ibid., p. 40.

30. Ibid., p. 42.

31. Ibid., p. 44.

32. Ibid.

33. Ibid.

34. Ibid., p. 40.

35. Recent Supreme Court rulings have both validated and contradicted this assertion. In June 2000 the Court ruled in *Mitchell* v. *Helms,* by a six to three margin, that it is constitutional for the government to provide computers and other educational materials to religious schools. Stephen Lazarus, Social Policy Research Associate at the Center for Public Justice (CPJ) wrote: "The Court is beginning to acknowledge more fully the rightful place of religion in schools in American Society." (Stephen Lazarus, "One Step Forward," *Capital Commentary,* 17 July 2000, p. 2, from the web site of CPJ: www.cpjustice.org/CapCom/ARCHIVE/7.17.00.html.)

Keith Pavilschek, a fellow at CPJ, agrees, but only in part. In a phone interview he said, "The Court has certainly been more willing, in a string of decisions, to allow a permissible attitude for aid and funding for parochial and Christian schools and, more generally, to allow a narrower understanding of the establishment clause in not striking those [decisions] down. But," he said, "the Court is becoming more restrictive of the visibility of religion in public schools and increasingly unwilling to allow public religious expression because it gives the impression of an endorsement."

Pavilschek cites the ruling in *Santa Fe* v. *Doe* (June 2000) that outlaws prayers and other religious expressions by students, even voluntary student-led prayer, during extracurricular activities.

He agrees that a paradigm shift has taken place in the courts, and acknowledges the willingness to support religiously-based organizations that serve a broader public good. He is less optimistic, however, about religious expression generally in the public schools. See his article, "Public Schools, Prayer and Creatures of the State," *Capital Commentary*, 3 July 2000 from the cpj web site: www.cpjustice.org/CapCom/ARCHIVE/7.3.00.html.

36. Hanna Rosin, "Winning by the Book," *Washington Post*, 21 June 1999, sec. A, p. 3.

37. Ibid.

38. Ibid.

39. Ibid.

40. Camille Paglia, "American Poison," *Salon.com*, 28 April 1999, p. 2. www.salon.com/people/col/pagl/1999/04/28/camille/index.html.

41. Ibid., p. 3.

42. Richard Russo, "How 'I' Moved Heaven and Earth," *New York Times Magazine*, 17 October 1999, p. 87.

43. Paglia, "Poison," p. 2.

44. C. S. Lewis, *The Abolition of Man* (New York: MacMillan, 1947), p. 39.

45. Friedrich Nietzsche, *The Will to Power* (New York: Vintage, 1968), p. 10.

Chapter 8

1. C. S. Lewis, *The Problem of Pain* (New York: MacMillan, 1962), p. 24.

2. The study was published in a series of four articles between April 9 and 12, 2000. The lives of 102 killers were examined.

3. Ford Fessenden, "They Threaten, Seethe and Unhinge, Then Kill in Quantity," *New York Times*, 9 April 2000, sec. A, pp. 1, 20, 21

4. Ford Fessenden, "How Youngest Killers Differ: Peer Support," *New York Times*, 9 April 2000, sec. A, p. 21.

5. Ibid.

6. Laurie Goodstein and William Glaberson, "The Well-Marked Roads to Homicidal Rage," *New York Times*, 10 April 2000, sec. A, p. 12.

7. Ibid.

8. William Glaberson, "Man and His Son's Slayer Unite to Ask Why," *New York Times*, 12 April 2000, sec. A, p. 22.

9. Ibid.

10. Goodstein and Glaberson, "Well-Marked."

11. Ibid.

12. Glaberson, "Man and His Son's."

13. 7 April 2000.

14. Dave Cullen, "Goodbye, Cruel World," *Salon.com*, 14 December 1999, pp. 1, 2. www.salon.com/news/feature/1999/12/14/videos/index1.html.

15. Peggy Lowe, "Facts Clarify But Can't Justify Killers' Acts," *Denver Post Online*, 12 March 2000, p. 3. www.denverpost.com/news/shot0312c.htm.

16. Dan Luzadder and Kevin Vaughan, "The Biggest Question of All," *RockyMountainNews.com*, 14 December 1999, p. 2. The article says, "In the months ahead, Battan would come to see this as the quintessential philosophy of the two boys." www.rockymountainnews.com/shooting/1214coll.shtml.

17. Lowe, "Facts."

18. John Whitehead, "Who's Afraid of the Exorcist?" *Gadfly*, October 1998, p. 15.

19. Ibid.

20. Ibid., p. 37.

21. John Whitehead, "Love Story, an Interview with *Exorcist* Author William Peter Blatty," *Gadfly,* October 1998, p. 19.

22. Ibid., p. 20.

23. Spoken by Craig Scott on a television special aired in Denver on 20 April 2000.

24. Valeen was speaking at a Torchgrab rally held in Littleton, 6 August 1999.

25. Mark 5:1–20; some Bibles refer to the region of the Gerasenes instead of the Gadarenes.

26. N. T. Wright, *The Lord & His Prayer* (Grand Rapids: Eerdmans, 1996), pp. 71, 72.

27. Ibid., p. 74.

28. Quoted in *She Said Yes* (Farmington: Plough, 1999), p. 106.

29. Television special.

30. Testimony of an unnamed student on the video made by Cassie Bernall's youth group shortly after the shooting.

31. Ibid.

32. William Safire, *The First Dissent: The Book of Job in Today's Politics* (New York: Random House, 1991), p. 14.

33. Ben C. Ollenburger, "If Mortals Die, Will They Live Again? The Old Testament and Resurrection," *Ex Auditu* 9 (1993): 29–44. Ollenburger presents this traditional view in a survey of the entire Old Testament; still he asserts that even in the Old Testament it is God—not death—who reigns. Likewise, in addition to this passage in Job, the books of Daniel and Ezekiel also offer glimmers of insight that provide a basis for hope in the afterlife.

34. The interpretation hinges upon the verb *niqqepu,* in verse 26a, which can be rendered either to "strip off"—as in "after my skin is stripped off" (suggesting a resurrected body) or "shriveled up" and so "marred beyond recognition."

35. John E. Hartley, *The Book of Job,* The New International Commentary on the Old Testament, (Grand Rapids: Eerdmans, 1988), pp. 292–293.

36. Wright, *The Lord,* pp. 69–71.

37. Ibid.

Chapter 9

1. Excerpts as they appear here are verbatim accounts Darrell Scott read to me from Rachel's journals in July 1999, unless otherwise noted.

2. Beth Nimmo and Darrell Scott, *Rachel's Tears* (Nashville: Thomas Nelson, 2000), p. 164.

3. Craig was speaking at a Teen Town Meeting held in Littleton shortly after the shootings.

4. "Isaiah's Last Moments," *Extra Daily News* (online), 22 April 1999, p. 1. www.extratv.com/cmp/spotlight/1999/04–22f.htm recounting the interview Craig Scott and Michael Shoels conducted on NBC's *Today* show with Katie Couric, 22 April 1999.

5. Additional excerpts from the Couric interview were taken from Laura Berman's, "Classmates Say Goodbye to Fun-Loving True Friend," *Detroit News* (online), 25 April 1999, p. 2. www.detnews.com/1999/nation/9904/25/04250081/htm.

6. Taken from the funeral transcript of Pastor Bruce Porter as it appeared on the Web site of Leadership U at www.leaderu.com/common/funeral/html.

7. J. Bottum, "Awakening at Littleton," *First Things* (online version), August/September 1999, p. 3. www.firstthings.com/ftissues/ft9908/articles/bottum.html

8. Diocletian (A.D. 284–305) was one of four tetrarchs who each ruled "corners" of the Roman Empire. The others included Galerius (selected by Diocletian) and Maximian and Constantius Chlorus (selected by Maximian, and father of the Christian emperor Constantine); the latter was the only one who did not undertake the systematic persecution of the Christians, and in fact helped to rescue many.

9. Paul L. Maier, *Eusebius, The Church History* (Grand Rapids: Kregel, 1999), p. 298.

10. Ibid., pp. 300–302.

11. "Perpetua" in Musurillo, pp. 126–27 as cited in Joyce E. Salisbury's *Perpetua's Passion* (New York: Routledge, 1997), p. 138.

12. Ibid., p. 142; citing Musurillo, p. 129.

13. Ibid., p. 147; citing Musurillo, p. 131.

14. Bottum, "Awakening," p. 3.

15. Ibid., p. 2.

16. Ralph P. Martin, "Martyr, Martyrology," in *The New International Dictionary of the Christian Church*, ed. J. D. Douglas (Grand Rapids: Zondervan-Regency, 1978), p. 638.

17. Herbert Lockyer, *Last Words of Saints and Sinners* (Grand Rapids: Kregel, 1969), p. 138.

18. They are Generational-cycle watchers who have cowritten many books on trends in generations, the most recent being *Millenials Rising* (New York: Vintage, 2000).

19. Phone interview, Fall 1996.

20. Staff and wire reports, "Churches Grow After Tragedy," *Denver Post Online*, 17 July 1999, p. 1. www.denverpost.com/news/shot0717.htm.

21. Lisa Miller, "Rebels With a Cause," *Wall Street Journal*, 18 December 1998, sec. W, p. 1.

22. "Teenagers Embrace Religion but Are Not Excited About Christianity," *Barna Research Online*, 11 January 2000, pp. 3–4. www.barna.org/cgi_bin/PagePress Release.asp?PressReleaseID=42

23. Leslie Petrovski, "Teens Find Unconventional Religion," *Denver Post Online*, 28 April 1999, p. 2. www.denverpost.com/life/teen0428c.htm.

24. "Teenagers Embrace," p. 4.

25. 8 May 2000.

26. John Leland, "Searching for a Holy Spirit," *Newsweek.com*, 8 May 2000, p. 2. www.newsweek.com/nw-srv/printed/us/so/a19272-2000apr30.htm.

27. Miller, "Rebels," sec. W, p. 14.

28. These observations came out of the research I did for my book *Generation 2K* (Downers Grove: InterVarsity Press, 1999), particularly chapters 5 and 6.

29. This popular song in contemporary Christian music circles includes the lyrics, "I'm going to heaven; we're going to heaven; our tickets are all paid to heaven that God made, so good-bye blue Monday, no pain on Sonday."

30. dc Talk and The Voice of the Martyrs, *Jesus Freaks* (Tulsa: Albury Publishing, 1999), pp. 34, 35.

31. Leland, "Searching," p. 1.

32. Spoken at the Torchgrab youth rally held in Littleton in August 1999.

33. Jim Jones, "'It Was All God,' Says Teen who Defied Ashbrook," *Fort Worth Star-Telegram*, on-line version, 1 October 1999, p. 1. www.star-telegram.com/news/doc/1047/1:99fwshoot174/1:99fwshoot174100199.html.

Chapter 10

1. The poems appear in the self-published book, *Screams Aren't Enough,* O'Neill Publishing, 2000.

2. This is a short excerpt from the poem used with permission from Devon Adams.

3. Dan Haley, "Protesters Fell Church's Trees," *Denver Post Online,* 27 September 1999, p. 2. www.denverpost.com/news/shot0927.htm.

4. Ibid.

5. Jeff Kass, "Angry Parents Cut Down 2 Trees," *RockyMountainNews.com,* 27 September 1999, p. 3. www.rockymountainnews.com/shooting/0927trees.shtml.

6. Haley, "Protesters," p. 2.

7. The Klebolds issued four statements, the Harrises two.

8. Peggy Lowe, "Harrises, Klebolds Apologize," *RockyMountainNews.com,* 15 April 2000, p. 1. www.rockymountainnews.com/shooting/0415lett2.shtml.

9. Ibid.

10. Katie Kerwin McCrimmon, "Two Continue a Life Planned for Three," *Rocky Mountain News,* 16 April 2000, sec. R, p. 9.

11. Gary Massaro, "'Someday It Would Be Nice To Laugh,'" *Rocky Mountain News,* 16 April 2000, sec. R, p. 10.

12. Kevin Simpson, "Voices of Columbine: The Family of Lauren Townsend," *Denver Post,* 16 April 2000, sec. I, p. 14.

13. Kieran Nicholson, "Voices of Columbine: The Family of Corey DePooter," *Denver Post,* 16 April 2000, sec. I, p. 12.

14. Kevin Vaughan, "Two Families Search for Serenity," *Rocky Mountain News,* 16 April 2000, sec. R, p. 4.

15. Ibid.

16. The Christopher Awards "salute media that remind audiences and readers of all ages and faith and of no particular faith, of their worth, individuality and power to positively impact and shape our world."

17. Susan Besze Wallace, "Voices of Columbine: The Family of Cassie Bernall," *Denver Post,* 16 April 2000, sec. I, p. 12.

18. Kieran Nicholson, "Voices of Columbine: The Family of John Tomlin," *Denver Post,* 16 April 2000, sec. I, p. 15.

19. Ibid.

20. Lowe, "Harrises," p. 1.

21. "Lord Reign in Me," text and music by Brenton Brown, Vineyard Songs (UK/Eire) 1998.

22. John Updike, "The Future of Faith," *New Yorker,* 29 November 1999, p. 88.

23. Job 40:4 NLT.

24. C. S. Lewis, *The Great Divorce* (New York: MacMillan, 1946), p. 7.